Death and Bereavement Across Cultures

All societies have their own customs and beliefs surrounding death. In the West, traditional ways of mourning are disappearing, and although Western science has had a major impact on how people die, it has taught us little about the way to die or to grieve. Many whose work brings them into contact with the dying and the bereaved from Western and other cultures are at a loss to know how to offer appropriate and sensitive support.

Death and Bereavement Across Cultures provides a handbook to meet the needs of doctors, nurses, social workers, hospital chaplains, counsellors and all those involved in the care of the dying and bereaved. Written by international authorities in the field, this important new text:

- describes the rituals and beliefs of major world religions;
- explains their psychological and historical context;
- shows how customs are changed by contact with the West;
- considers the implications for the future.

Death raises questions which science cannot answer. Whatever our personal beliefs we can all gain from learning how others view these ultimate problems. This book explores the richness of mourning traditions around the world with the aim of increasing the sensitivity and understanding which we all bring to the issue of death.

Edited by **Colin Murray Parkes**, Consultant Psychiatrist at St Christopher's Hospice, **Pittu Laungani**, Reader in Psychology at South Bank University and **Bill Young**, Consultant Child and Adolescent Psychiatrist at St Christopher's Fellowship, London.

Death and Bereavement Across Cultures

Edited by
Colin Murray Parkes, Pittu Laungani
and Bill Young

London and New York

First published 1997
by Routledge
11 New Fetter Lane, London EC4P 4EE

Simultaneously published in the USA and Canada
by Routledge
29 West 35th Street, New York, NY 10001

Reprinted 1998, 2000.

Routledge is an imprint of the Taylor and Francis Group

Typeset in Times by LaserScript, Mitcham, Surrey
Printed and bound in Great Britain by
T.J.I. Digital, Padstow, Cornwall.

British Library Cataloguing in Publication Data
A catalogue record for this book is available from the British Library

Library of Congress Cataloguing in Publication Data
Death and bereavement across cultures/edited by Colin Murray Parkes,
    Pittu Laungani, and Bill Young.
Includes bibliographical references (pp. 244–51) and index.
    1. Death – Psychological aspects. 2. Bereavement – Psychological aspects.
3. Death – Cross-cultural studies. 4. Bereavement – Cross-cultural studies.
5. Mourning customs.
I. Parkes, Colin Murray. II. Laungani, Pittu. III. Young, Bill.
BF789.D4D343   1996
306.9 – dc20   96-7558

ISBN 0–415–13136–7 (hbk)
ISBN 0–415–13137–5 (pbk)

Contents

Notes on contributors

Uwe P. Gielen, Professor of Psychology, St Francis College, Brooklyn Heights, New York, USA.

Gerdien Jonker, Dusseldorfer Strasse 4, 10719 Berlin, Germany.

Pittu Laungani, Reader in Psychology, South Bank University, London, UK.

Ellen Levine, Director of Psychosocial Oncology Research, Medical Center Research Institute, San Francisco, California, USA.

Danai Papadatou, Associate Professor of Psychology, University of Athens, Greece.

Colin Murray Parkes, Consultant Psychiatrist, St Christopher's Hospice, Sydenham, UK.

Paul C. Rosenblatt, Professor of Anthropology, College of Human Ecology, St Paul, Minnesota, USA.

Tony Walter, Lecturer in Sociology, University of Reading, Reading, UK.

Bill Young, Child and Adolescent Psychiatrist, St Christopher's Fellowship, London, UK.

Harold Ter Blanche, Grimsby Health Trust, District General Hospital, Grimsby, South Humberside, UK.

Part I

A conceptual framework: historical and cultural themes

Chapter 1

Introduction

Colin Murray Parkes, Pittu Laungani
and Bill Young

The twentieth century has seen major changes across the world. Many of these changes are beneficial. Improvements in medical care and nutrition have enabled most people in industrial countries to survive to old age. Improvements in mobility enable us to travel the globe and, for those who stay at home, the mass media of communication bring information and entertainment to fill the leisure hours that have been freed up by relief from drudgery.

Government and the rule of law have replaced the family and the neighbourhood as the main source of security and made it safe for people to leave the homes where they were born and travel to distant cities for their work. Instead of following our parents and relying on them for knowledge, Westerners are sent away from home to be educated. Self-reliance and independence are predominant virtues and the older traditions of obedience and respect for elders have faded in a world in which the knowledge of the elders is soon obsolete. Instead we have a cult of youth which overvalues the attributes of sex appeal and expects the old to emulate the young. And just as old people are assumed to be redundant, so the traditions, customs and beliefs that previous generations held to are assumed to be irrelevant to the world today. Dietary laws which protected people from harm in the days before refrigerators, methods of healing which have been superseded by modern medicine and the worship of tribal gods when the tribe has been absorbed into a larger society are all seen as irrelevant in the modern world. And if they are, we may be tempted to junk the lot.

On the other hand, all traditional beliefs and rituals must exist for a reason and many of those reasons may still apply. It is a peculiarly twentieth-century attitude to assume that because something is old it can't be true, good or useful. In times gone by its very antiquity was taken as evidence of its value.

This is nowhere more obvious than it is in an area of human experience about which science has taught us nothing – death. Despite all the advances of modern science 100 per cent of people still die. Ivan Illich has termed this 'the ultimate form of consumer resistance'. Science may delay death but it can neither prevent it nor can it tell us anything about what, if anything, lies beyond death or what we can do to prepare for that transition. This does not prevent people from behaving as if, even now, scientific medicine could provide a solution to the problem of death. Doctors and nurses tend to collude with this and most Westerners still go to a hospital to die, many of them in the naive belief that scientific medicine will prevail over death. Once in hospital nobody mentions the possibility that the disease may prove fatal; death is treated as a guilty secret. As one patient put it, 'I'm glad I'm not dying of anything *serious*!' It seems that modern man has created a new myth and new priests and acolytes (the doctors and nurses) to maintain the illusion that he can live forever.

Of course, our attempts to sweep death under the carpet have also given rise to a counter-culture, what Geoffrey Gorer terms the 'pornography of death' which, as with other taboo subjects, makes it the subject of jokes and fascination (Gorer, 1965). The horror film is an example of a genre which enables us both to approach and to distance ourselves from this area of experience by distorting and fictionalizing it.

Along with a decline in our ability to face death comes a decline in trust in the rituals that accompany and follow death. Traditional mourning customs have been largely abandoned and the rituals of cremation or burial of the dead have lost much of the emotional significance which, in the past, often made them a source of support for the bereaved rather than an ordeal. At least, so it is claimed by the psychiatrists and counsellors who are called upon to give help to bereaved people and who are themselves attempting to apply scientific methods to the solution of the problems created by science.

This does not mean that science is wrong and should be abandoned, but that there are still areas of human experience to which science has little to contribute. These include some of the most important and challenging aspects of life. How each of us approaches the prospect of our own death and the death of those we love remains a tremendous question which each generation must tackle afresh. Each generation and each society has come up with its own solutions to the problem of death and has enshrined them in a complex web of beliefs and customs which, at first glance, seem so diverse as to be impossible to digest. Yet there are common themes that run through all of them and even the differences become easier to understand when they are considered in the light of the historical context in which they have arisen.

Our enquiries, which will be developed in more detail in this book, lead us to conclude that all societies see death as a transition for the person who dies. How people prepare themselves for this transition and how the survivors behave after a death has occurred varies a great deal but even here there are common themes. Rosenblatt, Walsh and Jackson, in their important book *Grief and Mourning in Cross-Cultural Perspective* (1976) compared the accounts given by anthropologists of grief and mourning[1] in seventy-eight different societies (selected as representative from a pool of 186 world cultures). Crying, fear and anger are so common as to be virtually ubiquitous and most cultures provide social sanction for the expression of these emotions in the funeral rites and customs of mourning which follow bereavement. In this respect, Western cultures, which tend to discourage the overt expression of emotion at funerals, are highly deviant. They differ from most other societies and from our own society as it was a hundred years ago.

The fact that we are deviant does not necessarily make us wrong. Maybe mourning is a waste of time and energy and the best thing is to pull up our socks and get on with our lives. Maybe we are right to ignore death. If there is nothing we can do about it perhaps we should treat it as if it doesn't exist. When somebody dies we should get rid of the body as quickly as possible and carry on as if nothing had happened.

This is the logical view. It accords well with a pragmatic view of life which seeks practical solutions to practical problems. It is very different from the superstitions of religion, the pretensions of art and poetry and the unsubstantiated theories of psychiatrists and psychologists.

And yet, and yet, there are few of us who are prepared to discount altogether those aspects of life which are concerned with spirit rather than mind, feeling rather than doing and emotion rather than thought. We continue to prize the art, poetry, literature and music of bygone times and we particularly prize those that treat of death. Indeed there are many who prefer these traditional art forms to the arts of the today. Mozart's *Requiem* and Michelangelo's *Pietà* are enduring sources of inspiration and enlightenment despite, or perhaps, because of their concern with death.

---

1 In this book we shall use the term 'grief' to cover the psychological reaction to bereavement and the term 'mourning' for the public display.

'The heart has its reasons which the reason knows not' (Pascal, 1670) and one does not have to be a Mogul to appreciate the beauty of the Taj Mahal or an Elizabethan to enjoy Shakespeare's tragedies. But it does help to have some understanding of the 'languages' of architecture and English.

If art can transcend generational and national boundaries, the same cannot be said of religion. Despite current attempts at ecumenicity between the many sects of the Christian church, the rites and beliefs of other people seem alien or, at best, quaint. We allow licence to poets but no such licence is allowed to priests. Those who hold most passionately to the truths of their own religion often deride the beliefs of others. Accusations of 'mumbo jumbo' are made and 'holy wars' may even result.

One reason for this is the logical incompatibility of many belief systems. If human beings go to heaven or hell when they die they cannot also be reincarnated. If God is a man he cannot also be a woman, or a sun or a red kangaroo. Faced with these inconsistencies we either cling to our own 'true' faith and denigrate the rest, or we lose faith in all religions.

Most students of comparative religion take a different view. They see each faith as comprehensible in the time and place in which it has arisen. The search for meaning in life and death must take place within a particular historical and geographical context. It would be surprising if the context did not influence the form of our thinking. But there may still be fundamental consistencies, themes and truths that appear and reappear in one culture after another. Jung spoke of these as 'archetypes' and related them to his idea of a 'collective unconscious'. The editors of this book are, perhaps, more prosaic than Jung and prefer to leave open the underlying nature of these phenomena. We shall treat them in much the same way that we treat dreams and poetry, as having meanings that we can glimpse but not pin down. The better we understand the cultural context the more evident that meaning.

Psychology, because it deals with much that is subjective and unmeasurable yet tries to be systematic and logical, occupies an uncomfortable no man's land between art and science. Psychologists themselves vary in their commitment to one or other 'camp'. At one end of the spectrum are the behaviourists who concern themselves only with behaviour which they can measure, at the other extreme are those who distrust measurement and rely on intuition and empathy as their source of knowledge. The editors of this book take no such extreme positions. We recognize both the value and the limitations of the science of the mind and we also recognize that intuition, common sense and subjectivity, with all their inherent fallibility, add much to our understanding of those realms of humanity that cannot be understood by any other means. We prefer to be inclusive rather than exclusive, eclectic rather than narrowly focused, and soft- rather than hard-nosed scientists.

It could be argued that we are stepping outside our own areas of expertise in studying cross-cultural issues at all; surely this is the province of the anthropologist and the sociologist. While recognizing the validity of this we believe that we can justify ourselves. As editors we see it as our role to ensure that our distinguished contributors, who each brings his or her own special expertise to the book, will take full account of the current knowledge of the psychology of death and bereavement and will write in a way that is useful to those who are working with the dying and the bereaved. Two of the editors are medical practitioners and psychiatrists, one (Parkes) has long experience of helping dying and bereaved adults, the other (Young) specializes in the care of children and families. Our third editor (Laungani), an experienced psychologist, is an immigrant to Britain whose personal experience of crossing the cultural divide from Hindu India to Christian England ensures that the cultural biasses of the others will be kept in check.

Between us we have attempted to make sure that the contributions of our distinguished authors are comprehensible to non-specialists, well informed about the 'heart' and its reasons, and useful to those whose role it is to bring comfort and support to the dying and the bereaved of all nations.

We are not so arrogant as to imagine that doctors and nurses are always giving care and patients and their families receiving it. Caring is always a two-way traffic and, in the end, all benefit. Life, being an incurable disease which always ends fatally, the main difference between us and our patients is the likelihood that they will die before we do. One is reminded of the old rhyme:

Doctor, Doctor shall I die?
Yes, my child, and so shall I.

We are all in the same situation and need to learn from each other all we can in order to make sense of it. Serving dying and bereaved people from other races and creeds provides us with the privilege of learning from them. We should not expect that our expertise is greater than theirs but that does not mean that there is nothing we can do to help them. Times of death and bereavement are times when people need people and the mere presence of another person who cares is important. If, in addition, we have sufficient knowledge of and sympathy for the other person's culture to be able to understand what they need from us we shall have a great deal to offer. At least we can prevent some of the painful and unnecessary suffering that can follow when members of the caring professions impose their own cultural norms on others at times when they are extremely vulnerable.[2] At best we may contribute to make death a transcendent event for those who die and those who survive.

SUMMARY

☐ In the Western world, government and the rule of law have replaced the family and the neighbourhood as the main source of security.

☐ Just as old people are assumed to be redundant so the traditions customs and beliefs that previous generations held to are assumed to be irrelevant to the world today.

☐ All traditional beliefs and rituals must exist for a reason and many of those reasons may still apply.

☐ Science may delay death but it can neither prevent it nor can it tell us anything about what, if anything, lies beyond death or what we can do to prepare for that transition. This does not prevent people from behaving as if, even now, scientific medicine could provide a solution to the problem of death.

☐ Modern man has created a new myth and new priests and acolytes (the doctors and nurses) to maintain the illusion that he can live forever.

☐ Along with a decline in our ability to face death comes a decline in trust in the rituals that accompany and follow death.

☐ Each generation and each society has come up with its own solutions to the problem of death and has enshrined them in a complex web of beliefs and customs which, at first glance, seem so diverse as to be impossible to digest. Yet there are common themes that run through all of them.

☐ All societies see death as a transition for the person who dies.

☐ How people prepare themselves for this transition and how the survivors behave after a death has occurred varies a great deal.

2 Perry (1993) relates how authorities in an American hospital called the police who sent a riot squad to arrest a group of African American mourners who were 'crying loudly and wailing' outside the hospital to which a mortally wounded teenager had been admitted. A community leader subsequently complained, 'The hospital doesn't understand how black people grieve.'

☐ Crying, fear and anger are so common as to be virtually ubiquitous and most cultures provide social sanction for the expression of these emotions.

☐ Western cultures, which tend to discourage the overt expression of emotion at funerals, are highly deviant.

☐ Despite current attempts at ecumenicity between the many sects of the Christian church, the rites and beliefs of other people seem alien or, at best, quaint.

☐ Each faith is comprehensible in the time and place in which it has arisen.

☐ As psychologists, we recognize both the value and the limitations of the science of the mind and we also recognize that intuition, common sense and subjectivity, with all their inherent fallibility, add much to our understanding of those realms of humanity that cannot be understood by any other means.

☐ Serving dying and bereaved people from other races and creeds provides us with the privilege of learning from them.

Chapter 2

Culture and religion

Colin Murray Parkes, Pittu Laungani and Bill Young

The word 'religion' derives from the Latin *religare* which means 'to bind' and, traditionally, it is that body of ideas which binds a society together. More recently it has come to have a more specific meaning as the 'recognition on the part of man of some higher, unseen power as having control of his destiny, and a being entitled to obedience, reverence, and worship . . .' (*Shorter Oxford Dictionary*, 1970). This unseen power is usually referred to as 'God' in monotheistic, or 'the Gods' in polytheistic societies. As such it is distinct from the term 'culture' which, in the usage of sociologists and anthropologists, has come to mean the 'social heritage of a community' (*Fontana Dictionary of Modern Thought*, 1977), that is, the sum total of the possessions, ways of thinking and behaviour which distinguish one group of people from another and which tend to be passed down from generation to generation. Thus the term 'culture' now includes 'religion' although there is a sense in which religions, because they may be shared by people from many groups, can be said to transcend cultures.

Sociologists have written about popular culture, media culture, mass culture, minority culture, ethnic culture, aboriginal culture, black culture, white culture etc.: the list is almost endless. To make matters more confusing, since we have subgroups to every group we also have 'subcultures'. For the sake of simplicity we have limited our use of the term in this book to the main large ethnic and religious groupings that our readers are likely to meet in the course of work within the English-speaking world.

Difficulties arise, not only in the multiplicity of cultures and subcultures, but also in the characteristics which are thought to distinguish them and which easily lead to cultural stereotyping. Thus early visitors to other lands commonly picked on one characteristic which, to them, stood out as distinctive and often shocking because it seemed so much at variance with their own beliefs; tribes would be branded as 'cannibals', 'pagans', 'devil-worshippers' or 'ignorant savages'. This implanted in the minds of would-be conquerors a conviction of their own superiority which justified the conquest and subjugation of the 'inferior' race.

ANTHROPOLOGY AND CULTURE

Anthropologists, who are the pioneers in the study of cultures, have themselves been guilty of this abuse. The early writings of anthropologists were speculative, naive and even absurd (Harris, 1968). In fact Sir James Frazer, who wrote the twelve volumes of the classic, *The Golden Bough* (1890), which was a study in magic and religion across all societies in the world, boasted that he never met nor indeed visited any of the lands of the people of whom he wrote (Beattie, 1964)! Visiting the lands and living for extended periods with the peoples of those lands about whom volumes were written was considered to be a superfluous activity. Analyses of other societies were based largely on the available writings of colonial administrators, missionaries, historians and the like, and of course on preconceptions and stereotypes.

In addition to this arrogant naivety, anthropology, as Bock (1980), Harris (1968) and several others have pointed out, was also blatantly racist in its formulations. Differences between negroes (as they were referred to) and Europeans were often explained in terms of naive and ill-founded theories. Some anthropologists subscribed to the polygenist theory, which attributed racial differences to acts of special creation by God (Harris, 1968). A belief in the polygenist doctrine not only justified white supremacy but became a ground for accepting and justifying slavery in Europe and in America. The polygenists saw themselves as being apart from those who subscribed to the monogenist theory which holds that all humankind is derived from a common pair of ancestors. It is interesting to note that the subscribers of the monogenist doctrines, particularly those in the 'Bible belt' areas of the southern states in America, also justified slavery by accepting the theme of degeneration in the Book of Genesis. In both cases the negroes and members of other non-white races were seen as being inferior.

Darwin's theory of evolution added another dimension to these controversies. From now on the 'superior' nations became entitled to kill their enemies in the interest of 'survival of the fittest'. Non-

European and non-white societies came to be judged as being backward, primitive, inferior, etc. and, therefore, less fit to survive.

Such judgements are dangerous. Their dangers lie in their occasionally unintentional but frequently intentional promotion of appalling cruelty, savagery and, in extreme cases, genocide, a word coined to describe acts of the 'cultured' leaders of Nazi Germany. The world has already witnessed the devastating consequences of negative stereotyping which are continuing in Rwanda, Bosnia and Somalia. It is important to pay heed to the wise words of George Santayana: 'Those who do not remember the past are condemned to relive it' (1905–6, vol. I, ch. 12).

Although most of the pejorative evaluations concerning racial differences have currently fallen out of favour in the West, from time to time they keep resurfacing in different guises; arguments related to racial differences in schizophrenia, in measured IQ, etc., reappear in prestigious journals and books (Herrnstein and Murray, 1994).

It was not until the late nineteenth century that anthropology began to acquire some academic respectability. Anthropologists, led by the charismatic Franz Boaz (1911), started to undertake ethnographic field studies. Sensitive to the criticisms of ethnocentrism and racism with which the discipline had become tainted, Boaz paid special attention to research methodology. He insisted on maintaining the highest standards of scientific rigour, exhorting his colleagues to do the same. One of the ways by which this could be achieved was for the research worker to adopt a pure, non-judgemental attitude of scrupulous detachment and objectivity. All personal biases, subjective predilections, educated guesses, stereotypes, etc., had to be jettisoned – before undertaking a voyage to another country. They had no place in Boaz's research methodology, for such factors impeded the pursuit of objective scientific goals. He was also opposed to any form of premature theorizing and eschewed the construction of theoretical models *before any facts had been painstakingly gathered*. Facts, he believed, ought to speak for themselves. The greatness of Boaz lay in that he provided a much needed new model. Arm-chair theorizing gave way to the systematic collection of ethnographic data. Field studies, using a variety of techniques, came to be equated with anthropological research.

In his zeal to rid anthropology of subjective biasses and prejudices, however, Boaz threw the proverbial baby out with the bathwater. From now on anthropologists became fearful of drawing any firm conclusions or deriving any theories from their work, which was largely confined to describing the enormous range of human societies. Attempts to draw conclusions by comparing one society with another or with the human race as a whole were disallowed.

This form of extreme rigour is open to serious criticism (Chalmers, 1985). Firstly, facts seldom speak for themselves – they become meaningful when interpreted, and any interpretation is always in the light of a theoretical or conceptual framework, however vague it might be (Popper 1963 and 1972). Facts which do 'speak' for themselves, e.g., those found in a telephone directory, tell us little of any great value. Facts are used to *test* a theory, not to generate one. Secondly, Boaz's insistence on the purity and neutrality of observations, is also mistaken. All observations are theory-laden.

The influence of Boaz has not waned. Anthropologists in general, even to the present day, follow in his footsteps. The study of *whole* societies – describing a society in its totality – is still at the centre of their discipline. Although the findings from anthropological studies are not without value, their reluctance to draw conclusions by comparing one culture with another has seriously limited the value of their work to psychologists and others who seek to make generalizations about the human condition. This has meant that, although there are numerous accounts in the anthropological literature about funeral and mourning customs in many different societies, anthropologists have contributed very little to our understanding of the psychology of grief and loss.

PSYCHOLOGY AND CULTURE

Does psychology fare any better? It was in the late 1950s that cross-cultural psychology emerged as a discipline in its own right (Jahoda, 1970). Given that Britain had established a large number of colonies all over the world, it is strange that British psychologists were unwilling to undertake cross-cultural research. The curious moratorium was lifted after the Second World War, and the 1950s saw a burst of sustained activity in the subject. What progress has been achieved in the last forty years of research?

Cross-cultural psychology and anthropology have never enjoyed a good working partnership. They have usually gone their own separate ways. This is because of their differing approaches. Psychologists tend to be more concerned about testing explicitly formulated hypotheses rather than constructing social systems on the basis of detailed observations. Like all disciplines, cross-cultural psychology too is guided by several inter-related assumptions. The one which is of concern to us is the belief in *cultural variation*.

Societies vary with respect to their ecology, their means of survival, their socio-cultural system, their individual system, and their interindividual system (Triandis, 1980). Between them these allow us to understand the nature of variation in different societies and in so doing permit us to go beyond a descriptive classificatory system and pose fundamental theoretical questions concerning the causes of such variations. For instance, the death of an elderly person in a Hindu family is not just a private family affair. It affects the family's immediate relatives (the *baradari*), their sub-caste (*jati*) and the local community of which the deceased was a part. Any one who knew the deceased in any significant capacity is obliged to come to the funeral. Not to come to the funeral is more than a mere breach of social etiquette. It is an extremely serious social transgression. In contra-distinction to a Hindu funeral, a middle-class Anglican funeral is often seen as a private family affair. Only those specifically invited are expected to attend the funeral. A church service led by the vicar normally precedes the funeral. After the funeral the mourners, only if invited, may partake of the hospitality offered by the family of the bereaved. Condolences are offered and gradually the mourners leave. The bereaved are left on their own. No further attempt is made to intrude into their grief, which is seen as being private and personal.

These are simple descriptions. They serve an important function in helping us to understand the manner in which social customs are performed in different societies. The aim of scientific research, however, is to go beyond description and attempt an *explanation*. Such a level of analysis would attempt to tease out how these differential social customs came into being, what functions, if any, they serve, and the conditions under which they are likely to be perpetuated, or modified, or disappear altogether.

What constitutes a culture? It is suggested that all cultures possess a set of core (primary) features and a set of peripheral (secondary) features: the core features constitute the essential requirements of any culture. The peripheral features, although important, may vary from culture to culture. The primary features of a culture are as follows:

1 A past history (recorded or oral).
2 A dominant, organized religion within which the salient beliefs and activities (rites, rituals, taboos and ceremonies) can be given meaning and legitimacy. These include beliefs and ceremonies about death.
3 A set of core values and traditions to which the people of that society subscribe and which they attempt to perpetuate.

4 Regulated social systems, communication networks, including regulatory norms of personal, familial and social conduct.
5 Artifacts unique to that society, e.g, literature, works of art, paintings, music, dance, drama, religious texts, philosophical texts, etc.

The secondary features of a culture are as follows:

1 It should, to a large measure, have a common language or group of languages.
2 Common physical and geographical boundaries within which people of that particular society live, from which they may venture abroad but to which they will feel drawn to return.
3 A relatively fixed pattern of housing and other living arrangements.
4 Socially accepted dietary, health and medical practices.
5 A shared moral and legislative system.

Of these various features the most important is normally religion. It is this shared commitment to something more important than the individual and the family which provides both a rationale for society and a set of moral imperatives without which societies lose a major source of security.

With these thoughts in mind we turn now to a consideration of how the main world cultures have come into being. Since these have been inextricably linked to particular religious faiths it is these that will provide the focus of our discussion.

THE HISTORICAL DEVELOPMENT OF WORLD RELIGIONS

Most of us tend to think of a religion as a fixed and unchanging set of beliefs, a faith which is exclusive and incompatible with other faiths. This view is fallacious. All of the main world religions have changed in their systems of belief over time and under the influence of the various cultures into which they have spread. The most pronounced changes in religious faith have occurred at times when the cultures have been undergoing similar pronounced change. These are most likely to occur at times of conquest.

   Although contact with other faiths has often led to conflict, it has also led to modifications and compromises which have allowed people of different religions to get along together and, in many places, to adopt each other's beliefs. As a consequence of this, people who subscribe to a particular religion in one part of the world may have very different beliefs and rituals from those of people of the same religion who live in other places. Thus many of the beliefs and observances of a Buddhist in Japan resemble the beliefs and observances of a Japanese Shinto more closely than they do those of a Buddhist in Sri Lanka.

To understand these cultural and historical differences we need to trace the history of the spread of the main religions across the world. While little is known for sure about the prehistoric religions which caused Neanderthal people to bury their dead in distinctive ways it seems reasonable to assume that the religions of the hunter/gatherers were not very different from those found among similar small-scale societies today. Faced with the uncertainties of a natural world in which success at hunting, fishing and scavenging can never be assured and in which man is only one among several species competing for the same limited food supplies, it is not surprising that such tribes tend to focus their religion on the task of controlling this natural world. Typically they adopt polytheistic, animistic beliefs, seeing good and bad spirits in all the natural world and attempting to control these by magic and folk medicine. Those that have no settled home cannot have temples or churches and those that do can seldom afford them, nor can they afford the expense of a priesthood. Lacking any written dogma their beliefs are communicated by word of mouth and remain relatively unsophisticated.

Subsistence farming allows more settled communities to arise whose worship is much concerned with the fertility of the soil. Homes require household gods who are often located on the hearth where fire is a particularly valuable form of magic. Religious functions were, and in many tribal societies still are, the responsibility of the elders, but there is still no priesthood and an oral tradition limits the communication of a sophisticated dogma.

Only with the development of large-scale societies living in towns and cities did it become possible for priests and other ritual specialists to develop, places exclusive to worship to be built and, eventually, a written form of dogma to be recorded and passed on. For the first time it became possible for an entire nation to adopt one faith and for church and state to become intertwined. The state religion of ancient Egypt was promoted by a priestly system supported by the priest king, the Pharaoh. Unlike most later religions it persisted with very little change for 2,000 years. This reflected the unusual stability of a rigid political system in which a hierarchy of gods and goddesses bore a striking resemblance to the earthly hierarchy which maintained them. The pharaohs themselves were assured of an afterlife in an agricultural community resembling Egypt into which they were launched from spectacular tombs complete with chariots, slaves and treasure.

The Egyptians' religion perished with their dynasties and the first large-scale religion which has persisted to this day is that of the Hindus in India. This is a very different religion from that of the Egyptians and its persistence reflects its flexibility and capacity to adapt to a wide range of circumstances. Hinduism takes so many forms that a cynical writer once said that the only thing that Hindus have in common is their Indian nationality and their veneration for the cow. The name Hindu means 'India' and the cow, in that country, has long remained the symbol of Mother Earth.

The next long-lasting religion to arise was Judaism. Originating as a tribal god, the God of the Jews was unusual in being their only one (most tribes had a number of gods). This national god eventually became seen as the only true God, and the Jews as his chosen people.

The next to arise was Zoroastrianism. Zoroaster's dates are uncertain but his core belief was a powerful idea, namely, that religion is a personal faith in which each man must choose between good and evil and be rewarded or punished after death regardless of his wealth or status. This belief was adopted by Cyrus the Great, who conquered the Babylonian Empire and replaced it with the Persian Empire in the mid-sixth century BC. Cyrus was a tolerant ruler who liberated the Jews from their exile in Babylon and made no attempt to proselytize. Even so Zoroastrianism spread rapidly across the Persian Empire and its influence was felt even more widely.

It is probably no coincidence that several great world religions originated within fifty years of each other at about that time. Siddhartha Gautama (the Buddha), Vardhamana Mahavira (the founder of Jainism), Confucius and Lao Tze (Taoism) all challenged existing priestly authority and established their own followings. The first Hindu Upanishads were written and themselves reflected a major change; the Vedanta or end of Veda, Veda being the domination of the Brahmin priesthood which had been established to bolster the power of Aryan conquerors.

In the years which followed classical Hinduism emerged, Buddhism spread across south India into Sri Lanka and Burma, Confucianism became established alongside Taoism in China and Judaism became consolidated as a religion based on the Bible. Zoroastrianism itself dwindled with the fall of the Persian Empire but lingers on in parts of India to this day.

While religions can be spread by conquest they can also arise as a reaction against it. The solidarity of the Jews was maintained in the face of repeated persecution and enabled Jews to hold to the idea that they were the chosen of God who would one day be liberated by the advent of a great leader or Messiah. Successive claimants to the title attempted to lead uprisings with disastrous consequences to their followers but one such, Jesus of Nazareth, suggested that the Kingdom of God was not on this earth but the next and that liberation would be achieved by loving one's enemies rather than by hating them. This extraordinary doctrine did not prevent him from being executed by the Roman authorities under pressure from the Jewish priesthood.

Christianity soon died out as a Jewish sect but not before it had been taken up by small groups of Roman citizens who, in the fourth century AD, persuaded the Emperor Constantine to support their unpolitical and non-racial religion, amongst the numerous other religions of the Empire. Thereafter Christianity spread across Europe and, eventually, the globe. It did not deter its proponents from fighting their enemies but did tend to encourage a separation of military and religious leaders, with the latter then able to shake their heads in horror at the cruelties and injustice of imperialist conquest, while benefiting from its consequences.

Another great leader who came to be seen as a Messiah was Muhammad, a wealthy Arab citizen of the trading centre of Mecca who, about AD 610, became convinced that he had received messages from God which he must pass on to his followers. He too preached the resurrection of the dead and God's judgement on each person according to his works. He saw himself as one of a succession of Semitic prophets which included Moses and Jesus. Within a few years he had attracted a large following and he subsequently united the nomadic Arab tribes and successfully led an uprising which left him and his successors as Caliphs of Islam. They, in turn, brought about the Muslim world which was both a state and a religion. In addition to most of the northern half of Africa, in the fifteenth century this included Spain and, in the sixteenth and seventeenth, Mogul India.

While Jihad, or Holy War, is one of the good works by which a Muslim can enter paradise, Muslim rulers have, in the past, proved tolerant of other faiths, particularly those monotheistic faiths that have a common origin with their own, Judaism and Christianity. The expansion of the French and British Empires during the eighteenth and nineteenth centuries brought about a decline in Islamic influence which has been partially balanced by the discovery of oil in the Middle East during the current century. The creation of the Jewish State of Israel, however, has fed antagonisms that were already present and threatens to undermine the relationship.

In all of the great world religions there is a variety of sects which tend to emphasize different ways of practising the faith. Divisions tend to grow up between conservative and liberal elements: between those who seek a personal relationship with God and those who prefer to appoint priests as intermediaries; between those who seek intellectual justification for their beliefs and those whose faith comes from their emotions or 'heart'. There are those for whom mysticism and magic are at the root of religion and others who are highly suspicious of these. There are people who give ritual and prayer a central place and others who see them as unimportant.

As we have seen, the great world religions have evolved in diverse ways according to the particular beliefs of the people of power and influence in each place and time. One of the deepest divisions is between people who tolerate faiths other than their own and those who oppose them. In Japan, today, there is a high degree of tolerance, such that people often make use of rituals derived from several faiths. Thus most people will choose to have a Shinto wedding and a Buddhist funeral. In this atmosphere of tolerance a bewildering number of new faiths have come into being in recent years. In the past this kind of confusion has sometimes given rise to a backlash in which those in power attempt to impose a single faith on their followers.

The twentieth century has seen more social change across the world than any other century and it is hardly surprising that many of the faiths that were formerly relatively static are now changing. Democracy, with its emphasis on personal liberty, has encouraged religious tolerance, and the increased ability to travel and the mass media of communication have created a 'global village' in which we are repeatedly being made aware of the people who live in other cultures than our own. At the same time the dominance of the air waves by Anglo-American culture is ensuring that this new freedom will lead to an extraordinary degree of uniformity. Jeans and sweat shirts are the dress of young people in Malaysia, Beijing and Moscow as well as New York and London. Young people today, in many parts of the world, watch the same soap operas on television, listen to the same music, view the same films and read many of the same books. Explicitly religious programmes are not popular, and most media deliberately avoid religious themes for fear of offending the audience. While this protects the audience from indoctrination it also encourages the split which already exists between the sacred and the secular.

With all our tolerance, and perhaps because of it, we are in danger of losing one of the most important attributes of religion, respect for the sacred. Modern man, with all his cleverness, is in danger of losing that reverence for the awesome spiritual mysteries of the universe which is evident in the worship that is central to most religions.

In the chapters that follow we shall examine in turn the ways in which death and bereavement are treated and thought about by the proponents of each of the great world cultural and religious groupings. We hope that this will not only inform but also help us to confront the greatest and most awesome mystery of all, the mystery of death.

SUMMARY

- [ ] Religion is recognition on the part of man of some higher, unseen power having control of his destiny, a being entitled to obedience, reverence and worship.
- [ ] Culture is the sum total of the possessions, ways of thinking and behaviour, which distinguish one group of people from another, and which tend to be passed down from generation to generation.
- [ ] We have limited our use of the term culture, in this book, to the main large ethnic and religious groupings that our readers are likely to meet in the course of work within the English-speaking world.
- [ ] The characteristics which are thought to distinguish cultures easily lead to cultural stereotyping.
- [ ] Early visitors to other lands commonly picked on one characteristic which, to them, stood out as distinctive and often shocking because it seemed so much at variance with their own beliefs. This implanted in the minds of would-be conquerors a conviction of their own superiority which justified the conquest and subjugation of the 'inferior' race.
- [ ] The early writings of anthropologists were speculative, naive and even absurd.
- [ ] Belief in the polygenist doctrine not only justified white supremacy but became a ground for accepting and justifying slavery in Europe and in America.
- [ ] Darwin's theory of evolution was used by the 'superior' nations as justifying killing their enemies in the interest of 'survival of the fittest'.
- [ ] In the twentieth century anthropologists became fearful of drawing any firm conclusions or deriving any theories from their work, which was largely confined to describing the enormous range of human societies.

☐ Although there are numerous accounts in the anthropological literature about funeral and mourning customs in many different societies, anthropologists have contributed very little to our understanding of the psychology of grief and loss.

☐ Societies vary with respect to their ecology, their means of survival, the socio-cultural system, the individual system and the inter-individual system.

☐ The primary features of a culture are: (1) a past history, (2) a dominant, organized religion, (3) a set of core values and traditions, (4) regulated social systems and (5) artifacts unique to that society. The most important is normally religion.

☐ The secondary features of a culture are: (1) a common language or group of languages, (2) common physical and geographical boundaries, (3) a relatively fixed pattern of living arrangements, (4) socially accepted dietary, health and medical practices and (5) a shared moral and legislative system.

☐ All of the main world religions have changed in their systems of belief over time and under the influence of the various cultures into which they have spread. The most pronounced changes in religious faith have occurred at times when the cultures have been undergoing similar pronounced change. These are most likely to occur at times of conquest.

☐ Although contact with other faiths has often led to conflict, it has also led to modifications and compromises which have allowed people of different religions to get along together and, in many places, to adopt each other's beliefs.

☐ People who subscribe to a particular religion in one part of the world may have very different beliefs and rituals from those of people of the same religion who live in other places.

☐ Hunter/gatherers tended to focus their religion on the task of controlling the natural world. Typically they adopted polytheistic, animistic beliefs.

☐ Subsistence farming allowed more settled communities to arise whose worship was much concerned with the fertility of the soil.

☐ With the development of large-scale societies living in towns and cities it became possible for priests and other ritual specialists to develop, places exclusive to worship to be built and, eventually, a written form of dogma to be recorded and passed on. It also became possible for an entire nation to adopt one faith and for church and state to become intertwined.

☐ The first large-scale religion which has persisted to this day is that of the Hindus in India. Its persistence reflects its flexibility and capacity to adapt to a wide range of circumstances.

☐ The next long-lasting religion to arise was Judaism. Their national God eventually became seen as the only true God, and the Jews as his chosen people.

☐ Zoroastrianism is a personal religion in which each man must choose between good and evil and be rewarded or punished after death regardless of his wealth or status.

☐ Several great world religions originated within fifty years of each other in the mid-sixth century BC – Buddhism, Jainism, Taoism and the Hindu Upanishads were written down. All challenged existing priestly authority.

☐ Religions can be spread by conquest or, as in Judaism, arise as a reaction against it.

☐ Jesus of Nazareth suggested that the Kingdom of God was not on this earth but the next and that liberation would be achieved by loving one's enemies rather than by hating them. In the fourth century AD, the Emperor Constantine supported Christianity which then spread across Europe and, eventually, the globe.

☐ Muhammad, in AD 610, received messages from God. He preached the resurrection of the dead and God's judgement on each person according to his works. He subsequently united the nomadic Arab tribes and successfully led an uprising which left him and his successors as Caliphs of Islam. They, in turn, brought about the Muslim world which was both a state and a religion.

☐ In all of the great world religions there is a variety of sects which tend to emphasize different ways of practising the faith. Divisions tend to grow up between conservative and liberal elements: between those who seek a personal relationship with God and those who prefer to appoint priests as intermediaries; between those who seek intellectual justification for their beliefs and those whose faith comes from their emotions or 'heart'; those for whom mysticism and magic are at the root of religion and others who are highly suspicious of these; people who give ritual and prayer a central place and others who see them as unimportant. One of the deepest divisions is between people who tolerate faiths other than their own and those who oppose them.

☐ Democracy, with its emphasis on personal liberty, has encouraged religious tolerance and the increased ability to travel and the mass media of communication have created a 'global village' in which we are repeatedly being made aware of the people who live in other cultures than our own. Explicitly religious programmes are not popular, and most media deliberately avoid religious themes for fear of offending the audience. While this protects the audience from indoctrination it also encourages the split which already exists between the sacred and the secular.

☐ We are in danger of losing one of the most important attributes of religion, respect for the sacred.

Part II

Major world systems of belief and ritual

Chapter 3

Grief in small-scale societies

Paul C. Rosenblatt

His wife dead, Ambe'na Doko said, 'My feelings [are] like a crazy person. My head [isn't] thinking in a fixed way. What it [is] that I [am] thinking in the house, I don't know. I never [think] about the work in the fields. . . . My heart [is] very full' (Wellenkamp, 1991, p.127). Generalizing from Wellenkamp's description of ways of dealing with death among the 350,000 Toraja of Sulawesi in Indonesia, we would expect that as his wife was dying Ambe'na Doko would have heard her conversing with the souls of the dead and would have responded to her request for a luxury food such as palm wine. When she ceased breathing, she might have been cradled in his arms. Messengers would be sent to tell other relatives of the death. Although the Toraja try to maintain emotional equanimity and believe that intense sorrow may endanger one, it is permissible and even desirable to express intense grief through crying, calling out to the dead, and sobbing for a limited time period at the funeral, while near the body or an effigy of the body, or when first returning home after the death.

We would expect that the body of Ambe'na Doko's wife, Indo'na Doko, would be kept in the house for many weeks prior to the funeral. During that time, preparations would be made and an auspicious date selected for the funeral. Indo'na Doko would not be talked about as dead but perhaps as 'the person with a fever' or the 'sleeping person'. Her body would have been offered food and drink, and be told when a household member was leaving or had returned home. During this time, some people might have been offended by the odours of decomposition. However, the family would not have complained, out of respect for the deceased, nor would they have complained about the visiting souls with which they must contend, nor express much, if any, of the grief they felt. Her death, though unacknowledged prior to the funeral, would have polluted her village and prevented anyone in the village from engaging in certain rituals. When the funeral began, she would finally be labelled 'dead'. The funeral, lasting days or even weeks, would involve gradual moving of her body from the house, to the houseyard, to the burial site. Food offerings and sacrifices of pigs and water buffalo would have been made. The gravesite would be prepared, the remains of other deceased at the gravesite would have been rewrapped and damaged coffins repaired. This attention to the remains of other dead would be understood as an expression of continuing love and respect and also as earning assistance from the spirits of those deceased. At the conclusion of the funeral, the body of the deceased would have been entombed in a cliffside burial cave.

With the onset of the funeral, a formal mourning period began. Ambe'na Doko wore black and abstained from certain foods. During the funeral period Ambe'na Doko slept next to his wife's body at night and kept close to the body during the day, participating in offerings to her soul. With the end of the funeral, a few days after the burial, the official mourning ended and the taboos were lifted for all family members except Ambe'na Doko. People expected him to try not to dwell on her death or think of her face. However, he probably dreamed of her aiding him, a dream which he thought of as actually communicating with her soul. Unlike many other Toraja, Ambe'na Doko continued to grieve, to feel very much upset, and to be preoccupied with his wife's death long after the funeral. People tried to find him a new wife, but he told Wellenkamp, 'When people come bringing women here, I don't accept them. I refuse them! Because . . . I think within my heart, I imagine in my eyes or in my heart, that my wife is probably within the house' (1991, p.132).

Within (and sometimes straddling) the two hundred or so countries of the world are thousands of distinctly different societies, each unique in culture, language, religion and much else. Consisting of anything from a few hundred people to millions, there are thousands of societies, like the Toraja, partially or entirely outside of the major religious traditions.

Within almost any nation state there is considerable cultural diversity. For example, one might think of Mexico as Catholic and monocultural, but it includes many smaller-scale societies that, although more or less linked to Mexican economy and society, are distinctly different from one another and from what can be taken as the dominant national culture of Mexico. Many people in each of those societies speak Spanish only as a second language or do not speak Spanish at all. They may, at home, speak Mam, Tzotzil, or some other indigenous language. Some will have little or no knowledge of Catholicism, and many who consider themselves more or less Catholic will practise a Catholicism blended with indigenous spiritual beliefs and practices. Similarly one could look at India, Indonesia, the Philippines, Nigeria, the United States and many other nation states and find in them an impressive array of societal groups.

The distinction between small-scale and other societies is artificial in many ways, but it is helpful in pointing the reader to the diversity of societies within national boundaries and the limits of knowledge about the great religious traditions in understanding the spiritual beliefs and practices of many people in the world. This chapter focuses on people from small-scale societies, generally those with a population under, say, 1,000,000 and typically with a population under 100,000. That such people exist in vast numbers and will be encountered by any practitioner who deals with culturally diverse clients is a key reason for a chapter like this.

For the practitioner, one consequence of this diversity is that knowing somebody is from a certain country may not be of help in identifying the person's native language or culture. One cannot presume, for example, that somebody who is a native of India speaks Hindi or English, is an adherent of any of the major religions, or understands and experiences grief like any other Indian one has ever met.

I don't know if a resident of Great Britain, the United States, or Canada will ever meet a Toraja, but one is likely to meet people from southeast Asia, Indonesia, Malaysia, Singapore and Melanesia who share some of the Toraja beliefs and values, for example, the value of emotional control. This chapter cannot teach the reader about the specifics of thousands of small-scale societies, but it can use examples from some of those societies to sensitize the reader to working with people from many of these societies. Indeed, one will probably never meet many people from any specific small-scale society. Nonetheless, one can make beginning preparations to be of help should the opportunity arise.

Should one defer to experts? In a geographic area with a large concentration of people who could be considered members of a given small-scale society there may be some psychologist, nurse or physician who is considered an expert on dealing with people from that society. (For example, in my own metropolitan area there are a few health care providers considered expert at dealing with the Hmong, who have come from southeast Asia. and with their American-born children and grandchildren). But often there is no expert, or the person who is defined as an expert may not be available or may not be expert at what one must deal with. So expecting to rely on experts is often a mistake.

Expertise in dealing with someone from another society is always qualified by the limits of one's experience and knowledge. Even if one has dealt a number of times with bereaved people from a given small-scale society, one cannot presume that one's experience will help in understanding the next bereaved person from that society. Many societies are internally diverse, with various people following very different traditions and having very different understandings of death. Moreover, quite a few people in the world function with a mix of cultural traditions. For example, a Toraja may be Christian but may also maintain indigenous ways that are distinctly not Christian (Adams, 1993).

Sometimes the blending of traditions does not pose a particular problem for a would-be helper. In the case of the Christian Toraja, for example, indigenous notions of soul and dreams are maintained in those areas in which Christianity says little, so the blending of approaches is not particularly in conflict (Adams, 1993). However, there are other instances of the blending of indigenous beliefs with major religious orientations where the indigenous beliefs are defined, by at least some local people, as directly opposed to the major religious orientation – for example, the blending in highland Ecuador of Catholicism with indigenous beliefs in deaths caused by envy, bewitching, evil spirits, or possession by devils (Crain, 1991). So dealing with the blend of traditions may be challenging for a would-be helper. However, many people who blend traditions expect to seek help from more than one source. Thus, one should not be surprised if a person seems fully open and available to the kinds of help one can provide and yet also turns to sources of help (for example, a spiritualist) that may seem at odds with what one is offering.

CULTURAL APPROACHES TO DEALING WITH DEATH

Each culture has its own approaches to dealing with loss. These may be more or less standardized but almost always involve a core of understandings, spiritual beliefs, rituals, expectations and etiquette. In many societies, the requirements for dealing with a major loss are played out over the entire lifetime of a survivor – for example, in rituals, what is worn, how one is addressed by others, and one's rights and obligations to participate in various community activities.

There are no pan-human categories for understanding death; how people think about death is everywhere culturally embedded. One reaction to finding that one's own categories do not fit the realities of others might be to consider their ways to be uneducated, misinformed, superstitious, less developed, or in some other way faulty. But such ethnocentrism is unhelpful. In trying to offer understanding and assistance to people from societies other than one's own, there is no justification for privileging one's own reality over that of the people one wants to understand and help. The more useful course is to become adept at learning, respecting and dealing with another person's reality, no matter how discrepant it is from one's own.

Defining death

For many people in Euro-American societies, a person is either dead or alive, but for people in many small-scale societies there may be an assortment of categories and gradations of dead. For example, in some societies a person may be grieved as dead whom most Britons would count as alive. In some societies a person may even participate in his or her own death rituals. On the other hand, in most societies, the person whom many British or American professionals might count as dead might still be considered to be a communicating, acting presence among the living.

In trying to understand how death might be defined as a series of stages or as ending in categories that still involve communication with the living, it is helpful to understand that for most people in many small-scale societies, death is a transition (Glascock and Braden, 1981). The transition takes time, may well involve the help of the survivors or survivors-to-be, and may involve a series of steps. In some cultures, the metaphors for the transition involve a long journey (and funeral rituals provide assistance with the journey, including providing the dying/dead with supplies for the journey). In other cultures the metaphor for transition might involve elevation to successively higher spiritual planes, stages of greater integration into a spiritual world, or stages in moving towards physical and emotional distance from the living. It is also helpful to note that in most, if not all, small-scale societies death is not a transition to nothingness but to some other state (Glascock and Braden, 1981). In many cases, people understand that the deceased will continue to have an impact on the living and continue to communicate with the living. Whether as nearby spirit, god, benevolent presence or sorrowing entity trying to bring the closest survivors along on the trip to another world, the deceased can be understood as real and potentially or actually present.

Death rituals

In many societies, death rituals are far more elaborate and are extended over quite a bit more time than is common in Euro-American societies. The rituals occurring at the time of what Westerners might call physical death may last for days, weeks, months or years. They may require isolation of the bereaved, the wearing of special mourning clothing or special markings, and may require actions that seem to some outsiders to be pointlessly destructive or unpleasant – for example, tearing one's clothing, not bathing, tearing at one's skin, beating oneself or shaving one's head. In quite a few societies, the rituals for dealing with a death are spread out in a series of ceremonies that span months or even years. For example, there may be a ceremony at each transition of the deceased to a more distant, higher, more completely dead state; there may be death ceremonies on the anniversary of the death; and there may be an unearthing and reburial of the remains of the deceased months or years after the physical death. Often there is a final funeral ceremony (Rosenblatt, Walsh and Jackson, 1976) marking the end of mourning, the transition of the central mourners into new statuses and roles, and perhaps marking the transition of the deceased to a final state.

Westerners who are accustomed to a single funeral ceremony may not appreciate that the additional rituals that are common in small-scale societies are likely to have enormous religious, social and personal significance for the survivors and may be necessary to help the deceased, to guard against harm from the deceased, to heal and alter the relationships of the living and for many other reasons. People outside a culture may fail to appreciate the ritual activities that are necessary – whether it be loud wailing, angry inquisitions, ways of handling and dealing with the remains (for example, recurrent wrapping and unwrapping of the decomposing body), animal sacrifices, destroying the property of the deceased, requiring a newly widowed person to marry a person community authorities have selected for him or her, tearing clothing, falling into a stupor, or something else outside the experience of sense of decorum of many in the Euro-American world.

A person from a society with elaborate death rituals who is resident, say, in England or the United States may lack institutional support for engaging in necessary death rituals. Employers and school officials may not tolerate long or recurrent absences to engage in the proper practices. There may be no tolerance of special dress, of shaving the head, of self-mutilation, cessation of bathing and the like. Those outside the mourner's culture are not likely to know what to say or do. If anything, there may be attempts to mute or entirely stop practices that seem alien. In the society at large there may be no tolerance for certain rituals. For example, community authorities and neighbours may not tolerate destroying the property of the deceased, animal sacrifices, laying out the deceased at home for days or weeks following the death, or loud and continual wailing. One might think that all that is necessary to support a bereaved person from another society is to say the right words, but there may need to be enormous change in the society as a whole to provide that bereaved person with what is needed.

Rituals can be understood in many different ways. Often a key to them seems to be that they define. They define the death, the cause of death, the dead person, the bereaved, the relationships of the bereaved with one another and with others, the meaning of life, and major societal values. Not engaging in rituals or having them shortened or undermined can leave people at sea about how the death occurred, who or what the deceased is, how to relate to others, how to think of self and much more.

Modern medicine defines the cause of the death and in doing so provides a sort of death ritual. The bereaved from a small-scale society may have their own ways of defining the cause of death. To take one example, Brison (1992) has provided a description of elaborate inquests carried out by the Kwanga of Papua New Guinea. Some Kwanga are Christian, but even many Christian Kwanga, who are committed to rejecting the sorcery system that is so often thought to be a cause of death, participate in community inquests, accepting the reality of sorcery and realizing that they could be suspected of engaging in sorcery.

Ritual specialists

Some small-scale societies have no ritual specialists who deal with a death. However, many adults in such societies may know how to deal ritually and spiritually with a death. There are many other small-scale societies in which ritual specialists, people with special information, skills, power, rights, etc., have a part in or lead in carrying out the death rituals. To a Western physician, clergy person, or other Western 'ritual specialist', a ritual specialist from another culture may seem to be a competitor in the rituals of dealing with death. For example, a ritual specialist from another society may want to engage in tense discussion about who might have been responsible for the death or may want to inspect the body for meaningful signs. Such activities may seem bizarre, inappropriate and offensive to a Western ritual specialist. A ritual specialist from a small-scale society may also seem to be unworthy of respect by the standards applied to Euro-American ritual specialists. For example, a ritual specialist from another society may seem to be uneducated, may speak English badly or not at all, may be dressed shabbily or outlandishly by the standards of a Westerner, and may say and do things that do not fit the reality of most Westerners. Yet the Westerner's reality and rituals are no more universal or deserving of respect. There are no worldwide standards for determining whose view of how to deal with death is most valid. Moreover, if one wants to be supportive of the bereaved, one must value their reality, including their ways of understanding and making use of their own specialists.

Another reason to appreciate and value ritual specialists from another society is to realize that people from that other society bring to Western ritual specialists their respect, fear, etc. learned in dealing with their own ritual specialists. A person from another culture who has learned to be silent and patient in dealing with familiar ritual specialists will bring those dispositions to an encounter with a nurse, physician, hospital social worker, etc. from Western culture. The person will also bring expectations. For example, if ritual specialists in the person's own society never ask a bereaved person questions or never expect payment, there may be difficulty for the bereaved when a Western specialist asks questions or expects payment.

People are not necessarily knowledgeable about their own culture, particularly in areas in which ritual specialists work. Thus, a bereaved person from a culture that uses ritual specialists to deal with death may not be able to say much about death rituals or their meanings in his or her own culture (for example, see Hill, 1992, writing about the knowledge Chinese immigrants to Thailand have of their own funeral rituals). Thus, a person whose coping with death requires the help of ritual specialists may be particularly distraught and confused when dealing with a death without the help of an appropriate specialist.

Emotional expression and control

In many cultures, at least some people cry when a death occurs (women more often than men in the majority of cultures). Anger and aggressive verbal or physical attacks are less common than crying, cross-culturally, but still occur in a significant number of cultures (by men more often than women in the majority of cultures where anger and aggression are cultural patterns at a death). There are cultures where self-mutilation is part of the emotional expression at a death, and cultures where catatonic immobility is common. There are, however, no emotions or emotional expressions that are universally present at death. Even within cultures where there is a great deal of patterning to emotional expression in bereavement, some people will not follow the pattern.

What emotions are felt, how they are expressed, and how they are understood are matters of culture. Moreover, the distinction many Westerners draw between feeling and thought is also a matter of culture. It is clear from anthropological research in various cultures that emotions might better be called matters of feeling/thought than matters of feeling (see, for example, Wikan, 1990, writing about Bali, and Lutz, 1985, writing about Ifaluk of Micronesia).

Variations among cultures in defining a death may be understood as, in part, variations in cultural approaches to defining the meaning and cause of the death. Defining a death as a gift of the gods or as God's bringing the deceased to a glorious and peaceful place at God's right hand may be understood as, among other things, an approach to making the emotions of bereavement more upbeat. In another culture, a death may be understood as the result of somebody's malevolent act. Even a death that a Westerner might see as not caused by anyone else – say, a cancer death or a death due to an accidental fall – may be understood as caused by someone, for example someone who may have cursed the deceased from a distance. In cultures where deaths are seen as caused by others, the emotions of grief may include a great deal of rage, determination to identify the attacker and desire for revenge. Almost any feeling imaginable may be a part of grief in some culture.

English-language emotion words like 'grief', 'anger', 'sadness' and 'crying' do not necessarily translate well into the language of another culture, nor do the emotion terms that describe typical reactions to loss in another culture necessarily translate well into English. Lutz (1985), for example, talks about the concept of *lalomweiu* on the atoll of Ifaluk. *Lalomweiu* is a loneliness/sadness that involves, among other things, excessive thinking/feeling about a person who, because of separation or death, is missing. It is an emotion expressed in part through the disruption of other social ties – for example, not paying attention to others while they are talking. In children, *lalomweiu* can lead to illness. Another Ifaluk emotion term that is used a great deal when a loss has occurred is *fago*, which is a blend of compassion, love and sadness.

The grief of someone from a culture where the emotions of bereavement are quite different from those in one's own culture may seem insincere or artificial, or may seem to result from a failure to understand what death really is. A Westerner may have trouble understanding and accepting a grief heavily laden with joking and laughter, murderous rage, wailing and lamentation that go on for months, or mute unresponsiveness. However, for the bereaved, the expression of emotions may be totally sincere and heartfelt, may fit what that person understands about death and grief, and is likely to be for that person the most desirable way to act.

I know of no society in which the emotions of bereavement are not shaped and controlled, for the sake of the deceased, the bereaved person or others. If one does not know the cultural background of a person who is making efforts to control emotions in ways that seem foreign by the standards of one's own culture, one may assume that one is seeing the expression of an individual personality or individual psychological problem. However, it is best not to separate individual from culture. For example, a Toraja may work hard to avoid a hot or choked emotional state because such a state is a violation of customary practices and may be punished by the ancestors or the spirits with illness, misfortune or even death (Hollan, 1992; Wellenkamp, 1988). As Hollan says, feeling such emotions a Toraja is likely also to feel confused and dizzy and may faint or experience episodes of depersonalization; thus, a Toraja is likely to engage in various strategies for avoiding strong emotion. Hollan distinguishes self-directed emotional control strategies (for example, reminding oneself of the dangers of strong emotion or consciously suppressing certain thoughts) from other-directed strategies (for example, speaking politely and respectfully to a person who might otherwise be upset). Imagine the trouble a well-intentioned but ignorant Western psychiatrist or clergy person might make for a Toraja grieving someone accidentally killed by another. Although the Toraja have an indigenous concept of grief catharsis (Wellenkamp, 1988), encouragement to express feelings may be seen by a Toraja as an invitation to disaster and an impolite failure to help with emotional control. But for the Westerner, the Toraja's suppression of thoughts and distancing of feelings may seem pathological.

'Religious' beliefs

It is a mistake to assume that any category from one's own culture applies neatly to several thousand other cultures. The Western category of 'religion' may be inappropriate to apply to the beliefs and actions that people in other societies display at the time of a death, during funeral rituals, or when referring to the deceased or the spirit of the deceased. In various cultures 'religion' may blur into what a Westerner might call 'science', 'health care', 'preventive medicine', 'farming', 'law', 'art', 'music', 'poetry', or something else. But let us say, for the sake of advancing this discussion, that we can determine for a society a set of commonly held beliefs about the nature of the world and the relationships of the living with the dead that is in some sense like what many in the English-speaking world call 'religion'. One thing we almost certainly can expect to learn about the 'religious' beliefs and practices of another society is that there are beliefs in the spirits of the dead. Almost all societies have such beliefs (Rosenblatt, Walsh and Jackson, 1976). In quite a few cultures the spirits of the dead are thought to act in the world of the living, communicate with the living, and are present (more so shortly after the death than later) in the world of the living. Thus, for many people in the world death does not end relationships. Even in the United States, many people experience what might be called 'sense of presence', a sense that somebody who was close to one and who has died is in contact with one. Thus, one should not be surprised if someone reports interactions with the deceased.

Types of death

In many cultures different kinds of deaths are understood differently and dealt with differently. The meaning of death, the rituals called for, the emotions felt, the extent to which others are involved, how the body is to be disposed of, and one's ultimate relationship with the deceased may vary depending on such factors as whether a death is a suicide, a drowning, the death of a child, a miscarriage, a woman's death versus a man's, a death in childbirth, a violent death, a death far from home, a death in the house versus outside, whether the deceased is a parent or grandparent, or whether the deceased had reached a specific ritual status. Thus, even if one knows something about how a 'typical' death is dealt with in a society, for example, how the death of the Toraja woman Indo'na Doko was dealt with, one may not be prepared to understand what is going on when some other kind of death occurs in that society.

As an illustration of factors that vary with the type of death, consider how the Shona of Zimbabwe understand and deal with the death of a child (Folta and Deck, 1988). Though many Shona belong to a Christian denomination, their understanding of a child's death may hinge on traditional beliefs. A child's death may result from diagnosed diseases such as measles, 'natural' causes as Shona understand them (for example problems with specific organs), failure to follow the proper birth rituals, incorrect burials following previous deaths in the family, the anger of a spirit from a clan other than one's own, witchcraft (often by jealous people close to the child's mother), or parental breaking of taboos (for example, adultery by the child's mother). Shona mothers may try religious, modern medical, and ethnomedical approaches in hopes of preventing a child death. The death of a young child is not dealt with as the death of an older child or an adult would be. A mother will be prevented from grieving extensively if the child was very young and from holding a public funeral. But the mother will still be likely to experience grief and to cry (at least privately or silently). A mother might be angry with God or the child, or may perceive that someone is at fault and be preoccupied with how to take revenge against that person. Some women are blamed by husband or in-laws and some blame themselves. The valuing of fertility and the problems of being seen as an outsider by husband and in-laws may lead to physical abuse, distancing by in-laws and husband, or to divorce. The grief that is unacknowledged may lead the woman to work less at chores her husband and in-laws expect her to carry out, and this too may lead to abuse, distancing and divorce.

Generational differences

It is not uncommon for there to be marked generational differences in dealing with death. Where there are generational differences, typically it is the older generation that seems more observant of the rituals and more dedicated to the cultural meanings and emotional forms that have been dominant in the culture. Perhaps that is especially so in immigrant communities. The younger generation may have been strongly influenced, for example, by schooling in the new country, employment, age peers from other cultures, and contact with television, to assimilate 'modern' ways. The younger generation may also have been deprived of exposure to activities, rituals and much else that would lead them to be adherents of the ways of their elders.

An outsider who wants to understand and help people from a small-scale society must be sensitive to the possibility of different needs, expectations, standards and practices in different generations. Thus, what is appropriate in dealing with an elderly Hmong-American may not be appropriate in dealing with a young Hmong-American. Another thing to keep in mind is that often one's informants about a culture and one's translators are younger people, people who have had a chance to become bilingual and, perhaps, bicultural. Younger informants may not know or understand some of what a member of the older generation may say or experience, or may choose to censor some of what they fear might seem to an outsider to be outlandish. On the other hand, a younger person who seems to be relatively Westernized in dress, language and the etiquette outsiders expect may actually be as fully traditional as an older person when it comes to dealing with a death.

The cultural embeddedness of ways of dealing with death

Cultural approaches to dealing with death are embedded in larger and well articulated aspects of culture and society. For example, for the highland Ecuadorean peasants studied by Crain (1991), beliefs about the cause of death were connected to relations with land owners and officials of development agencies, differential integration of men and women into wage labour and speaking Spanish, the uses of modern medicine and Catholicism as political forces, and traditional patterns of exchange in the community. Beliefs and practices concerning death should thus not be thought of as matters of taste but as vitally connected to much in a person's life. To understand cultural ways of dealing with death fully may require extensive knowledge of the culture's history, economics, politics, social class system, residence patterns and much more. Even the hybrid beliefs that many people hold, for example blending indigenous notions about grieving with beliefs from a great religious tradition, should be understood in this light. The hybrid beliefs may reflect ongoing political and social processes, for example conflict between forces connected to the two traditions.

Another aspect of the cultural embeddedness of ways of dealing with death is that cultures vary in who has the right or obligation to grieve, who is defined as the principal mourner, and who is seen as experiencing the most loss with a given death. One cannot, for example, assume that a new widow or widower feels the rights, obligations or feelings of a principal mourner for a deceased spouse. One cannot assume that the person who is wailing most loudly or supported most attentively by others from her or his culture is a close relative of the deceased. For example, Toraja may grieve intensely at a funeral for someone who was not close to them, either out of sympathy for the principal mourners or because the death reminds them of their own major losses (Wellenkamp, 1988).

TYPES OF SMALL-SCALE SOCIETIES

It is tempting to try to come to terms with the plethora of small-scale societies by classifying them. Indeed, from a distance an outsider interested in how societies deal with death might feel justified in classifying societies as animistic, fetishist or the like. Such classification might be useful in helping an outsider see that there is a logic to how a people deal with a death. However, the classification risks creating a barrier between the outsider and the people of the culture of interest. It seems more helpful to assume that whatever a people does has meaning and value to them and then to try to understand it as they understand it. In a sense, the crucial task of an outsider who wants to be of help is to understand the cultural realities of the bereaved, not to fit what they do into a framework that makes sense in terms of the outsider's culture.

THE MEANINGS OF 'WESTERN' APPROACHES TO DEALING WITH LOSS

For a Euro-American practitioner, there are standard ways of supporting bereaved people that are as much culturally embedded as the ways the bereaved people of an exotic culture grieve. It is risky to assume that the supporting actions that are commonly used in Euro-American societies are appropriate in dealing with people from another culture.

Talking

A standard way of dealing in the West with grief is to talk. Therapists, nurses, clergy, etc., ask the bereaved to talk and offer them listening and talk. Talk about a death, one's feelings, or one's past relationship with the deceased is appropriate for some people from some cultures. But for others, talk of certain kinds is inappropriate. For example, talk may disrupt one's hard-won efforts to feel what is appropriate in one's culture, and disrupting those feelings may be perceived as risking one's health or safety. In some cultures talk is acceptable, but one must never mention the name of the deceased – perhaps because it makes it likely that the spirit of the deceased will return to bring one to the world of the dead. In such cultures, there must be careful circumlocution in order to avoid mentioning the name of the deceased. In some cultures talk is acceptable as long as it does not focus on oneself. The possibilities are innumerable. A would-be helper needs to know what sort of talk, if any, is appropriate for a person from a culture the helper does not know well. In fact, even in the West there are many who do not readily talk about loss and grief. Although a practitioner might consider such a person to be in trouble, defining the seeming resistance to talk as pathological or a potential source of pathology, that way of understanding those who do not talk is open to question (Stroebe, Gergen, Gergen and Stroebe, 1992).

Another aspect of cultural differences in talk is that what is important about life, death and grieving differs markedly from culture to culture. The issues that are discussed and the metaphors that come up may be foreign to a Westerner but entirely appropriate in the bereaved person's own culture. For example, a Toraja would care intensely about what a death means for the practice of smoke ascending and smoke descending rituals (Wellenkamp, 1991). In a sense, death rituals, including eulogies and ritual lamentations, point to and create the realities that people will discuss when talking about a death. A helpful outsider would do well to respect those realities. For example, in trying to help a Toraja, one might do well to understand what smoke ascending and smoke descending rituals are and why those are matters of importance.

Treating 'grief pathologies'

Many Westerners who work at helping the bereaved have notions of grief pathology – for example, grief that is never expressed, grief that goes on too intensely for too long, grief that is delayed, grief that involves delusions, grief that involves threats to others, grief that involves self-injury. One may think of grief as a human universal and grief pathologies as also universal, but the reality is that grief is quite different from culture to culture. So what, if anything, is considered a grief pathology differs widely from culture to culture. A mother in the slums of Cairo, Egypt, locked for seven years in the depths of a deep depression over the death of a child is not behaving pathologically by the standards of her community (Wikan, 1980). A bereaved Balinese who seemingly laughs off a death is also behaving appropriately by the standards of her culture (Wikan, 1990). Similarly, in another society a person who is possessed by the spirits of the dead may be in line with what is entirely understandable and quite common in bereavement in her own society.

This is not to say that grief pathology is solely a notion of Western psychology. There are indigenous notions of grief pathology in many small-scale societies, and along with those notions, indigenous notions of treatment. For example, in some areas of Mexico or Central America a death may cause *susto*, a soul loss due to magical fright, which Houghton and Boersma (1988) argue produces symptoms quite like the classic symptoms of grief described by Parkes (1972). In cultures where *susto* is a familiar affliction, there are cultural ways of helping the *susto* patient. As Houghton and Boersma indicate, the ways may focus on restoring the departed spirit, but some of the actions may not be so different from those of a Euro-American grief counsellor. Wellenkamp (1988) recounts an instance where Toraja village leaders were willing to violate a rule about holding certain memorial services in order to help a bereaved mother whom they feared would experience a not 'satisfied/content' heart and might die of grief. As Wellenkamp asserts, the Toraja have clear notions of pathological grief, including the dangers of not crying after the loss of someone close to one or of a grief that goes on too intensely beyond the initial funeral. Among the Toraja, pathological grief is thought to produce both illness and distracting thoughts that block one from dealing with important responsibilities.

I have heard therapists, physicians and nurses in the United States assert that now that someone is a resident of the country that person should behave in ways that fit the country. Typically, I think, what is meant is that the newcomer should behave according to the culture of the speaker, not according to any of the hundreds of other cultures that can be found in the United States. Although I am not opposed to someone changing beliefs and practices to fit into a new country of residence, I think it is not usually helpful to expect someone who might need help to fit one's own culture, and to judge pathology based on one's own cultural standards. It makes much better sense to try to accept and even appreciate the person's own cultural beliefs and practices and to provide help that makes sense within that framework.

GRIEVING IN AN ALIEN WORLD

There may have been a time when almost anyone could grieve in a monocultural community, a community where everyone the person met understood things the same way and had similar ideas of how to deal with a death. That time, if it ever existed, is in the past. Hundreds of millions of people have been forced to flee their homelands or have been driven to multicultural cities by economic forces, war, government terrorism, overpopulation, the actions of colonial powers and a host of other factors. Nowadays bereaved people often grieve where many around them do not grieve their way and do not understand (or perhaps even respect) what they understand. This means that many around one cannot be of much help, cannot do what in one's rituals others are supposed to do, do not know the etiquette for dealing with one's grief, and may not even be able to speak a language one can understand. Moreover, the same processes that caused one to move among strangers may have robbed one of contact with many of the friends, relatives and community members who, in one's home community, would have helped one carry out the rituals and would know the proper ways to deal with and support one's grief. Ritual specialists and members of one's family may have been scattered by the same economic and political forces that drove one away from one's home community or may have been killed in warfare or government-sponsored exterminations. All that may make grieving a lonely endeavour. It also may mean that one's grief for a specific death may be tangled in grieving for all one's other losses (see, for example, Boehnlein, 1987, writing about Cambodian refugees whose religious grounding is typically a mix of Buddhism and folk religion). A practitioner must be alert to these complexities and provide help that is responsive to them. For example, to support a Timorese grieving for a child who just died, one must also be attuned to the genocidal forces that have devastated eastern Timor.

Barriers to performing the appropriate rituals

If proper grieving involves engaging in certain rituals and being able to feel, think, and do certain things in a social environment that supports those endeavours, being in an alien social environment can be very difficult for the bereaved. Part of the problem is the absence of people. Many Westerners think of grieving as an individual action, and much of grief therapy is individually focused. Yet the mourning rituals of many societies are complex, elaborate, spread out over months or years, and generally require collective participation. Often a mourner must interact with specific others in specific ways – for example, patterned wailing with others or exchanges with specific kin of the deceased. Outside the public rituals, there may be more private observations of mourning that, again, require others. For example, in some cultures in which the most bereaved persons are isolated from others for long periods of time, there is a culturally patterned dependency on others for help in acquiring drinking water, food, firewood and the like. No amount of words exchanged with a therapist may suffice to substitute for absent partners in carrying out mourning customs.

Moreover, proper grieving may require things as well as people, and those things may not be available when one is away from one's home community. Mourning may require foods, species of flowers, or other objects not available in one's new location. The rituals may also require contact with the soil of one's home community or with specific geographic locations in or near that community. If, for example, one cannot visit the graveyard of the ancestors or use a pot of soil from the home fields of the deceased, the death rituals in which one engages may feel hollow and one may feel sad, frightened, or embarrassed that one cannot do the right thing for the deceased (or to defend against them if failure to follow the appropriate rituals makes the spirits of the dead dangerous).

For a person living far from home, a death can set off grief for deaths that occurred at the time the person was driven from his/her homeland, for the home left behind, for a lost way of life, for a time when his/her language was the only language the person could hear, or for other things related to leaving. Consequently, one of the barriers to performing appropriate rituals in a new homeland is that one may feel overwhelmed by the totality of one's losses. In a sense, the problem may be that one scarcely knows what to grieve or may lack rituals to deal with the bitter losses of war, of government-sponsored 'disappearances', of expropriation of farmland, etc., that led to one's needing to move.

Poverty

Often a bereaved person from a small-scale society is economically much poorer than the professionals who might offer help. Some practitioners may feel that a person and the person's culture are to blame for the person's poverty. But being born into poverty, especially a poverty that is driven by national and international political and economic forces, makes escape into middle-class affluence very difficult. It is important for a practitioner who wants to be helpful not to be blocked by prejudices related to economic differences.

Poverty can also be an issue when the bereaved make efforts to deal with their loss in ways that make sense to them culturally, socially and religiously. Lack of economic resources may block the bereaved from doing certain things – for example, carrying out necessary rituals, travelling to be with other family members or to a place of special spiritual importance, or disposing of property that customarily would be given away, abandoned or destroyed during proper mourning.

Large wealth differences can also create confusion about the limits of help. When a would-be helper has far more economic resources than a person who is bereaved, what are the appropriate limits in providing help? If I am willing to listen to a bereaved person and to say kind words, why should I not also be willing to give money for a necessary animal sacrifice or for airfare back home. The issue is complicated by cultural differences. Such expenditures of money, especially for a stranger, may be out of the question in my own culture but may be entirely appropriate in the culture of the person to whom I am offering emotional support.

The multiple reality problem

Living where there is more than one understanding of death, grief, the spiritual world, and the proper rituals can be debilitating. It is easier to believe the proper beliefs, follow the proper rituals and feel the proper feelings when everyone agrees that they are proper. But living where different people have different beliefs, rituals and feelings, doing what is appropriate by the standards of one's culture of origin may be difficult. Instead of the familiar ways of acting and feeling being right, being expected by all around one, and being demanded by the spirits, they are just a few of many possibilities and may seem no more justifiable than doing something very different. Perhaps that is part of why so many people are multicultural. Perhaps too that means that some people have a 'pathology' of grieving that comes with questioning their culture of origin and realizing that many other ways are valid. Such people may feel paralysed and engage in nothing or they may engage half-heartedly in a given set of rituals. Their alienation may mean that they remain stuck in a kind of grief limbo. For them, someone may help, even someone who does not know their culture at all well, by legitimating investment in a specific culturally based set of rituals and expression, with full investment, of emotions that are appropriate by the standards of one of their cultures.

GUIDELINES FOR OUTSIDERS

What is an outsider to do in trying to help? Perhaps the first step is not to stereotype. One can know things about the other's culture, know that certain beliefs and practices are common, but one should not assume that all people who come from that culture are alike. One's knowledge can be an asset. Knowing that people from a given culture believe that the spirit of a deceased person is linked to personal possessions of the deceased or that the spirit is dangerous to people the person loved while alive may be helpful. But one must not assume that everyone from that culture holds those beliefs.

Dealing with one's own ethnocentrism is not a simple matter. It is perfectly human to have a visceral reaction to, say, a bereaved Toraja who covers her head with a cloth as she wails loudly. It is also easy to assume that people who are expressing feelings in ways that are foreign to one are not feeling genuine feelings. However, the concepts of authenticity and inauthenticity are themselves cultural constructs, and even if those concepts have some sort of meaning in the small-scale society of a person one wants to help, they may be much more important in Euro-American cultures than in some other cultures (Rosaldo, 1984). So the emotional expression and action of someone in another culture might be judged in that person's own culture by standards very different from those having to do with authenticity. Moreover, the markers for authenticity in Western cultures might mislead one about the grieving of someone from another culture. For example, in the West an abrupt transition in emotional expression – for example, from deep grief to cheerfulness – discredits the prior emotion. However, in other cultures the definition of emotions, the ways people learn to express emotions, and their ideology about grieving may make the abrupt transition easy, necessary and perfectly authentic. Nor does the fact that someone's grieving is channelled by culture mean anything about whether that grieving is genuine. It probably is best for one to suppress feelings that another's expression of grief is inauthentic and to accept it as authentic.

In dealing with one's own ethnocentrism, plausible explanations of what others do can be helpful. Learning that what people from another culture do makes sense to them and fits their culture may make it easier for an outsider to accept what they do and believe. However, it is important to remember that the concept of 'help' comes out of Euro-American cultures. To the extent that we only offer what we consider help and make no effort to understand what the person we want to help would want from us, we may not be of much help.

The practitioners I know who are most successful in dealing with people from a culture very different from their own are generally specialists in dealing with a specific culture. Through many practice encounters, through reading, through international travel, through participation in local rituals, through language learning, and much else, they have become expert in how to help people in a specific other culture. They have also become brokers, interpreters and 'bridges' between their own culture and this other culture, working with physicians, nurses, psychologists, police, funeral directors, social workers and others.

The 'generalists' I know, people who are good at working with a diversity of cultures, are good at learning, good at findings others who can help them, good at avoiding ethnocentrism, comfortable working with social and practice standards different from the ones that would be 'right' in their own culture. In a sense, one of their great strengths is not that they know what to do but that they know how to find people who can help them to know what to do, that they know how to seek help, and that they know how to evaluate the advice they get and to learn quickly from a mistake.

It is often of great value for an outsider who would like to be of help to say and do things that are appropriate in the culture of the other. For example, it may be appropriate and even necessary that one not cross one's legs during a ritual or not touch a person who is experiencing spirit possession. However, often an outsider is not expected to engage in what insiders do and risks offending by offering an inauthentic version of the insider actions. It may help immensely to have competence in the language of the bereaved person, to know things about that person's culture, and to be open to being a learner, but often what is most helpful is to be authentically human. At times, a genuine and caring offer of sympathy, shared tears, or a hug has more meaning than stilted efforts to try to act like people in the other person's culture. This chapter advocates sincere and determined openness to the cultural realities of others, but it also is supportive of efforts that are authentic and caring in cultural idioms that are distant from the culture of the bereaved.

LESSONS TO BE LEARNED FROM OTHER CULTURES

One can find, in the ways many small-scale societies deal with grief, valuable lessons for Euro-American societies. For example, societies with final funeral ceremonies occurring months or years after an initial funeral ceremony may do relatively well at preventing interminable intense grieving (Rosenblatt, Walsh and Jackson, 1976). Societies in which there is a clearly defined etiquette for people to follow in dealing with a bereaved person may have few problems with the feelings of being abandoned that many bereaved Americans report. The possibilities for useful reform at the cultural level seem numerous, but they also would be hard to engineer.

As a helper, one can find wisdom and good ideas in the rituals and beliefs of cultures other than one's own. In working with a bereaved person from another culture, it may be enormously helpful to promote the person's participation in the death rituals of her or his own society. The person may simply need encouragement, but the person may also need help finding people from her or his own culture who are knowledgeable about death rituals or who have the materials (prayer books, ritual clothing, special foods, etc.) that may be necessary to carry out the rituals properly.

Sometimes it is even helpful to bring in knowledge from a culture different from one's own and from the culture of the person one hopes to help. For example, if a bereaved person wants to honour a dead parent but lacks the resources or knowledge to do it properly by the standards of her or his own culture, it may be inspiring to learn how people in some other culture accomplish such honouring.

Death rituals and beliefs from any society can be used as a metaphor to help oneself or others to come to terms with a death. For example, knowing something about how much love and care people in some societies demonstrate in dealing, over the years, with the remains of a deceased loved one may help to make cemetery visits more meaningful. Or knowing how many cultures require mourners to be in seclusion, helped by others to accomplish basic everyday living tasks, may make it more comfortable for someone who is bereaved to ask others for help. From this perspective, whether or not one will ever actually have to deal with bereaved people from a given small-scale society, one may still find it personally useful and useful in helping others to know the specifics of death rituals and beliefs from a given society. That knowledge will help one to see alternative solutions to common problems in bereavement and to find new paths for thinking about how to come to terms with a loss.

SUMMARY

- ☐ There is a very great number of small-scale societies having a wide range of beliefs and religious practices.
- ☐ Knowing somebody is from a certain country may not help us to understand how they experience grief.
- ☐ Often there is no expert available to help us to understand a particular culture.
- ☐ Many people who blend traditions expect to seek help from more than one source.

- ☐ Each culture has its own approaches to dealing with loss.
- ☐ There are no pan-human categories for understanding death.
- ☐ We must become adept at learning, respecting and dealing with death and loss from the perspective of the other person's view of reality rather than our own.
- ☐ For most people in small-scale societies death is a transition or journey which takes time and may require a series of steps on the way to some other state. During this journey the deceased are often assumed to continue to communicate with the living.
- ☐ In many societies, death rituals are far more elaborate and protracted than those common in Euro-American societies. They may require actions that seem to outsiders to be pointless, destructive or unpleasant.
- ☐ Often there is a final funeral ceremony marking the end of mourning, the transition of the mourners into new statuses and roles, and the entry of the deceased into a final state. This may have enormous religious, social and personal significance to the bereaved.
- ☐ Immigrants from these cultures may lack institutional support for engaging in necessary rituals particularly from employers and school officials. Sometimes deliberate attempts may be made to stop practices which are seen as abhorrent.
- ☐ Rituals define the death, the cause of death, the dead person, the bereaved, the relationship between the bereaved and others, the meaning of life and major societal values. Failure to undertake them in full may leave people confused about all of these.
- ☐ Some small-scale societies have no ritual specialists. Those that do may find their ritual specialist undervalued or treated as a competitor by the ritual specialists of the host country.
- ☐ Support to the bereaved includes respecting their ritual specialists.
- ☐ Persons from other cultures may expect to treat and be treated by our ritual specialists in the same way as they treat and are treated by their own. This may create problems.
- ☐ People are not necessarily knowledgeable about their own culture, particularly about the areas for which ritual specialists are needed.
- ☐ In many cultures some people (particularly women) cry when a death occurs. Anger and aggression are less common but widespread.
- ☐ There are no emotions that are universally present at death. What emotions are felt, how they are expressed, and how understood, are matters of culture.

☐ In cultures in which death is seen as caused by others, the emotions of grief may include a great deal of rage, attempts to identify the attacker and a desire for revenge.

☐ Words like grief, anger, sadness and crying do not necessarily translate well. Neither do the words used after bereavement in other cultures translate well into English.

☐ Emotions expressed by people from another culture may seem insincere or artificial and lead to unfair condemnation, denigration or attributions of sickness or personal deviance. It is best not to separate individual from culture.

☐ In other cultures 'religion' may blur into 'science', 'health care', 'preventive medicine', 'farming', 'art', 'law', 'music' or 'poetry'.

☐ Almost all societies believe in spirits of the dead. These are usually thought to be present, communicate and act in the world of the living. Thus, death does not end relationships.

☐ Different kinds of death give rise to different beliefs, emotions and rituals.

☐ It is not uncommon for there to be marked differences between generations in their ways of dealing with death. These need to be understood and sensitively handled by caregivers.

☐ Cultures vary respecting who has the right or obligation to grieve.

☐ Rather than imposing classificatory systems, it is more helpful to assume that whatever a person does has meaning and value to them and then to try and understand it as they do.

☐ It is risky to assume that the supporting actions commonly used to support bereaved people from Euro-American culture are appropriate to people from another culture. This includes what, if anything, it is appropriate to talk about after a death.

☐ There are indigenous notions of grief pathology in many small-scale societies and indigenous notions of treatment. But what, if anything, is regarded as pathological grief differs widely from culture to culture.

☐ We should try to accept and even appreciate other persons' cultural beliefs and practices and to provide help that makes sense within that framework.

☐ Immigrants may have lost their social support systems and their ritual specialists at a time when they have suffered many losses. Practitioners must be sensitive to these complexities and provide help that is responsive to them.

☐ Proper grieving usually involves other people and objects with whom the mourner must interact in specific ways. No amount of words with a therapist can replace such people and objects.

☐ Poverty may impair a person's ability to carry out proper rituals and may lead to rejection by or refusal of help by others.

☐ Immigrants may become alienated from their culture of origin and suffer from the lack of their traditional support systems when they experience a loss. It may help if we encourage them to engage in the rituals and express the emotions that are appropriate to their culture.

☐ Plausible explanations of what others do are helpful in dealing with our own ethnocentrism.

☐ Often outsiders are not expected to engage in what the insiders do and may cause offence if they offer an unauthentic version. A genuine and caring offer of sympathy, shared tears, or a hug may have more meaning than stilted efforts to act properly.

☐ Final funeral ceremonies may reduce the risk that mourning will become perpetual.

☐ Knowledge of the beliefs and rituals of small-scale societies may help us to find alternative solutions to common problems and new ways of thinking about loss.

Chapter 4

Death in a Hindu family

Pittu Laungani

This paper is concerned with understanding the beliefs, attitudes and values which Hindus (in India and those living abroad) in general have towards death and bereavement. We shall examine too the rites, rituals and ceremonies associated with death. To set the scene it is necessary to make a few assumptions.

Let us first assume that we are dealing with a high-caste Hindu family. Such an assumption prevents us from getting tiresomely involved in trying to distinguish between different sects and denominations within Hinduism. Having established a high-caste pattern we can then use this as a basis for comparison with other castes, sects and circumstances (particularly those that affect immigrants to other lands).

The second assumption is to invite the reader to undertake a sensitive and imaginative flight of fantasy. For the purposes of our discussion we shall imagine that a real death (in so far as one can imagine a real death) has occurred in a Hindu family in Bombay. The reader is transported to the bosom of the family, where he or she becomes privy – as a detached observer – to all that follows.

The third assumption is more a *caveat* than an assumption. It should be recognized that the major purpose of this paper is to discuss the issues surrounding death and bereavement in a Hindu family: it is not a paper on Hinduism. It therefore needs to be emphasized that only those aspects of Hinduism which are relevant to our understanding of death and bereavement will be discussed. For a comprehensive account of Hinduism, the reader is referred to, among others: Chaudhuri, 1979; De Riencourt, 1960; Radhakrishnan, 1923/1989; Stutley, 1985; Zimmer, 1989.

Mr Bishwanath Pandey has been ailing for some time. (Pandey, it should be noted, is a Brahmin surname. Brahmins, by virtue of their birth, are placed at the top of the caste-system; the three other castes below them in a hierarchical order are the Kshatriyas, the Vaishyas and the Sudras.) In the last three years his condition has deteriorated considerably, and it seems certain that he does not have long to live. His three sons and two daughters too have arrived at the same conclusion. Mrs Pandey, however, believes otherwise. She is unshaken in her belief in her husband's recovery. In keeping with ancient Hindu religious traditions, she undertakes severe fasts for the welfare of her husband. She is convinced that her prayers and her fasts will propitiate the gods, who will heed her pleas, intercede on her behalf, and restore her husband's failing health. A stream of astrologers, fakirs, pirs, sadhus, sooth-sayers, yogis, call upon her with increasing regularity, nurturing her pious hopes. Notwithstanding her own failing health, she spends long hours sitting by the family shrine, singing bhajans (devotional songs), reciting mantras (prayers) from the Vedas, and slokas (verses) from the holy texts, including the Gita.

It is Mrs Pandey's ardent wish that she should predecease her husband. The thought of living out the rest of her life as a widow with the consequent loss of status which widowhood brings upon Hindu women disturbs her intensely. Although convinced that she would be well looked after by her three sons, she would rather she died 'in the hands of her husband', who would then perform all expected funeral rites. Her belief concerning the eventual recovery of her husband has come to acquire the tenacity of faith. It is steadfast. It remains unassailed by unvoiced doubts which pervade the atmosphere of gloom in the house. Her children know that their father does not have long to live, but are unwilling and even unable to communicate the knowledge to their mother. The knowledge of their father's impending death does not make it any the easier for the family members at home to 'accept' the eventuality with equanimity. Although from time to time they try to talk about it, they merely skirt round the edges, referring to it in vague terms. None of them is really willing to envisage a life without their father, who has been the head of the family for over fifty years.

The eldest son, Vikram Pandey, is overwhelmed by the prospect of becoming the head of the family upon his father's demise. It is not a role into which one is initiated gradually. However, he takes the precaution of ordering vast supplies of provisions, including flour, ghee, rice, pulses and other essentials, which will be needed when the time comes. His sister, who lives in England with her husband and their three children has also been informed. She, in her turn, has made the necessary arrangements to fly out to Bombay at a moment's notice.

Their father is never left on his own in the hospital. During the day the room overflows with an unending stream of visitors who come to pay their respects. After visiting hours, the three sons take it in turn to spend the night in the hospital with their father. The private hospitals in India seldom baulk at the idea of relatives of patients staying the night in the hospital. If the patient's room is not large enough to accommodate another bed, the relatives spread mattresses and curl up on the wooden benches in the hospital corridors.

Muffled sounds reach your ears from each room as you walk along the corridor of the hospital: a passing trolley, the regular footsteps of nurses striding down the corridors, the occasional moans of a patient in pain or discomfort, the clatter of instruments, the bustle of visitors wandering in and out of rooms – each sound, with its own distinctive quality. Suddenly, without warning, you hear loud, shrieking wails from a room at the end of the corridor.

Mr Bishwanath Pandey has died. Surrounded by grieving relatives lies the frail and wasted body of the old gentleman – perhaps in his mid-seventies. The room is crowded with people of all ages, including a couple of children of not more than 6 to 8 years of age. Presently a young doctor arrives and takes control. He approaches the eldest son of the deceased and puts his arm around his shoulders in silent sympathy. No words are exchanged. Gradually the room falls silent. People wait expectantly. Vikram, the eldest son, has only a vague awareness that they are all waiting for him to decide what to do next. He has now become head of family, a role for which he has had no proper initiation.

Although the relatives – particularly the late Mr Pandey's wife – are reluctant to part from the deceased, they are persuaded to go home. Vikram is aware of the rules of the hospital. It is only after all the hospital bills have been settled in full that the hospital will issue a death certificate and finalize arrangements for the release of the body. This done, as dictated by custom, the body is brought home in an ambulance. It will remain at home until the funeral.

At home, there is now a reversal of roles and the women take charge of the altered domestic arrangements. They have already had their cleansing baths and changed into their funeral dresses, white saris. Most of them, in particular the widow, will wear funeral whites until at least the first death anniversary of Mr Pandey. In keeping with Hindu tradition, the glass bangles of the deceased's widow are broken, and the red 'sindoor' – the wedding mark – which she has worn on the centre parting in her hair since she first married, is wiped off, indicating an abrupt change in her status.

Strict attention is paid to the altered cooking arrangements which are now called for. Not all Hindus are strict vegetarians. During this period, however, great care is taken to observe a strict vegetarian diet at home and outside. Any cooked meat (including eggs) lying at home is either given away or discarded.

Sleeping arrangements in the household are radically altered also. Mattresses from all beds are removed and placed on the floor; everyone is expected to sleep on the floor for the twelve days of the funeral. Exceptions are made for the very old and the infirm.

A decision is taken regarding the place where the body, when it arrives from the hospital, will be kept, until the time of the funeral. This place is swept, cleaned and made ready for the purpose. Since the Pandeys come from an affluent background (in keeping with extended family norms, they all live together in a large house) the deceased's bedroom has been allocated for the purpose. When it arrives, the body will be placed, not on the bed, but, as dictated by ancient custom, on the floor.

The men are involved with other equally serious concerns. Copies of the obituary are drafted and sent out to newspapers. A list of relatives who live in Bombay and outside, and those who live abroad, is compiled. Where possible, the people concerned are informed by telephone.

A team of cooks and cleaners is hired for the entire twelve-day period. Their job will consist primarily of cooking, cleaning, and feeding all the funeral guests who will begin to arrive within the next day or two. Most of the close relatives will stay for the entire duration of the funeral ceremony, and some even longer.

The family decide to arrange a twelve-day religious ceremony at home. This involves a relay of priests staying at the house for all the days of the ceremony, reading from sacred texts, reciting holy verses from the Gita, and singing devotional songs of Kabir and Ravidas, to the accompaniment of music.

Although the Pandeys belong to the priest-caste themselves, they nonetheless have their own family priest. Mr Sharma has been with them for several decades, and attends to all their religious needs, ranging from births, christenings, casting of horoscopes, to engagements, marriages and, latterly, deaths. To supplement his variable income, Mr Sharma, like other priests, is also attached to the local temple in an advisory capacity. He is summoned, and upon his advice appropriate steps are taken to arrange the twelve-day religious ceremony, starting on the following morning.

It is expected that all the members of the family of the deceased, their neighbours, friends and relatives will participate in the prayer meetings, which are held twice a day, at sunrise and at sunset. For a person to participate in the prayer meetings it is obligatory for the person concerned to have performed his/her morning ablutions. One is expected to sit at a prayer meeting only when one is in a state of physical and spiritual purity.

Such is the close affinity between Hinduism and Sikhism that many Hindu families engage Sikh priests instead of Hindu priests for the entire duration of the ceremony. The Sikh priests read from their holy text, the Granth Sahib, recite poems from Hindu religious texts, preach sermons from the *Puranas*, sing a variety of devotional songs of Kabir, Mirabai, Surdas, and even of the well-known Muslim sufis, such as Shaikh Nizam ud-din Auliya of the famous Chisti order of Sufis, which still has a foothold in parts of North India. One cannot but feel spiritually uplifted by the harmonious confluence of Hinduism, Sikhism and Islam during the twelve days of grief and mourning.

From a financial point of view, it is obvious that a twelve-day religious ceremony at home can cripple a family of more than moderate means. But since a religious ceremony of such an extended period is seen as an act of supreme piety and ensures the repose of the departed soul, the families that can afford them seldom baulk at the extra expenses which such ceremonies entail. Those that cannot, may even borrow money in order to perform the act of piety, or are assisted by the members of their baradari (sub-community).

The household awakens before dawn the following day; there is work to be done. A curious sight meets the eyes in the courtyard. All the three sons of the late Mr Pandey are seated on wooden stools. They all sit bare-chested – their sacred thread suspended diagonally across their chest and shoulders – awaiting the clippers of the barber! It is customary for the sons and the grandsons of the departed father to have their heads completely shaved, with just a tuft of hair left on the crown, and so a barber has been summoned to shave the heads of all the three sons. Mr Vikram Pandey, although a 'Westernized' Indian, educated abroad and now in charge of a large engineering organization in Bombay, should willingly defer to the hallowed custom which calls for the offering of one's hair to the departed soul may be surprising.

All of them are having their hair cut *outside* the house. Barbers traditionally come from the lowest caste, the Sudras, and are not normally allowed into the homes of high-caste Hindus for fear of polluting the household by their entry. A state of spiritual pollution is undesirable and the affected family would be expected to engage in a complex set of religious rites and rituals to 'purify' their house once again.

As the day progresses, the courtyard is transformed into a communal kitchen. An army of cooks, cleaners, helpers has appropriated a large corner of the courtyard, where coal fires have been set up. One can see mountains of vegetables being washed, cut, chopped, diced, and cleaned, daal (lentils) being boiled in gigantic cauldrons, onions being fried, rice being washed, dough being kneaded – there is a great bustle of activity.

Soon, other workmen arrive. As instructed, they spread sheets and durri carpets on the floor in the courtyard, which will soon be turned into a large refectory, to feed all the funeral guests. Many of the guests have already started to arrive. The more affluent ones have flown; others, accompanied by their children, have come on the train. While the newly arrived children fight and befriend one another, the adults file upstairs into the house, to pay their respects to the members of the Pandey family, offer their condolences, and have a glimpse of the body, which arrived from the hospital in the early hours of the morning. The body lies on a sheet on the floor, and is covered by a thin white cotton sheet. The face, drained of all colour, and in *rigor*, remains uncovered.

The mourners who have just arrived sit cross-legged on the floor beside the body, their palms joined together, in silent prayer. Despite the overhead ceiling fan which whirs monotonously, the heat is quite overpowering. Some mourners fan themselves with newspapers, and in so doing disturb the flies that have settled on the deceased's uncovered face. A few cry openly, tears streaming down their faces. A few mumble prayers, reciting slokas from sacred religious texts. They all gaze at the inert body in intense sorrow. An elderly woman who, it turns out, is the sister of the deceased, and has only just arrived from Delhi, wails disconsolately until she is led away gently by the other members of the family. Occasionally, a child wanders into the room, and stands to watch. No one attempts to turn the child away. The child, bewildered and intimidated by the large group crowded in the room, scampers away.

After they have had their glimpse of the body, the mourners rise and leave the room, making room for the others awaiting their turn. On leaving the room the mourners split into two groups: the women congregate in one room, the men in another. Some wander down into the courtyard.

Presently, lunch is announced. It is served in relays: the children and the men are fed first. The mourners assemble in the courtyard. A canvas canopy has been erected – complete with fluorescent lights – as a temporary protection against the piercing heat of the afternoon sun. In the night, after all the guests have eaten their dinner, the canopied courtyard will be turned into a dormitory; bedding and mattresses will be unrolled, where most of the male members attending the funeral will retire for the night.

Vikram Pandey, along with his two younger brothers, all dressed in their white kurtas and dhotis, their heads shaven, their foreheads glistening in the dazzling sunlight, greet all their guests deferentially. The guests sit cross-legged on the durri carpets, in neat rows. The chief Brahmin cook, Maharaj as he is often called, beckons his army of attendants who, upon receiving his signal, walk along each row, ladling out the food from large metal containers onto the leaf-plates, placed in front of each guest. The attendants, some with pots of rice and daal, others with potatoes, cauliflower, and mixed vegetables, others with chappatis and parathas, walk up and down each row, offering second or third helpings to those who need them. No guest is ignored. No request is denied. The meal ends with a variety of sweets which are offered to each guest – ladoos, pedas, and a variety of barfis. The Pandeys, aware of the importance of social approbation, conduct themselves with impeccable decorum and dignity.

The family priest consults his almanac to determine the most auspicious time for the funeral; he suggests that the funeral procession should leave home soon after nine the following morning. The body in the meantime is kept on large slabs of ice. The unusual delay gives the last of the guests the opportunity to arrive in time for the funeral.

The widow of the late Mr Bishwanath Pandey sits in a room, surrounded by her well-wishers. Out of deference to her grief, she has been relieved of all responsibilities and decisions which, until recently, as head of the family, she would have had to take. The responsibility – in a very subtle but not unnoticeable way – has now been passed on to Vikram Pandey's wife. It will not be long before she acquires the final symbol of authority – the keys of the household.

Early next morning, amidst the crying and the wailing, amidst the sounds of the bhajans and kirtans being sung by the priests who have been engaged by the family, amidst the clatter and the noise of the household awakening from its fitful slumber, the male members of the family gather together to undertake all the funeral arrangements.

At this point, the tasks are distributed. The relatives who have had some past experience in constructing biers take over. All the materials needed for the bier – rolls of jute matting, coir, several yards of white and red muslin, thick bamboo staves, ropes with which the body will be secured when it is placed on the bier – have been neatly stacked in one corner of the room. They were acquired the night before.

The family priest, Mr Sharma, has brought with him all the ingredients required for the prayers: ghee, cotton-wool, camphor, vermilion paste, coconuts, rice, joss-sticks, nutmeg, cinnamon sticks and a variety of other necessary condiments. The servants, as instructed, have just brought in vast quantities of garlands and seasonal flowers – including marigolds, roses, jasmine – which will be used to adorn the body as soon as it is placed and secured on the bier. The heavy, dank smell which had pervaded the room disappears soon after the flowers and garlands are removed from their leafy packets. The fragrance of the flowers blends with the smell of joss-sticks, burning by the little prayer temple in the corner of the room.

The body is removed from the slabs of ice on which it has lain for the whole night, and placed on the floor. Very gently, with tears streaming down their faces, the three brothers take it in turn to wash their father's body with tepid water mixed with perfume, attar. The others stand by, watching, silently. Then they take it in turns to oil and anoint the body.

Soon the body, with its face uncovered, is wrapped in muslin, and is placed on the bier; it is held secure by the ropes and garlands of flowers which are interwoven around it. No sooner does the sonorous chanting of the priest reach the ears of the household than the entire congregation gathered in the hall-way, on the stairs, and in the other rooms, joins in the chanting. The women cry and weep without restraint – a few with increasing hysteria, particularly the daughter who has only just arrived from abroad.

To the accompaniment of the chant *Ram Ram Satya hai, Sat naam, Satya hai* (God is truth, in God is truth), the bier is lifted by the three brothers and their uncle – the principal pall-bearers – and carried down the stairs into the courtyard. The courtyard is crowded with hundreds of mourners, who all wait patiently. All the women, including the widow, who is inconsolable, gather for their last darhsan, their last glimpse of the deceased. They cry, they weep, they wail; they are unwilling to be parted from their loved one.

Presently the women are pacified by the family members. Slowly, tearfully, unwillingly, the women part from their loved one. They turn back into the house. For none of the women, not even the widow, is expected to accompany the coffin to the crematorium.

At last the funeral procession is ready to leave. The priest, swinging an earthenware pot which contains the sacred fire which was lit earlier, chants the words, *Ram Ram Satya hai, Sat naam, Satya hai*, as he heads the procession. The mourners, chanting in unison, follow. From time to time, individual mourners ease the burden of the pall-bearers, and shoulder the coffin for a short distance, only to be replaced by other mourners. Each mourner is eager to shoulder the coffin. It is seen as an act of great piety – to shoulder the dead one on his or her last journey.

On the road, the passing traffic slows down. Passers-by, motorists and cyclists carefully overtake the funeral procession and on seeing the coffin, they slow down and join the palms of their hands in silent prayer. People standing on balconies or in shop windows, on either side of the road, do the same. To witness a funeral procession is a good omen. In the heat and the rush of the morning traffic, the two-mile journey to the crematorium takes about an hour.

As soon as they reach the gates of the crematorium, the priest takes charge. He bids them stop outside the gates of the crematorium. The coffin is lowered to the ground. Relieved of their burden, the pall-bearers wipe the sweat off their faces. The priest chants a few mantras, invokes the gods, turns and offers prayers to the four corners of the earth, seeking blessings for the quiet repose of the departed soul.

The coffin is lifted again, and they enter a large quadrangle. Someone rushes off to fetch the crematorium attendant. A few of the mourners, overcome by the heat, sit on stone benches in the shade. Vikram Pandey produces the death certificate, which the crematorium attendant glances at cursorily. Care is taken to avoid any physical contact with the crematorium attendant, in case one is polluted by physical contact with an untouchable. Crematorium attendants traditionally come from the lowest caste, the Sudras. They are considered to be the lowest of the lowly among untouchables because of their polluting occupation. Eventually, the procession enters the burning ghat, where the body will be cremated.

There are six burning ghats in this particular crematorium. Four are already in use. The mourners of four other cremations look at the Pandeys in mute sympathy. No words, no greetings are exchanged. The singeing heat from the funeral pyres has driven all the mourners into taking refuge in a dark room about thirty feet away from the ghats. Occasionally, the crematorium attendant ventures out, approaches a particular pyre, and stokes the burning logs with a metal rod. Thick, belching smoke rises from the blazing fires and stings one's eyes; occasionally, a burning log sputters and crackles, and, a ball of fire, drops with a thud to the ground. It could be a limb. The bodies, which have been packed tightly between the heavy logs of wood, are not easily visible from a distance.

The Pandeys have been allocated the ghat in the far corner of the crematorium. The logs – sandalwood has been used at the bidding of the Pandeys – have already been piled at least five feet high on the ghat. The pall-bearers once again lift the body and place it on top of the logs. The three Pandey brothers, at the request of their priest, smear the body with ghee. Ghee is poured on the face, in the nostrils and in the ears of the corpse. More sandalwood logs are then placed on top of the body.

The priest beckons the Pandey brothers to approach them. He recites several slokas in Sanskrit and, after all the prayers have been said, he hands the eldest of the Pandey brothers a lighted torch. It is Vikram Pandey's sacred duty, his dharma, as the eldest son, to light the funeral pyre. He bows before his father's body, and in a voice choking with emotion, repeats the lines after the priest. He then brings the flaming torch close to the body. It catches instantly. The torch is then passed to the other two brothers, who do the same. By then the other mourners reach the pyre, and each of them offers the burning torch to the body.

Within minutes the fire rages, and the scorching heat drives them hastily into the dark room, where they sit among the other mourners, who have been sitting there before them.

Now that the cremation rites have been completed, the mourners who have attended the funeral approach Vikram Pandey, offer their condolences, and beg their leave. The Pandeys and their close relatives – all those who are staying with the Pandeys – sit and wait. They will all wait until they hear (or claim to hear) the sound of the skull cracking open. (There is an ancient belief among Hindus that when the skull cracks open, the soul of the dead person is released.) Vikram Pandey, however, would prefer to wait in the crematorium until his father's body has been totally reduced to ashes, so that the ashes can be gathered and deposited into a container. The others are unwilling to wait that long. They know from past experience that it would mean staying in the crematorium for at least eight to ten hours. The ashes, he is told, will be collected by the attendant and stored in a jar or an urn, which will be carefully labelled and kept in the crematorium for the next twelve days. The urn will be collected on the twelfth day when it is time for their father's final rites to be performed on the banks of the holy river Ganges in Varanasi, or Hardwar, or Nasik, or wherever the tributaries of the river Ganges flow in confluence. In accordance with ancient Hindu customs, the ashes will be immersed in the river Ganges to ensure the spiritual salvation of the deceased.

While the mourners wait in the crematorium, fresh preparations are in progress at home. An army of servants and daily helpers has been on the march since dawn: bedding and mattresses have been rolled up and put away, to be unrolled again at night; the remains of the morning breakfasts for all the guests (in some cases, individual requirements due to health or other reasons have had to be catered for) have been cleared, menus for lunch and dinner have been decided. Above all, huge drums of water have been warmed and kept ready in the courtyard. A small partition has been erected to permit a person to bath in relative privacy. A Hindu bath usually consists of a person filling a lota, a pitcher, from a bucket of water, and pouring the water over his body. The mourners upon their return from the cremation grounds, will all be in a state of spiritual impurity, or pollution. They would all without exception be expected to have a ritualistic purifying bath, change into a fresh set of white clothes and undertake brief prayers before they are allowed to sit down to the communal meal. After lunch, the guests are free to do their own bidding.

As well as the informal, individual visits by neighbours, relatives and other well-wishers, the Pandey family prepares itself for the formal public condolence meeting. In some communities, it is referred to as the markha ceremony, in others, the utthama ceremony. It has been scheduled for six in the evening. The notification for this formal meeting was sent out to all the national newspapers. No formal invitations are sent out to funeral guests. The notification in the newspapers serves as an open invitation to all those who wish to offer their condolences to the Pandey family. This gathering is considered to be of such importance that no relative, no well-wisher – in fact, no one who has known the Pandeys in any capacity – can afford to ignore it without incurring communal misapprobation.

By five-thirty the three brothers and all the relatives assemble in the courtyard. Within the next half hour or so, all the mourners and the well-wishers begin to arrive. By six, the courtyard is crammed with people, with the late-comers trying to jostle their way in.

The three Pandey brothers, dressed in their white kurtas and dhotis, their heads covered with white Gandhi caps, rise from their chairs. There is silence. They stand firmly and look at the crowd facing them. One by one, each mourner approaches them, bows his head, whispers his condolences to each of the three brothers. Each mourner displays the palms of his hands, with fingers pointing towards the earth, and departs. The symbolic interpretation of this gesture – empty-handed we come, empty-handed we go – is self-evident. Within fifteen minutes all the mourners have offered their condolences and departed. The general condolences meeting is over.

The subsequent days fall into a ritualistic pattern. Just before dawn, the priests appointed by the family start to sing the early morning devotional bhajans. The family awakens to the strains of devotional music, and soon after their morning ablutions, joins in the kirtan and the prayers which follow. Their neighbours and their friends who live close by, make their daily appearance. To hold the attention of his congregation, the priest from time to time narrates a popular story from the *Puranas* or the *Mahabharata*, or from any of the scores of Hindu religious texts, embellishing his stories with themes of topical interest. All his stories contain a clear, simple and poignant moral message. They all extol ancient Hindu virtues of obedience, respect, honour, compassion, and doing one's duty in accordance with one's dharma.

Although the day-to-day running of the household is delegated to the women, the men in the house keep themselves occupied in different ways. They look after and pay for the provisions and groceries required for the feeding of all their guests, they hire extra hands, respond to the letters of condolences which arrive, and receive the stream of well-wishers who visit them at all hours of the day. During these twelve days, the men seldom leave home. Vikram supervises all the activities which require his attention, and from time to time stays with his widowed mother, to share their mutual grief. In keeping with strict Hindu customs, he avoids any physical or sensual pleasures, shuns any form of physical adornment, remains unshaven, and will remain so until the final rites have been performed.

The women on the other hand spend the later part of the morning supervising the daily chores and activities of the household. When the morning chores are done, all the the women await the hour of four. Around that time, other women – friends, neighbours, relatives, well-wishers – begin to arrive. Slowly the house starts to fill with over fifty women who arrive at that hour every day. They all congregate in a room specially allocated for this meeting. The widow generally sits in the centre of the room, noticeable by all the women around her. They have all assembled to mourn and grieve for the departed soul. Usually an experienced mourner, possibly a widow herself, takes the lead. (In some instances – though not in this case – the services of a 'professional mourner' are sought in order to hasten the process of grieving.) She talks of the late Mr Pandey with consummate skill and persuades the bereaved members in the family, particularly the widow, to cry; one tear leads to another, one shriek is followed by another, and soon the room reverberates with piteous wails and lamentations, which can be heard by the men, who have gathered at the same time in another room.

This is an ancient custom, hallowed by tradition. As the days slip past one can see its 'therapeutic' value. The daily crying, the weeping, the wailing and, in some instances, breast-beating, has a startling effect on the mental well-being of the bereaved family. Most of the members of the family are now able to talk of the deceased without restraint. Obviously, it has been a source of intense security and comfort for the bereaved persons. What the bereaved person has realized – and has been made to realize – is that he or she is not alone with death. It is touching to see how the members of the extended family, and indeed of one's entire community, one's baradari, have stood by the bereaved persons and have offered whatever help and support has been needed.

Plans for the twelfth-day ceremony and the subsequent immersion of the ashes into the river Ganges are now discussed freely and openly among the members of the family. The family priest has also been invited to participate in these discussions. After some debate it is agreed that Vikram, being the eldest son, would need to go to Hardwar, where he would, with the assistance of the local priest, perform the final funeral rites. This decision is also in keeping with the requirements in the will made by the late Mr Pandey. In it, he had decreed that upon his death, his final funeral rites would need to be performed by his eldest son, his ashes would need to be immersed in the Ganges and, after all the funeral rites had been completed, arrangements would have to be made to feed 350 needy mendicants.

With the exception of Vikram Pandey, everyone appears to be pleased with the decision. He has reservations. He has never been to Hardwar before. He does not know how he will locate Mr Shastri, their local family priest. No one knows where Mr Shastri lives; all Vikram has is his name – which is not an uncommon Brahmin surname. And how will he find 350 mendicants to feed?

In Hardwar, Vikram Pandey's reservations turn out to be unfounded. Locating their local family priest, Mr Shastri, presents no problems. Vikram learns that each local priest in Hardwar keeps a record of his own benefactors, or clients. In some instances, the records go back over two hundred years. As soon as Vikram Pandey announces his own family name to a group of priests he encounters on the banks of the river, they are able to identify correctly his own family priest. Word spreads and within a short time, Mr Shastri finds Vikram.

Vikram is astonished at being shown a complete genealogy of his own family; the records go back to over one hundred and fifty years ago! Priesthood being an inherited profession, these records are passed on from father to son; Mr Shastri has inherited these records from his father. He will, in turn, pass them on to his son, who will then become the family priest of the future Pandeys. Whenever a member of the Pandey family visits Hardwar, the records are up-dated.

Mr Shastri agrees to perform the final funeral rites and promises to locate 350 (more, if need be) beggars, who will be fed after the funeral rites have been performed. They arrange to meet the following morning at the banks of the river Ganges, where they will sit and perform the final funeral rites.

Early next morning they meet as arranged. As instructed, Vikram has brought with him a set of clean white clothes which he will have to wear after he has had a dip in the holy Ganges. He has also brought with him the metal urn which contains his father's ashes. A clean sheet is spread on the ground, which has been swept clean by the untouchable sweeper. Vikram sits on it, facing the priest. Dotted around the bank are several such religious ceremonies in progress. The chants and the incantations of the priests create sonorous cadences as they perform their respective ceremonies, praying for the repose of departed souls. Stray dogs and cows wander about, sniffing. Early morning worshippers stand on the banks, invoking the gods, before diving or dunking into the muddied waters of the cold, swiftly flowing river. Carried aloft by the wind, thick heavy smoke rises from the funeral pyres in the distance, staining the clothes which the women are washing along the bank. Beggars, eager for alms, hover in the distance, waiting for the ceremonies to come to an end.

Vikram does the priest's bidding. He undresses, and plunges into the river. The seal of the urn is cracked open, and to the incantations of the priest, the ashes and bits of charred bone are cast into the river. After Vikram has changed into the clean white clothes, the priest starts the ceremony. The priest lights a fire and offers the preliminary invocations to the god Ganesha. The ceremony has commenced. The prayers are said in Sanskrit. From time to time, the priest asks Vikram to repeat after him, which he does faithfully, but without a great deal of understanding.

After about an hour the ceremony comes to an end. The last funeral rites, as dictated by ancient custom, have been successfully performed.

The priest has also made the necessary arrangements for 350 beggars to be fed. A restaurant by the banks of the river has been contracted to undertake this last task. Word spreads, and by one o'clock, the courtyard outside the restaurant is teeming with beggars of all ages. Even at a rough guess one can tell that there are more than 350 people assembled in the courtyard. They rattle their metal dishes and their begging bowls in anticipation. Lunch consists of seasonal vegetables, such as cauliflower and potatoes, paneer and peas, daal, rice, chappatis, followed by traditional sweets: ladoos, and pedas.

Vikram has now performed all the rites related to his father's funeral. He pays Mr Shastri the agreed sum, receives his blessings, and returns to Bombay.

Let us at this point take a pause. The above narrative constitutes an opening point for a discussion of Hindu funerals, but it is not the whole story. Let us look at some general areas where questions may be raised.

Firstly, one might like to know: is the above narrative a true reflection of what happens in most, if not all, Hindu funerals in India? The reader will recall that at the start of the paper several assumptions were made, one of which was that the family chosen for our detailed description was a typical high-caste Hindu family. Does the family mirror to a large extent Hindu families of other castes in India? Or to put it in the language of sampling theory, is the family representative of the Hindu population? India's population is about 85 per cent Hindu, a total of just under 800 million. Given the diversity of linguistic, educational, climatic and economic factors, it is clearly impossible to provide a representative sample in one family.

The merit of the narrative lies in the fact that it articulates a set of fundamental principles related to death, the handling of death, and the rituals associated with death and bereavement among Hindus. It is those principles one is concerned with – not the variations in detail.

For instance, we have described a family of considerable affluence. If we were instead to describe a family of moderate means or a family from the slums of large metropolitan cities, or from a typical Indian village (it must be recognized that villages in India vary considerably in degrees of affluence, levels of education and size: it seems pointless therefore to refer to a *typical* Indian village) we would observe a variety of differences with regard to funeral rites. Such differences are differences in detail: to have your head shaved or not at the death of the elderly parent, to organize prayer-meetings extending over twelve days, to perambulate round the funeral fire three times or five times, to feed the needy, to scatter the ashes in the holy Ganges: such variations may be influenced by economic and other considerations. What remain constant, however, are the sets of values to which Hindus subscribe: for instance, it is the sacred duty (dharma) of the family and one's (sub-community) baradari to deal with death in their family in accordance with the teachings of the shastras, the sacred religious texts, to perform all the expected rites and rituals, to engage in acts of piety and charity so as to ensure the peaceful repose of the departed soul. It is these fundamental value systems which unite all Hindus and indeed the rest of the Indians in India, including the Muslims, Buddhists, Jains, Sikhs, Catholics, Parsees and other religious groups. It is this unity enjoined by core values which enables us to refer to Indians as a cultural group. A comprehensive theoretical model which examines the major value systems of Indians has been described at length elsewhere (Laungani, 1992; 1993a; 1993b; 1994; 1995) and therefore need not concern us here. Suffice it to say that several testable hypotheses clearly deduced from the model have been validated by rigorous empirical tests (Sachdev, 1992).

Thus, from a theoretical point of view, the answer to our question concerning the representativeness of our narrative to the Hindus as a whole is an unqualified yes.

Let us now turn to the situation in other countries. We shall take Britain as our example but similar problems exist in most Western countries. How far does our account of the Hindu funeral in India echo the situation in Britain? Are there parallels to be drawn? Sadly, no. In terms of the practical arrangements related to dying, the handling of the dead, the performance of funeral rites, etc., the two countries are divided by vast and seemingly insurmountable differences.

FUNERAL RITES OF HINDUS IN BRITAIN

It will be obvious from the above account that the ceremonies described above would be difficult to perform in other countries. The Ganges does not flow through Bethnal Green, the law does not permit bodies to be paraded through the streets without a coffin and burned on public pyres, and Western business customs do not allow a son to take twelve days off work in order to fulfil his obligations to a dead father. Some compromise is inevitable and most Hindus allow hospital authorities and funeral directors to decide how things should be handled. What is surprising, and indeed questionable, is the degree of compromise. It is as if the Hindu population of Britain were adopting the truncated rites of their land of adoption. The alternative, which is adopted by the orthodox few who can afford it, is to fly the body back to India for disposal, but this means that only those mourners who can afford the journey can take part in the rituals and it is, at best, a partial solution.

The differences become obvious even prior to death. In India, when it becomes clear that the person concerned is about to die, he/she is lifted out of bed and placed on the floor. In addition to the universal symbolism of 'earth to earth', there is a belief among Hindus that when death occurs it becomes easier for the soul to depart from the body when the body is placed on the floor. To assist in the process the relatives gather round the dying person, dip a basil (tulsi) leaf or two into holy water from the river Ganges and place it on the lips of the patient, to the accompaniment of hymns and holy songs. Since most Hindus in India die at home, such cultural rituals can be observed unimpeded. However most Hindus in Britain die in hospital. For obvious reasons no hospital would allow the dying person to be placed on the floor, nor would it permit relatives to gather round the dying person and sing hymns. However, the important rituals related to the sprinkling of a drop or two of Ganges water with a basil leaf on the lips of the dying person seems an innocuous practice and there is no reason why a thoughtful and enterprising hospital chaplain (and/or the ward sister) might not keep a supply of Ganges water (some Asian stores sell Ganges water in sealed metal containers; others sell it in litre bottles) and offer some to the relatives of dying patients. What a thoughtful gesture that would be, provoking enormous feelings of gratitude among the Asian community living in Britain.

Unlike in India, the deceased Hindu in Britain is seldom brought home. The body is transported by the funeral directors and is kept in their mortuary until the time of the funeral. As we saw earlier, it is beholden upon the close relatives to prepare the body for the funeral. But here the bereaved have no hand whatever in performing the extremely important last rites related to bathing, anointing and dressing the body. All that is left to nurses or undertakers, some of whom who have no awareness of Hindu customs. Few Hindus would dare defy them, yet virtually every Hindu in Britain becomes (or will become) a party – albeit an unwilling party – to such a violation. What the effects – both short-term and long-term – of such practices are likely to be on the recovery from their sad loss and on their eventual well-being is an unresolved issue.

Can anything be done? From the point of view of doctors, nurses, hospital administrators and others who are involved prior to a death the important thing is to consult the patient and family to find out what they prefer: some will not want to follow the customs of their native land, others will want to do so as far as is practically possible. Even the decision to allow the patient to die at home may be greeted as a welcome opportunity for the family (which at this time still includes the patient) to take control and follow tradition. If there is no opportunity for the patient to die at home then the provision of a private room where the family can gather, and a policy of interfering as little as possible with their care of the patient, is appropriate. When death occurs, nurses and funeral directors should leave the bereaved family to participate in the preparation of the body which, if the patient died in hospital can then be brought home, if that is their wish. The cultural importance of such a strategy cannot be overemphasized.

To outward appearances most Hindu funerals in Britain look rather like a Christian funeral. On the day of the funeral, the undertakers – dressed in black, in sharp contrast with the bereaved, most of whom are dressed in *white* – bring the body into the crematorium in a closed coffin. As was pointed out earlier, Hindus carry their dead on a bier – not in a closed coffin. It is also common for the undertakers to deprive the rest of the mourners of the devoutly wished for opportunity of becoming pall-bearers and thereby acquiring virtue. A vital act of virtue, so easily fulfilled, is as easily frustrated.

If the use of coffins is unavoidable, one might wish to suggest that funeral directors explore the feasibility of designing a coffin which might be more in keeping with Hindu customs and traditions. The pecuniary advantages of such entrepreneurial ventures could hardly fail to go unnoticed. Few Hindus would be likely to quibble over the extra cost of such a coffin.

Hindu funerals – once the auspicious time has been determined by the family priest – are not organized around a rigid time-schedule. They are chaotic and quite flexible. In Britain, however, time plays an extremely crucial role with regard to funeral arrangements. The day and the time of the funeral are arranged with the crematorium authorities by the funeral director rather than the family priest; he is expected to comply. The crematorium authorities insist that these time-schedules be strictly adhered to. The funeral must proceed like a well-rehearsed drill for fear of clashing with the next one ('If you have tears, prepare to shed them now – for it will soon be too late' is the message). Spontaneity and flexibility which are such characteristic features of Hindu funerals, are sacrificed to order and precision.

From a Hindu perspective, it appears that crematoria in Britain are designed to *conceal* funerals, rather than to express them. For instance, the incinerator into which the coffin is finally disgorged is concealed from view; the bereaved and particularly those family members involved with the performance of the last funeral rites, are seldom allowed to see the incinerator. Nor are they given the opportunity of lighting the flame. To see the coffin – at the press of a concealed button – slide off on an electronically operated carousel and drop into a concealed hole can be an unnerving and even grotesque experience. The mourners do not know where or how the cremation is taking place. There is no smoke to sting their eyes, nor the fire to singe their hair, nor the smell of burning flesh to bring the poignant immediacy and reality of the experience to their consciousness. They see nothing, they hear nothing, they feel nothing; there is just the dull realization that their loved one is being cremated by an anonymous, faceless bureaucratic *fiat*.

As far as the service itself is concerned, it is held in a room which resembles a church hall rather than a temple. The mourners do not sit cross-legged on the floor as they would in all parts of India; they sit in rows upon pews, and the priest conducting the service stands on a dais. The priest does not perform the funeral rites in the way in which they would be performed in India. Instead he preaches a sermon – very much as one would expect at a Christian funeral. The very setting is designed as though to keep crying to a minimum; sorrow, as instilled in the Western psyche, is to be borne in the silence of one's heart, not expressed openly in public. To burst into uncontrollable sobs is often considered hysterical, undignified and even rather vulgar. In restraint lies dignity: in fact, restraint *is* dignity. Such is not the Hindu way. (Nor, for that matter, is it the Indian way; nor the Asian way; nor the Eastern way). It is the Western way.

CONCLUSION

The problems, as we have seen, are not entirely insuperable. One of the more radical solutions to the problems articulated above is for the Hindus in Britain to come together, build their own crematoria and train their own priests to act as funeral directors. Such a solution would enable the Hindus to revive their hallowed cultural customs, some of which date back to 3000 BC. Yet it is often the 'fate' of immigrant populations to conform and accept – often with bitterness and sorrow – the dominant social norms of the host culture they have elected to adopt as their own. An unqualified willingness by the host community to respond sensitively to the fundamental values (religious, social and familial) of different cultural groups, and actively assist in their perpetuation rather than in their destruction, will eventually lead to the creation of a genuine pluralistic society based on trust and harmony. To achieve this it is necessary for persons of goodwill, compassion and power from both sides of the cultural fence to come together and express a willingness to pay urgent attention to these problems. Unless this is done, in the years to come the rituals, the traditions and the customs which give each culture its unique identity and meaning will be swept aside and will be replaced by gargantuan, monolithic, homogeneous cultural arrangements. And that would mean the death of a culture. The death of a culture is a far greater loss to humanity than the death of an individual: the latter is inevitable, the former avoidable.

The death of a culture is the death of civilization.

SUMMARY

☐ There is considerable variation between the observances of Hindus from different castes, regions and financial status.

☐ Close relatives, particularly wives, of seriously ill patients will pray, fast and call upon the help of astrologers and others in order to propitiate the gods and restore the patient to health. Few will accept the fact that death is approaching. Family and friends remain at the bedside throughout.

☐ It is the sacred duty (dharma) of the family and one's sub-community (baradari) to deal with death in their family in accordance with the teachings of the shastras, the sacred religious texts, to perform all the expected rites and rituals, to engage in acts of piety and charity so as to ensure the peaceful repose of the departed soul.

☐ When it becomes clear that the person concerned is about to die, he/she is lifted out of bed and placed on the floor. The relatives gather round the dying person, dip a basil (tulsi) leaf or two into the holy water of the river Ganges and place it on the lips of the patient, to the accompaniment of hymns and holy songs.

☐ When death occurs loud shrieks may be expressed.

☐ The body of the patient should preferably be sent home unwashed after death. The family will then carry out a ritual washing.

☐ The widow will wipe out her wedding mark (sindoor) and close female relatives wear white saris for a year after a death. Sons often have their heads shaved, apart from a small tuft of hair.

☐ The rituals of the funeral last for twelve days. They can cripple a family of more than moderate means. During this time family members sleep on the floor and eat only vegetarian food. Prayers are said, songs are sung and there are readings from the holy books.

Food is provided and friends join in the ceremonies, after formal ablutions, at sunrise and sunset. They visit the body which is shrouded in a white sheet on the floor with face uncovered.

☐ There is a harmonious confluence of Hinduism, Sikhism and Islam during the twelve days of grief and mourning. Many Hindu families engage Sikh priests, instead of Hindu priests for the entire duration of the ceremony.

☐ The body is anointed, garlanded with flowers and carried in procession to be cremated at the burning ghat where the pyre is ignited by the eldest son. Mourners chant and wail. Close relatives wait until they hear the skull crack open so that the spirit can depart.

☐ After further ablutions friends gather to wish condolences to the family using a ritual greeting. Tears are encouraged and professional mourners are sometimes hired to evoke these.

☐ At a further ceremony the ashes are scattered into the waters of the Ganges. Beggars are fed as a tribute to the dead person.

☐ Because it is difficult to carry out these rituals outside India, compromise is necessary when people die overseas. It is our view that the degree of compromise expected and accepted is often excessive. We advocate death at home wherever possible, or the provision of a private room in hospital, with a tolerant attitude to the family needs, when it is not. Those who can afford it prefer to fly bodies back to India. Those who cannot should have the services of a Hindu funeral director or one who can meet the special needs of this group.

☐ The death of a culture is the death of civilization.

Chapter 5

A death on the roof of the world
The perspective of Tibetan Buddhism

Uwe P. Gielen

Of all mindfulness meditations, that on death is supreme.

Shakyamuni Buddha

Thus think of all this fleeting world: a star at dawn, a bubble in a stream; a flash of lightning in a summer cloud, a flickering lamp, a phantom, and a dream.

The Diamond Sutra

To practise death is to practise freedom.

Montaigne

Among all the world's major religions Buddhism has traditionally been perceived as having an especially close affinity with death. In Japan, for instance, most funerals are conducted by Buddhist priests. In contrast, the native Shinto religion originally abhorred death, and Christianity has influenced Japanese ethics, education and wedding ceremonies much more than it has Japanese burial customs and beliefs associated with death and bereavement (Reischauer, 1988). In traditional China too, Buddhist priests were often looked upon as 'burial specialists'. In contrast, the Taoist monks were more likely to advertise their mysterious abilities to prolong a person's life. While some other world religions have also decried the vanity of all earthly things, it is Buddhism that has most persistently emphasized the pervasive principle of impermanence and the ceaseless transmutation of all existing beings and forces, the endless cycle of birth, death and rebirth, and the suffering (*dukkha*) that inevitably accompanies impermanence.

But religion must protect its believers from the terrors of finitude, meaninglessness and hopelessness, and so Mahayana Buddhism introduced the saving idea of a timeless, deathless, blissful Nirvana radiantly coexisting with and outside change, time, space, form, death and the world of suffering (*samsara*). In addition, many Buddhists have cherished more concrete ideas of salvation such as hoping to lead, after their deaths, blissful lives in the paradisaical Pure Land of Opame (Amitabha);[1] the Buddha of Boundless Light. For them, the idea of Nirvana may be psychologically too remote.

At the centre of Buddhist doctrine lies the concept of no-[substantial]-self (*anatta*), the idea that a person's perceptions of and attachment to his or her 'I' are both profoundly mistaken and the basic source of his or her suffering. Our self-interest and our tiny place in history grotesquely distort our ability to see things as they really are, rather than as how we wish or fear them to be. Our loves and hates are based on a kind of egocentric 'self-addiction' that traps us in a self-constructed cage of blind desires and baseless fears. But rightly conceived the 'I' is just as impermanent and illusory as anything else perceived by the senses. The Buddhist asks: 'Is life not like a bubble in a stream or a fleeting dream from which only the few awaken during meditation or, perhaps, at the hour of their death?'

VAJRAYANA BUDDHISM

The dream-like feeling of impermanence is especially keenly felt by traditional Tibetans. Closely akin to them are the Buddhist Ladakhis of Kashmir, Northwest India, who for many centuries have followed the tenets of western Tibetan Buddhism. They live in high-lying valleys surrounded by the soaring peaks of the Karakorum and the Himalayas, and on the bleak high plateaus situated north of these mountain chains.

The Ladakhi peasant, nomad, monk, or nun is no stranger to death which not infrequently has stalked him or her from infancy on. Prior to the 1950s, the chances of a Ladakhi or Tibetan reaching adulthood were probably no higher than 30–60 per cent, since infant and child mortality rates reached very high levels. As adults, not a few Ladakhis lost their lives to spreading epidemics, on hazardous trips across steep mountain passes, by falling into icy rivers, or by perishing in howling winter storms sweeping with enormous force across the barren landscape. Given these conditions Buddhist admonitions to be ever aware of the

1 In Ladakh and Tibet, deities are frequently known both by their Tibetan and their Sanskrit names, since Buddhism reached these regions originally from India. In the present instance, Opame is the Tibetan name, Amitabha the Sanskrit name. In Japan, Amitabha is better known as Amida.

possibility of sudden death have found a ready echo in the hearts of the Ladakhis. This has not made them morose, since few people face adversity as cheerfully as most Ladakhis do. A philosophical sense of humour, based on a fine feeling for the evanescence of all that exists, makes itself frequently felt in daily life.

Responding to Buddhist conceptions of liberation from the endlessly turning wheel of life, the prevailing difficult economic conditions and the harshness of the land, many Ladakhis and Tibetans became monks. In their town-like monasteries or as hermits in remote mountain caves they developed a special form of Buddhism called Vajrayana ('Diamond Way') or Tantric Buddhism. This esoteric form of Buddhism, especially as practised in the remote Himalayan corner of Ladakh, provides the special focus and background for this chapter. In this context, it should be noted that Vajrayana conceptions of death and rebirth differ significantly from those prevailing among the Theravada (Hinayana) Buddhists living in Sri Lanka, Indochina and elsewhere. For instance, while many Theravada Buddhists believe in 'instant rebirth' after death, Vajrayana Buddhists describe an intermediate *bardö* period lasting up to forty-nine days between death and rebirth.

The development of Vajrayana Buddhism was influenced by the special challenges that living on the world's highest plateaus posed to the hardy monks, nuns, peasants, caravaners and nomads. When the pious pilgrim crossed the endless stony deserts of the Chang Thang beneath the deep blue dome of the Tibetan sky, he or she experienced the infinite in its most direct and luminous form. Deeply aware of his puniness in Tibet's infinite open spaces or beneath her awe-inspiring peaks, he came to believe that the luminosity of the sky is a symbol of the luminosity of his own mirror-like mind. Gradually, the deep silences, the empty grandeur and the stark nakedness of Tibet's sacred landscape would work themselves into the pilgrim's heart and mind, supporting the conviction that a mysterious Voidness or Emptiness (*tongpanyi*) lay at the heart of all existence. At night he would find himself beneath a canopy of stars whose remoteness whispered to him of limitless space and endless time. In contrast to all this vastness, he experienced his ego or self as small and transient, as no more stable than the endlessly shifting clouds drifting lazily across the spacious sky. And so, Tibet's endless vistas would at once humble and uplift the pilgrim, slowly stripping from him the trivia of daily life, diluting some of his all-too-human egocentricity, liberating him from the tyranny of his desires, eroding his sense of time, filling him with awe, and setting him face to face with eternity (Tucci, 1967). As the pilgrim's larger self became absorbed into the rhythms and seasons of the landscape, his puny ego was put into its place. Life and death became relative for him.

Still, the pilgrim would ask himself or herself: 'Is there not something stable and permanent beneath and beyond all the vastness and the ceaseless change, such as the luminous, translucent stillness of the Mind that perceives the endless change but does not change itself?' To experience the overpowering inner light of 'Mind as such' became the ultimate goal of Tibetan meditation. As we shall see later, this Radiant Light of Pure Reality was also said to occur at the time of death, when consciousness was liberated to begin its reluctant flight from its now useless shell.

While at times monks and lay persons experienced outer reality as almost dream-like, as a series of floating, cloud-like images against a background of impermanence and death, the more highly trained among the monks searched for inner illumination leading to the mystic experience of Nirvana. Simultaneously and at a more easily graspable level of understanding, they saw in the surviving consciousness of the dead person the inheritor of the karmic residues of the past. After death, a person's karma, that is, the lasting moral impact of all of his actions in his previous lives, would provide the seeds for his rebirth in one of the many realms of existence. Like an irresistible Tibetan blizzard, the relentless red storms of negative karma would drive the surviving, free-floating consciousness of the dead person toward the beckoning womb of his or her future mother, who could be a person, an animal, or one of the many invisible beings populating the Tibetan symbolic world.

Higher Buddhism and Folk Buddhism

In all Buddhist countries, the 'Higher Buddhism' of the trained monks and meditators has mingled over the years with folk beliefs, resulting in various forms of 'Folk Buddhism'. This also occurred in Tibet and Ladakh where vivid native imagination and belief in magic-like forces blended with abstract Buddhist speculation to form a unique whole. Among most lay persons and not a few of the monks, the trained meditators' search for archetypal visions and the inner light was replaced by or existed side by side with the traditional Tibetan belief in the reality and power of countless invisible beings and forces that variously might be helpful, dangerous or indifferent to humans.

The ever-present armies of invisible beings included semi-anthropomorphic 'gods' (*lha*), sky-walking fairies, spirits of the sky, the mountains, the earth, the rivers and the house, cannibalistic ogres, dangerous witches, restless ghosts, eerie goblins and prowling demons who needed to be placated, or whose protection was sought. In the Tibetan semi-animistic worldview, there is little place for chance since all events are determined by the interaction of visible and invisible moral and natural causes. All events are in this sense 'meaningful' and point to a hidden, more encompassing reality which also manifests itself in dreams, during meditation, and during and after death. The transcendental world breaks through our normal states of consciousness especially when we experience the transitional *bardö* states. Besides our ever-changing states of consciousness during waking life, these 'between-states-of-awareness' include the state of dreaming, trance states during meditation, the experience of the inner light at the point of death and the two *bardö*[2] states experienced for several weeks after death.

From the villager's pragmatic point of view, it was the task of the religious specialists to perform the many rituals necessary to help the lay person survive and prosper in a field of powerful invisible forces. The most important rituals were those connected to a person's death: since death was seen merely as a point of departure separating one life cycle from the next, it became the all-important task of the monks to guide the deceased person's consciousness or 'spirit' (*nam shes*)[3] through the transitory *bardö* states towards a favourable rebirth. For this purpose, the monks would read the *Bardö T'ödröl* or *Great Book of Natural Liberation Through Understanding in the Between* (known in the West as the *Tibetan Book of the Dead*) to the deceased person's *nam shes*, which was believed to hover in the vicinity of the corpse (Evans-Wentz, 1960; Freemantle and Trungpa, 1975; Lauf, 1989; Thurman, 1994).

In the following, the reader is invited to take an imaginary trip to a little village in remote Ladakh, a traditional centre of western Tibetan Buddhism, to witness a death in one of the village's families, and to think and feel himself or herself into the psychology and theology underlying the *Bardö T'ödröl*. This slim book has in recent years been

2 The term *bardö* is used in two, sometimes confusing ways. Strictly speaking, *bardö* refers to the six in-between states of awareness listed in this paragraph. The term *bardö* may also be used to refer in a general way to the in-between state lasting from a person's death to his or her rebirth several weeks later. Confusingly, that period can also be divided into three (sub)*bardö* states.

3 Since this chapter is intended for the general reader, an informal transcription system has been adopted for Tibetan and Ladakhi terms. For instance, silent prefixes (which are common in Tibetan) have been omitted to avoid confusion.

the object of much discussion by both Westerners and Tibetans. Since among all world religions Buddhism is the most psychologically oriented, little violence is done to this age-old text if we look at it from a psychological point of view.

Traditional Ladakh and Tibet

Ladakh is located in the northwestern area of India and forms a part of the state of Jammu and Kashmir. About half as large as England, it has approximately 140,000 inhabitants. More than 99 per cent of the land is a high-altitude mountain desert, but barley, buckwheat, potatoes, turnips and walnut and apricot trees are planted in the valleys. Ladakh borders on Pakistan and on Tibet, the latter now forming part of China. The upper Indus valley forms the cultural centre of Buddhist Ladakh. Here are located many of the monasteries that traditionally have dominated the spiritual life of Buddhist Ladakh. There is one town, Leh, which has about 12,000 inhabitants. The other Ladakhis live in villages, although some nomadic pastoralists continue to roam the more remote, high areas. Most Ladakhis are farmers, craftsmen, small businessmen, government officials or members of the Buddhist clergy. They speak Ladakhi, an archaic Tibetan language. About 55 per cent of Ladakh's population profess the Buddhist faith while most other inhabitants of Ladakh belong to the Sunni and Shia traditions of Islam. The present chapter confines itself to the Buddhist population.

In terms of religion and culture, Buddhist Ladakh has been part of the wider Tibetan world for many centuries (Petech, 1977). The 'Tibetan world' includes approximately 6 million people living in China's Autonomous Region of Tibet, throughout various provinces of China, and in Bhutan, northern Nepal and northwest India. During and after the 1950s, the Chinese state tightened its grip on Tibet, destroyed its traditional social structures, levelled almost all of Tibet's monasteries and killed large numbers of people, especially during the Great Proletarian Cultural Revolution. Following an uprising in 1959 the Dalai Lama, traditionally the spiritual and political leader of Tibet, fled to India, where he formed Tibet's government-in-exile. Many high-ranking monks joined him and soon helped to spread Buddhist ideas to the Western world.

Today, Ladakh forms the last major bastion of western Tibetan Buddhism, which has survived there in pure form. If one wishes to understand Tibetan Buddhist beliefs and customs related to death and bereavement, the villages of Ladakh provide an ideal environment to pursue this endeavour.

A DEATH ON THE ROOF OF THE WORLD

It is a warm autumn evening, and the sun is slowly sinking behind the jagged peaks of the Inner Himalayas. Beyond the prayer flags on the roof of Wangchuck Chosphel's spacious house in Sakti village, a patchwork of yellowing barley fields and irrigation channels glitters in the last rays of the evening sun. In the far distance, a chain of snow-covered peaks rises to a height of more than 23,000 feet above the Indus river which winds its way through the mountain desert of upper Ladakh, the 'Land of High Passes'. An old woman is passing by Wangchuck Chosphel's home turning her prayer wheel, murmuring mantras, and sending the holy invocation 'Om! Mani padme hum!' to Tibet's compassionate protector deity, Chenrezig (Avalokiteshvara) in the lustrous, unwrinkled sky. From time to time, the merry laughter of young children drifts across the fields as they play with their homemade toys or turn into mischievous little human wolves chasing giggling little human sheep. But today, the house of Wangchuck Chosphel is not a happy place. Grandfather is battling with death, and it is clear to his family that his life is about to end.

Wangchuk Chosphel has lived a long and good life. A farmer in his younger days, he gradually withdrew in his later years from this world of illusion to prepare himself for the inevitable 'change of body' that lay ahead. Under the guidance of the monks and the *rinpoche* (abbot) from the nearby Trakhtok Monastery,[4] he has tried to empty his mind, so as to loosen the bonds and attachments which still tie him to the ever-turning 'Wheel of Life'. Unlike some of the better trained monks, Wangchuk did not learn to concentrate his mind one-pointedly by following the rigorous techniques of tantric meditation and yoga. Instead he has practised a kind of 'free-floating' meditation and has gone on several pilgrimages to holy places to gain religious merit and thus to improve his karma. For years, Wangchuk Chosphel has earnestly prayed for a favourable rebirth, but like most of his peers, he does not

4 Several 'lineages' or schools of Vajrayana Buddhism are represented in Ladakh and Tibet. They emphasize different deities, texts and rituals for the dead. Trakhtok Gompa (monastery) follows the ancient Nyingma tradition which incorporates certain magical practices going far back into Tibetan and Indian history. The *Bardö T'ödröl* in the translation by Freemantle and Trungpa (1975) belongs to this tradition, while Mullin's (1987) work represents the more commonly known Geluk tradition.

believe that after death he will be able to enter the cool bliss of a Nirvana beyond pain, evil, time and death. He hopes for a good rebirth instead.[5]

On clear days Wangchuk would sit in the sun and murmur his mantras (sacred invocations containing in their sound-essence the essence of a deity) while providing warm support and guidance for his son's children who play in the courtyard. Few sorrows shroud his heart, but old age has been stealing in on him, and time has been writing ever more wrinkles and lines into his kind face.

Having quietly said good-bye to his family, the hum of life is now receding in Wangchuk's drifting mind. He attempts to pray, but soon his mind is beginning to burrow through the tunnels of time and is getting lost in the winding corridors of his memory. For a moment the house grows still; only the muffled sobs of his daughter can be heard faintly through the walls of the family altar-room where Wangchuk is lying in his bed. Somehow, he feels the body's basic elements of earth, water, fire and air (which had supported his daily existence) collapsing one by one into each other, till finally the element of air dissolves into his consciousness. Visions start to flood his mind; terrifying images appear to him of crushing mountains, gigantic waves, scorched landscapes and howling storms. And now, Wangchuk Chosphel's consciousness is beginning to separate from his body. He is now travelling through the *bardö* of dying.

As the shock of Wangchuk's collapse hits his family, it becomes incumbent upon his lama or spiritual guide, the monks of the nearby monastery, other members of the his family's *phaspun* (a kind of mutual aid society), the local *önpo* (astrologer), and various family friends to provide the family with emotional and material support. Most importantly, Wangchuk's lama will soon arrive in the house and attempt to guide the dead man's consciousness (*nam shes*) on a steady path through the dangerous confusions of the *bardö* state.

His family belongs to a *phaspun*, a group of households whose members help each other during crisis situations, worship a common guardian deity and share a common cremation oven. And so a

---

5 Sympathetic descriptions of Tibetan Buddhism by Western interpreters (Govinda, 1960; Lauf, 1989; Thurman, 1994) tend to depict a highly sophisticated religion based on intricate metaphysics and abstract speculation about the ultimate nature of mind and reality. Buddhism at this level is fully understood only by a few of Ladakh's more highly trained monks; in contrast, some of the other monks can barely read and write. This chapter attempts to describe some Buddhist beliefs and practices as they are experienced by many of the people rather than only by a small elite of monks.

prominent member of the *phaspun* is sent to inform the nearby astrologer and Wangchuk's lama about his death. The astrologer soon sets to work to establish his death horoscope. Following an age-old astrological guide and basing his predictions on complicated calculations, he determines that the sinister messenger of death had arrived from the Eastern direction. Prescribing numerous prayers and religious ceremonies to ward off the threat of invisible but potent beings lurking around the house, he predicts that Wangchuck's spirit will be reborn in the human realm, and then computes the date for his cremation (Ribbach, 1940, 1986). But Wangchuk's spirit needs help on his perilous journey through the *bardö*, and so the astrologer will perform a series of rituals during the next few days to ensure a good outcome for Wangchuk's journey. The family will pay him well for his efforts.

In the meanwhile the *rinpoche* is attempting to return the *nam shes* (which after death had escaped from Wangchuk's body) to his body. By the power of the truth of the Buddha, the Buddhist teachings (*dharma*), the community of monks (*sangha*) and by the truth of the Destroyer of Death, he summons the consciousness from wherever it may have been wandering. He tears some hair from the top of Wangchuk's head, thus creating a symbolic opening for the consciousness to return. Visualizing the Buddha Opame as sitting on Wangchuk's head, the *rinpoche* shouts three times *Hik!* and then *Phat!*, thereby attempting to eject the consciousness a second time through the opening on top of Wangchuk's skull so that it can enter the spinal nerve of Opame, Lord of the Western Paradise. But there are some signs that the *rinpoche* has not been successful in guiding the spirit directly to the Pure Land of Opame: the upper part of Wangchuk's body remains warmer than the lower part, a sign that the *nam shes* has exited through a lower body opening. It has not taken rebirth in a celestial form inside a heavenly lotus flower in Sukhavati, the Pure Land of Joy in the Western Realms.

Several monks begin to chant their prayers. Addressing themselves to the all-knowing, all-seeing, all-loving Buddhas and *bodhisattvas* of all directions, they beseech them to descend to Wangchuk's house, to help his lonely, friendless spirit make the difficult migration across the gloomy wilderness of the *bardö*. 'Protect him who is unprotected! Be his ally', they pray to the compassionate ones, 'save him from being dragged down into the netherworld by the messengers of Shinje (Yama), Lord of Death. Turn him away from the red storms of *karma*; catch hold of him with the hook of your grace.'

In the meantime, relatives, friends and neighbours have begun to arrive in the house bringing with them butter tea and beer. They try to console the sobbing women in the kitchen, while Wangchuk's stony-faced son and several of the *phaspun* members begin preparations for the ceremonies. So much has to be done during the next few weeks! Several *phaspun* women are preparing food, and during the next few days a stream of visitors will flow through the house.

Reading the *Bardö T'ödröl*

In the quiet family altar-room the *rinpoche* begins to recite the *Bardö T'ödröl* to the dead man, hoping and believing that his consciousness has entered the first of three post-death *bardö* states, the *Chikhai Bardö*. He quietly speaks into Wangchuk's ears:

> O son of noble family, Chosphel Wangchuk! We are here to help you. Now the time has arrived for you to seek the way . . . the objective clear light of the first *bardö* will dawn . . . you will experience [ultimate] reality stark and [as] void-like space, your immaculate naked awareness dawning clear and void without horizon or center. At that instant, you yourself must recognize it as yourself, you must stay with that experience. This radiance is the mind of all the Buddhas, the awakened ones. Do not be afraid of it; recognize it as yourself.
>
> (Thurman, 1994, p.122)

Several times he repeats his instructions, appealing to the dead man's consciousness to recognize its (his) own Buddha nature in the luminous and vibrant emptiness of the Immortal Light, to unite with the indescribable transparency, and thereby to attain ultimate liberation and freedom from birth and death.

But the *rinpoche* knows that the best moments for the experience of ultimate reality as limitless light had occurred at the moment of Wangchuk's death, when his consciousness and body were beginning to separate – and that these precious moments have passed. Are not Wangchuk's experiences during and after death being determined by his karma, his thoughts and emotional states during the transition to the *bardö* states, the emotional atmosphere that surrounds him, and the prayers and skilful practices of the *rinpoche* and the quietly chanting monks? The *rinpoche* and the monks are doing everything they can to guide Wangchuk's consciousness toward the light path, but it is now falling into a dreamless swoon.

Four days after his death, Wangchuk's consciousness is suddenly recovering from its swoon. Having entered the *Chönyid Bardö*, he must now face a complete reversal of reality, a reversal of everything that until now had seemed familiar to him. Desperately he tries to cling to that which he takes to be real, but which is not. Hovering above his body, his former home, the 'illusory mental body' with its attached consciousness is now observing the living, not realizing that he has become disembodied and invisible. Wangchuk's wife is placing his favourite food before the corpse, and so he tries to speak to her. Hearing no answer, he grows annoyed at her but also feels a slowly growing, nameless fear. Floating past a mirror, he is puzzled when his reflection does not appear in it. Looking down on his body, he mistakes it for a pig in clothes. How can that be? His senses and understanding having become sharper than ever, he listens to the wailing women in the adjacent room. 'Who has died?' he asks himself, and a cold dread overcomes him. To his horror, he gradually discovers that it is he who has died. His life is slowly but steadily dismantled before his terrified, invisible eyes.

Coloured lights and piercing rays flash before his eyes, and thunderous sounds hit his ears. He is growing ever more frightened and angry. These karma-laden emotions serve him poorly, since they are forcing him to travel further down the road toward rebirth. As his body is about to be cremated, his consciousness enters a dreamlike state, becoming simultaneously the creator and observer of a vivid series of hallucinations and mind-projections. His 'illusory mental body' or 'desire body' is capable of instantaneous, unlimited motion as directed by his desires. Thought and action have become one with him. But though his thoughts instantly and magically become true, he cannot control them. It is not he who rules his thoughts, but it is his thoughts which rule him.

Cremation

The day has arrived when, following the astrologer's calculations, Wangchuk Chosphel's corpse is to be burned. A large number of relatives, visitors, monks and helpers have assembled in the house. The guests all bring their gifts: bread, beer, flour, biscuits and money. Together with other female relatives, Wangchuk's wife and daughter are sitting in the kitchen, crying, reciting mantras and singing sad songs, while lamenting Wangchuk's death and praising his virtues. A group of men are sitting in the next room drinking salted butter tea and beer made from barley. The monks and the astrologer perform their intricate ceremonies to guide the deceased on his way through the *bardö* (Brauen, 1980)

Wangchuk's body is placed in a sedan-chair covered with cloth on all sides and is carried by male *phaspun* friends to the cremation site. A group of richly attired monks playing oboes, drums and cymbals accompany him on this, his last earthly journey. As the flames engulf his body, the monks conduct a fire ritual to purify the deceased from all sins, attempting to burn away all attachments and obstacles that might interfere with his release from the round of life, death and rebirth. Their blessings, they hope, will soar to heaven and create a mind-created force-field favourable to his future destiny. Soon the monks return to Wangchuk's former home where they auction off his clothes and personal belongings. While Wangchuk's consciousness is now wandering through the *bardö*, his physical existence has come to an end.

Bardö visions

Wangchuk's lama is reading the *Bardö T'ödröl* to him:

> O son of noble family, Chosphel Wangchuk, listen: the whole of space will shine with a blue light, and blessed [Buddha] Vairocana will appear before you. . . . The blue light . . . of consciousness in its basic purity . . . luminous, clear, sharp, and brilliant, will come towards you . . . and pierce you so that your eyes cannot bear it. . . . Do not be frightened . . . it is the light-ray of Vairocana's compassion.
>
> (Freemantle and Trungpa, 1975, p.42)

Wangchuk is now experiencing a series of overwhelming visions of archetypal Buddhas. They first appear to him from his heart in their unbearably brilliant splendour, and next emerge from his brain in their terrifying forms as blood-drinking wrathful deities. His lama admonishes him to merge with these Buddhas, to dissolve into the brilliant rainbow light of their bodies, to recognize their images as the primordial, spontaneous play and radiance of his mind. But Wangchuk, bewildered and frightened by the shimmering lights, piercing rays and terrifying sounds, feels faint and dizzy as he rapidly falls into the lower realms of neurotic anxiety and self-induced suffering.

Because Wangchuk has been unable to recognize as his own projections the overwhelming visions of archetypal Buddhas in their serene and terrifying forms, his mental body and consciousness are now entering the grey twilight zone of the *Sidpa Bardö*. As his consciousness enters an ever more dreamlike state, his mind begins to curl back upon itself. Floating pieces of his identity and flickering phantoms appear before his inner eye; these are as real to him as a dream is to the dreamer. The phantoms represent the surviving witnesses to his former deeds. Unformed thoughts shape themselves into vivid hallucinations which move his illusory mental body around at will.

There now appears before him Yama (Tibetan: Shinje), Lord and Judge of the Dead, together with his minions. Consulting his infallible Mirror of Karma reflecting all of Wangchuk's good and bad actions, the stern judge pronounces his severe verdict. It is as if the mind of Wangchuk is punishing itself for some of his past deeds.

Still reading the *Bardö T'ödröl* to him, Wangchuk's lama attempts to explain this terrifying vision to him:

> Yama will tie a rope around your neck and lead you away. He will cut off your head, rip out your heart, pull out your guts, lick your brains, drink your blood, eat your flesh, and gnaw your bones. . . . Don't fear Yama . . . you cannot die. . . . Your form is the void itself. . . . The Yama-deities are your own hallucinations and themselves are forms of the void. . . . Voidness cannot harm voidness.
>
> (Thurman, 1994, p.175)

Some days later Wangchuk sees himself surrounded by the lights of the six *lokas*, that is, the six kinds of beings among whom he might find rebirth. The six lights invite him to be reborn among egotistic humans, envious titans, proud and sensual gods, ignorant brutes, greedy and hungry ghosts, or angry hell beings. He dimly remembers some of their shapes and characteristics from his former life, because he had many times seen them depicted on the monastery walls, where their vividly painted bodies filled up the Wheel of Life.

The Wheel of Life

Close to the entrance door of every large Ladakhi monastery one can find a painting of the Wheel of Life (*Bhavacakra*) which in a concrete, easily understandable form sums up the worldview of Vajrayana Buddhism. In earlier times, Wangchuk had sometimes stood in front of it with a friend who liked to point out to him the ominous parts of the painting depicting human beings suffering in the Buddhist version of purgatory. While they had smiled at the figures, they could not forget them.

The wheel depicts the six kinds of beings in the six zones of existence which together make up *samsara*, the realm of suffering, illusion and rebirth. Yama, Lord of Death holds the wheel between his claws and teeth, symbolizing that attachment to *samsara* represents a kind of spiritual death. Fortunately, every sentient being is born with the possibility of reaching enlightenment or Buddhahood, thus escaping the wheel of suffering.

At the hub of the wheel Wangchuk and his friend could see three theriomorphic symbols representing 'mental poisons'. These are said to turn the wheel (and thereby all existence), reproducing forever the karmic stages of birth, death, and rebirth. The three poisons are symbolized by a pig, a rooster or cock, and a snake. The pig symbolizes ignorance and illusion, the cock greed and lust, and the snake hate, envy and jealousy. The three animals bite each other's tails, reflecting intrinsic connections between the basic manifestations of the mental poisons, that is, of evil and sin.

The symbolic nature of the three animals is easily understood since they represent a kind of 'Buddhist id'. In a way similar to Freud's theory, a combination of blind sexual and aggressive impulses together with ignorance or repression forms the core of worldly human nature. But unlike orthodox psychoanalysis, Tibetan Buddhism teaches that we can overcome the basic impulses of greed, hate and attachment to egoistic goals by striving simultaneously for our own liberation and that of all other sentient beings. By recognizing and sharing universal sorrow, we overcome our egocentricity and become part of the ceaseless flow of life. More generally, liberation can be accomplished by following the basic teachings (*dharma*) of Buddhism; meditation, empathy for the suffering of others, nonattachment to the illusions of this world, and the fundamental insight that the self is a steadily shifting mixture of karmic factors. All life is transitory, and an attachment to the goods of this world chain a person to *samsara* and the steadily turning wheel of life. Greed, hate, illicit lust, envy, jealousy, egoism and ignorance make up the basic links of this iron chain. In this view, the end of desire is also the end of sorrow.

Because human beings are ignorant, they need models of perfection. In Vajrayana Buddhism, the saviour figure of the *bodhisattva* serves as such a model. *Bodhisattvas* are enlightened beings who, out of compassion for all sentient creatures, forgo their chance to enter the blissful. timeless state of Nirvana which would take them out of the wheel of life. Instead, *bodhisattvas* descend to the earthly realm where they become incarnated in *tulkus* and *rinpoches*, including the Dalai Lama and some of the abbots of Ladakh's monasteries. The Dalai Lama is a reincarnation of Chenrezig (Sanskrit: Avalokiteshvara), patron deity of Tibet and manifestation of the principle of compassion, a principle which pervades the teachings of Vajrayana Buddhism.

Although Wangchuk did not grasp certain details of the wheel (which can only be understood by the theologically trained monks), he had gained a deeply intuitive understanding of the basic interpretation of human nature and human destiny symbolized by the Wheel of Life.

Rebirth

It is now six weeks after Wangchuk's death, and his restless *nam shes* is floating like a leaf through the sky. The images and memories of his former existence have almost completely crumbled away, and he does not remember the piercing luminosity that had engulfed him at the hour of his death. There remains only a vague feeling that once he had almost been annihilated by a blazing, sun-like energy. Now clothed in the illusory body of a young child, he is driven here and there by the savage winds of karma created by his errant thoughts. They pursue him in the form of restless beings and inviting places. His terrifying ride takes him right through rocks and mountains, and so he is desperately searching for a womb that will provide him with shelter, peace and solidity.

In the village of Stok, the young couple Dolma and Tsering are making love. Buried beneath warm blankets to protect themselves against the icy autumn air, they search for each other's bodies. High above them in the piercing coldness of the night, Wangchuk's *nam shes* is filled with a vision of Dolma's opening 'lotus gate'. While resenting his future father, Tsering, he is irresistibly attracted to Dolma's gate and enters it to find himself in a gem-studded palace – or so Dolma's womb appears to him. As Dolma and Tsering unite, Wangchuk's substance-less, dream-like karmic body merges into the mucous intermingling of egg and semen. Wangchuk has found a new body; his karmic destiny has been fulfilled. He has been reabsorbed into the ceaseless cosmic flux of which he has been and will be a part.

Soon the black velvet of the sky is losing its lustre and a cold dawn rises above the snow-clad peaks of Ladakh. Below them, the village of Stok is beginning to warm up beneath the first rays of the golden morning sun. Tsering and Dolma rise, her mind filled with floating images of a dream dimly remembered. Dolma smiles: It was a good dream, perhaps an omen that she has conceived the long desired son. Her ardent prayers may have been answered! She listens to two old women cackling next door, while the birds are continuing their morning concert. A dog barks, and a door is slammed. Soon, Dolma and Tsering are out in the fields harvesting the barley which had been ripening during the brief summer months and is now ready to be cut. Village life is resuming its slow, steady rhythm. A new yet also very old life is on its way, but Wangchuk will remember nothing of his former existence.

In the coming months, more couples are making love, more babies are born, more old people die; and more invisible wanderers are blown across the barren landscape searching desperately for new wombs. Scared by the armies of illusion, they search for new houses of bones, with flesh and blood for plaster. Some of the 'lucky' ones are reborn as humans or gods, while less 'lucky' ones become dumb animals, greedy ghosts or angry hell-beings. The wanderers look for final release and freedom, a freedom they can gain only through hard spiritual practice and the compassion and wisdom that must be won through a long procession of lifetimes. For them, as for all sentient beings, the wheel of life has seemingly been spinning forever: life and death, death and life, life and death . . .

Grace-bestowing saviours

There is always hope and faith. Buddhism is not a harsh religion, and it does not preach eternal condemnation. A person's suffering ends the moment he or she has completely woken up from the delusions of this world, becoming a Buddha in the process. To seek Buddhahood is open to us all. Spiritually less advanced beings can always rely on help from the numina in the sky, the all-seeing, all-knowing, all-compassionate Buddhas and *bodhisattvas*. Mahayana Buddhism and its offspring, Tibetan Buddhism, emphasize the importance of the saving grace bestowed by countless *bodhisattvas*. Among them, Chenrezig and his female emanation, Tara (Dolma), come first in the hearts of the people.[6]

Somewhere high above Stok village, but also in the hearts and minds of its farmers and monks, in a timeless realm without form, reside the bliss-bestowing Buddhas and *bodhisattvas*. To help suffering creatures

6 When Avalokiteshvara entered East Asia, he was transformed into the Goddess of Mercy, Kuan-yin (Japanese: Kannon). In old China and in Japan, her temples could be found everywhere. She was the goddess to whom the people brought all their troubles, just as today Tibetans and Ladakhis pray to Dolma and Chenrezig in their hour of need.

they descend from their realms of bliss and incarnate in *tulkus* and *rinpoches* who assist the villagers in their hour of death. If the villagers' hearts are filled with pure compassion and faith, and their minds with lucid, spacious, one-pointed wisdom, the *rinpoches* (and the other monks) can help them overcome the relentless cycle of birth, death and rebirth, or at least assure them of a favourable rebirth.

Once, the Buddha Opame looked down on this world from his celestial abode, seeing that all beings were suffering endlessly. He felt great compassion for them, and from this thought the *boddhisattva* Chenrezig was born. Appearing on an island in the centre of Lhasa, he became the protector of Tibet. The Lord of Compassion vowed that he would not leave this world until all sentient beings had gained final release and liberation.

Preaching the Buddhist *dharma*, he led many beings to freedom but new beings without number arose and cried to him for help. To help Chenrezig better fulfill his task, Opame gave him eleven heads, a thousand arms, and an all-seeing eye in the palm of each hand. Now he could see and reach out to the numberless sentient beings asking for his help. As he cried out in despair for their suffering, a crystal teardrop formed on his cheek giving birth to Dolma (Tara), Tibet's saviouress. Today Chenrezig is incarnate in the Dalai Lama, the spiritual leader of the Tibetan people. Chenrezig's and Dolma's statues can be found in many of Ladakh's monasteries, their images engraved in the hearts of the people. They are certain that Dolma and Chenrezig's assistance, compassion and wisdom can be counted on by those in need, and especially by the dying on their twisting journeys through the *bardö* realm.

The *Bardö T'ödröl* and human destiny

In Ladakh as elsewhere, death stamps order on the seeming randomness of human existence and reduces everyone to his or her spiritual core. At death, humans assume their true identity which until then had been hidden beneath a thick crust of the trivialities of everyday life. The twisted grooves of their minds, having been shaped by the inextinguishable memories of their actions, give birth to hallucinations containing the psychological projections of a lifetime of experiences, desires, dislikes, fears and twisted imaginations. The sweet or bitter fruits of karma are always ripening. We alone are responsible for them. When we die the only things of worth we can take with us are the results of successful spiritual practice, and nothing more. Without spiritual practice, and assistance from others, there is only a small chance that we will be reborn into a state of happiness.

But help is nearby, if we only ask for it. It is clear to the Ladakhi that his destiny after death depends not only on his karma, but also on the emotional atmosphere surrounding him in his hour of need, the positive psychic energies created by the sincere prayers of his loved ones, the invisible flow of energies produced by the potent rituals and prayers of the monks, and the skilful guiding hand of his lama who himself must be pure and sincere. Together, these forces shape the fate of his surviving consciousness. Salvation, then, depends on efforts and forces emanating both from within and without the dying person.

The various Buddhist traditions have frequently differed about the question of whether self-created karma or divine grace determines the destiny of the dying person (Anesaki, 1963; Smith, 1991). The Theravada Buddhists of Sri Lanka and Indochina honour the last words of the Buddha: 'All things are impermanent. Work out your own salvation with diligence'; and so they emphasize that salvation depends above all on the person's own relentless efforts. In contrast, the followers of the Pure Land sects of East Asia believe that a person's last thoughts before his death determine his future fate. If at the moment of death he completely relies on the grace of the Buddha Amitabha, he will surely be reborn in the Western Paradise, no matter how sinful his life had been.

Tibetan Buddhism strikes a middle path between these two extreme possibilities: it argues that while karma steers our journey through the *bardö* realms, the prayers of loved ones and the skilful guiding hand of our lama are of equal importance. It is also true that a few religious 'virtuosi' in Ladakh and Tibet have aspired to Buddhahood 'in one lifetime' through their own relentless efforts, spiritual practice and many years of meditation. The popular biography of Tibet's eleventh-century poet–saint and hermit Milarepa portrays the disciplined struggle needed to achieve final liberation at the hour of death (Evans-Wentz, 1969). For him, as for all Buddhists, the practice of death also meant the practice of freedom. Today, as in Milarepa's time, one can find in some Himalayan caves anchorites who practise daily meditation on death, thereby hoping to win in one lifetime ultimate freedom from the bondages of attachment and karma. The people admire and support them, but few of them are able or willing to follow their demanding example.

The *Bardö T'ödröl* reflects the desire to write a positive death script in the face of the harsh doctrines of karma and rebirth. It serves as a priceless travel guide for the dying person and his (or her) surviving consciousness. The book provides a map of the inner landscape of the mind, thereby helping the deceased to recognize both his hallucinations and his fundamental nature. Hearing it assures the dying person that others have been on the same path before him, and that they have discovered a secure way through the wilderness of the unconscious mind. The person's ongoing consciousness is assured that heaven and hell, gods and demons are merely projections originating in the recesses of his own heart and mind – that they do not exist 'out there'. If calmly observed, the visions will self-destruct, illustrating the principle that by clearly recognizing and giving a name to the mysterious and unspeakable, humans can gain power over it.

By conquering time we also conquer death. Normally the dance of life and death appears to us superimposed on the background of the stainless mirror of Eternal Mind, but if we succeed in seeing through and beyond the illusory dance we will merge with the blazing mirror into a non-dualistic, translucent, calm and timeless reality beyond words and concepts. The images of life and death are merely dust dancing on the mirror, which must be cleared away before ultimate reality can appear in its purity. The promise is that once this has occurred, we will find an abiding peace beyond the ceaseless flux of life and death. To its believers, then, Buddhism delivers incorruptible value. It emphasizes the relentless flow of time, but then promises to conquer it.

The *Bardö T'ödröl* is not only a book to help the dying; it is above all a guide for the living. Like other traditional 'books of dead', it proposes that the art of living well and the art of dying well are one and the same. It also suggests a reversal of one's conventional notions of truth: whatever is concrete, externally visible, and therefore seemingly real is in truth only an illusion which sooner or later will fade away. In contrast, the innermost, hidden and indestructible layer of our heart–mind constitutes our true Buddha nature, and thus also our true identity. The more we become attached to the goods of this world, that is, the more 'realistic' we become in the wordly sense, the more our true identity disappears from our view. In truth, the so-called realist is altogether a prisoner of *samsara*.

Vajrayana Buddhism is above all a theory of mental states. According to it, we are nothing but our thoughts: usually they rule us, but we do not rule them. Just as Wangchuk's mental body had drifted helplessly across the landscape of Ladakh, driven by his thoughts, fears and desires, so we drift helplessly across our merging landscapes of life and death, driven by our thoughts, fears and desires.

We are Wangchuk, just as in some previous life he has been us. Our bodies are merely loaned to us; we should (but do not) feel that they can be as easily discarded as a pair of old jeans.

Nowhere on earth have the recesses of the unconscious mind been explored more creatively and more relentlessly than in the *Bardö T'ödröl*, and more generally on the roof of the world. Its symbols express a multifaceted, but ultimately inexpressible reality lodged in our hearts. The symbols are not themselves the reality; they can only point us towards it.

Ultimate reality cannot be fully known by the reflecting intellect. It can, however, be directly experienced during meditation and perhaps also at the hour of death. But then it may be too late, since without prior meditative practice and experience a person will hardly be able to recognize it in its purest and most enduring form. He will instead feel overwhelmed and threatened by its sheer splendour and power. From the Buddhist point of view, the person has then wasted his or her entire life and must begin all over again. What a waste of time!

POSTSCRIPT

Seven weeks have passed since Wangchuk's death. His wife Pema is sitting with the other family members in the altar room, listening to two murmuring monks reading the *Bardö T'ödröl* one more time for the welfare of the deceased. Butter lamps throw their flickering light onto Wangchuk's photograph which hangs above the family altar.

Pema's aching heart has slowly grown more serene during the last few weeks. During those weeks she has found much social support from her neighbours and family members, and thus has been able to share her sorrows with them, just as in the past she had shared theirs. Now Pema feels at peace, because she and her family have done everything possible for Wangchuk's wandering spirit.

After the monks have left she prostrates herself before the altar and begins her prayers:

I take refuge in the Buddha,
I take refuge in the *dharma* [the teachings; the truth],
I take refuge in the *sangha* [the Buddhist community].

A little later, Pema and her daughter step outside the family home. Behind them, the wind-beaten shapes of decaying stupas throw their ever-lengthening shadows across the snow-covered fields. The stupas contain the ashes and fading mortuary images of monks long since dead, vaguely reminding Pema of the sacred but decaying nature of all life. As the sun is sinking behind a wall of giant peaks, the deep sounds of gigantic copper trumpets drift from far-distant Chemdre Monastery across the darkening landscape, evoking the basic vibrations of the universe. On the other side of the valley, three tiny specks move with glacial speed across the steep mountain. Then everything is silent – so very silent.

Above Pema, a flower-galaxy of brilliant stars emerges across the darkly translucent sky, reminding her that Wangchuk's spirit might still be lost somewhere in this immense emptiness. Where might he be now, she asks her daughter. Has he found a new home in a human womb, or must he suffer rebirth among the lower beings? But soon her heart quiets: has not the all-knowing *rinpoche* told her that Wangchuk had lived a good life, and that he would certainly find refuge in a good human womb, if not final release?

Pema steps back into her home, the total annihilating power of death slowly drifting to the fringes of her consciousness. Just now, her daughter is telling her some good news: she has become pregnant. Spring is bound to arrive soon and life will blossom again! Pema fingers her prayer-beads:

> Om! Mani padme hum!
> Lord of Compassion, please let me hold my grandchild in my arms, before I too must cross the great divide!
> Protect my daughter and the little one who is now growing in her womb!
> Bestow your mercy on them!
> Om! Mani padme hum!
> Om! Mani padme hum!
> Om! Mani padme hum!

SUMMARY

- ☐ Buddhism has an especially close affinity with death. It emphasizes the principle of impermanence and the ceaseless transmutation of all existing beings and forces.
- ☐ Buddhism emphasizes impermanence, the cycle of birth, death and rebirth, and the suffering that accompanies impermanence.
- ☐ Religion must protect us from the terrors of finitude. Mahayana Buddhism introduced the saving idea of nirvana, a form of being beyond change, time, space, form, death and suffering.

☐ Some Buddhists also believe that they will, after death, go to a blissful life in the Pure Land of Lord Amitabha.

☐ A person's perceptions of and attachment to his or her 'I' are at the root of suffering. The 'I' is as impermanent and illusory as anything else produced by the senses.

☐ A dream-like feeling of impermanence is most keenly felt by Tibetan Buddhists and those from Ladakh (Vajrayana or Tantric Buddhists) where the harshness of life causes many to seek liberation from the wheel of life by becoming monks.

☐ Theravada Buddhists believe in instant reincarnation after death.

☐ Vajrayana Buddhists believe in an intermediate *bardö* period (up to forty-nine days) between death and rebirth.

☐ In contrast to the grandeur of limitless space and endless time the ego is small and transient.

☐ Behind vastness and change the pilgrim seeks the Radiant Light of Pure Reality, the Mind that perceives change but does not change itself.

☐ Two forms of Buddhism are the Higher Buddhism of the monks and Folk Buddhism. The latter includes belief in magic and countless 'gods' and other invisible beings who help or harm humans. Many rituals are needed to placate them and to advance the person's security in this world and the next.

☐ All events are determined by the interaction of visible and invisible moral and natural causes. The transcendental world breaks through our normal consciousness in dreaming, meditation trances, the experience of inner light at the point of death and the two *bardö* states after death.

☐ Tibetan monks guide the deceased person's spirit through the perilous *bardö* by reading from the Book of the Dead (*Bardö T'ödröl*).

☐ Buddhism is the most psychologically orientated of world religions and is open to interpretation in the contemporary language of psychology. Thanks to the presence of Tibetan refugees it is one of the fastest growing religions in England, Germany and the USA.

☐ An elderly or dying Ladakhi Buddhist withdraws from the world of illusion to prepare himself for death. He prays for a better reincarnation. An abbot (*rinpoche*) helps him to loosen the bonds of attachments to life.

☐ The spirit's progress after death is determined by his karma, his emotional state, the emotional atmosphere surrounding him, and the prayers and rituals of the monks.

☐ When death occurs local monks, members of the family's local society (*phaspun*) and an astrologer are called. His lama guides his consciousness (*nam shes*) and the astrologer prepares a death horoscope and prescribes prayers and ceremonies to ward off hostile influences.

☐ The rinpoche summons the *nam shes* back to the body before attempting to eject it a second time into the body of the Lord of Western Paradise (Opame). He is aided by the monks and *phaspun*. Relatives, friends and neighbours bring food and drink for the ceremonies, which continue for several days.

☐ The *bardö* is divided into three phases. During the first the *nam shes* is in a swoon. The *rinpoche* repeatedly enjoins it to enter the clear light of ultimate reality, to recognize its own Buddha nature. During the second *bardö* the *nam shes* recovers from its swoon and becomes aware, and frightened by, its own disembodied identity. It gradually becomes aware that it has died and perceives the dismantling of its life. Finally it enters the 'illusory mental body' of a child, a dream-like state.

☐ Cremation is carried out at a time determined by the astrologer as propitious. The body is carried in procession in a sedan chair by male *phaspun* friends to the site accompanied by musicians, monks, family and friends. The fire is seen as burning away attachments as well as sins. Clothes and personal belongings are then auctioned.

☐ Meanwhile the *nam shes* is experiencing overwhelming visions of archetypal Buddhas and wrathful deities. The Lord and Judge of the Dead (Shinje) pronounces his verdict. Some days later it meets the six lights (*lokas*) who try to persuade it to become reborn in their negative realms.

☐ These and other dangers can be resisted and liberation from the wheel of life attained by enlightenment, but basic impulses of greed, hate and attachment to egoistic goals must be overcome by striving for one's own liberation and that of all other sentient beings. By recognizing and sharing universal sorrow, we overcome our egocentricity and become part of the ceaseless flow of life.

☐ *Bodhisattvas* are enlightened beings who, out of compassion, forgo their chance to enter Nirvana to become reincarnated in *tulkus* and *rinpoches*. In Vajrayana Buddhism the *bodhisattva* Chenrezig is the patron deity and model of perfection. He is reincarnated as the Dalai Lama. His female emanation, Tara, was formed as a crystal tear in Chenrezig's eye.

☐ Six weeks after death the *nam shes* is still buffeted by the winds of karma; it searches for and finds the 'lotus gate' of a woman in sexual congress, entering her womb to become her unborn child. Less 'lucky' *nam shes* will become dumb animals, greedy ghosts or angry hell-beings.

☐ At death, humans assume their true identity. The only things of worth that we can take with us are the results of spiritual practice. But a person's destiny after death is not only determined by our self-created karma; it is also influenced by the positive energies emanating from the sincere prayers of loved ones and monks.

☐ Theravada Buddhists emphasise the importance of personal effort in achieving salvation, the followers of the Pure Land sects of East Asia emphasize reliance on the grace of the Buddha Amitabha at the moment of death and Tibetan Buddhism strikes a middle path allowing both karma and the prayers of others to play a part.

☐ The *Bardö T'ödröl* proposes that the art of living well and the art of dying well are one and the same.

☐ Following bereavement family members are given much social support by neighbours and extended family who share their sorrow. They may also be reassured by the *rinpoche* of the likely destination of the departed *nam shes*.

APPENDIX: SUGGESTIONS FOR FURTHER READING

Readers interested in a brief introduction to Buddhism might wish to begin with H. Smith (1991, ch.3). His book also contains a lucid chapter on Hinduism, alongside and out of which Buddhism emerged. A charming introduction to Tibetan Buddhism can be found in Lama Lo-drüp's (1982) book, while Lama Govinda (1960) and G. Tucci (1980) offer more elaborate and more conceptually orientated introductions to the same topic. G. Samuel's (1993) scholarly and detailed account includes an extensive bibliography on Tibetan Buddhism. J. Snelling (1991) provides a broadly conceived yet concise overview of Eastern and Western Buddhism. His book also contains much useful practical information including addresses of Buddhist institutions in Western countries. For more detailed histories of Buddhism in the West, consult R. Fields (1986) and N.R. Reat (1994).

Westerners have frequently headed for Tibet and Ladakh in their quest for spiritual knowledge and enlightenment. A classical account of such a spiritual journey has been written by the German-born Lama A. Govinda (1970); also interesting are the 'spiritual travelogues' of the

Greek mountaineer M. Pallis (1974) and the Indian-born English mystic poet A. Harvey (1983).

The reader interested in Ladakh will find in J. Rizvi (1989) a concise introduction to Ladakh's history, culture and people. J. Bray has translated into English a 'novel' by the German missionary S. Ribbach (1986) who describes the life-cycle of a typical Ladakhi farmer, his death included. U.P. Gielen (1993) and U.P. Gielen and D. Chirico-Rosenberg (1993) offer interpretations of the Ladakhi worldview, together with discussions of gender roles and other aspects of Ladakhi society. G. Tucci (1967), the former dean of Western Tibetologists, sums up a lifetime of work in his sympathetic, richly illustrated survey of Tibetan culture and society. For an easy-to-read, down-to-earth anthropological account of a Tibetan people living in the Himalayas see W. Chorlton (1982).

Several English translations of the various versions of the *Bardö T'ödröl* are available; of these R.A.F. Thurman's (1994) is perhaps the most useful one for the general reader. Sogyal Rinpoche (1992) is indispensable for a modern understanding of the broader context and the Tibetan attitudes that have evolved around death and caring for the terminally ill. Additional information about Tibetan approaches to death may be gleaned from G.H. Mullin (1987). For accounts of specific burial and death customs in Ladakh and Tibet, see M. Brauen (1980, 1982), C. Ramble (1982) and S. Ribbach (1940, 1986). C. Corlin (1988) presents a brief, lucid discussion of the symbolism of Tibetan mortuary rites and the *Bardö T'ödröl*. The philosophical puzzles of the Theravada doctrines of death and rebirth are lucidly outlined by C.B. Becker (1989).

A vivid introduction to the Ladakhi way of life and Ladakhi attitudes to death can be found in the two videotapes entitled *The Tibetan Book of the Dead. Part I: A Way of Life*, and *Part II: The Great Liberation*. They are available from Direct Cinema Limited, PO Box 10003, Santa Monica, CA 90410 (Fax: USA-[310] 396–3233).

The reader interested in Buddhist attitudes toward death developed outside Tibet and Ladakh may begin with Y. Hoffman's (1986) beautiful translations of Japanese death poems by Zen monks and Haiku poets. They are preceded by a concise introduction exploring the attitudes and customs surrounding death in historical and present-day Japan. P. Kapleau (1971) explores Zen perspectives on death and dying. For a broader history of Japanese religion including the various Buddhist traditions see M. Anesaki (1963).

Chapter 6

Jewish views and customs on death

Ellen Levine

It is told that on his death bed the Hasidic master Zusia of Hanipol began to cry. When his disciples asked: 'Are you crying because you are afraid that when you stand before the Holy Tribunal, they will ask you, "Why were you not like Moses?"' 'No', replied Zusia: 'Then why do you weep?' he was asked. The master answered: 'Because I am afraid that they will ask me why I was not like Zusia. Then what shall I say?'

Two of the most important commandments in Jewish tradition are to honour the dead and comfort the mourner. We honour the dead by treating the body with respect, by accompanying the deceased to the cemetery, and by honouring the memory of the deceased. We comfort the mourner by being available physically and emotionally for them individually and as a community, by enabling the mourner to grieve and pray in whatever way is best for them, and by helping them to return to life after the death of a loved one.

This chapter will focus on these two important commandments, starting with the care of the individual before and after death, and then focusing on the mourner and the grieving process according to Jewish tradition.

Jews are not a homogeneous group of people. To be Jewish means to share a common religion and historical background. Jewish communities exist in practically every country in the world. While the basic culture of Judaism is the same world-wide, there are many regional differences in how this culture is expressed. There are two broad groups: Ashkenazic and Sephardic Jews. Ashkenazic Jews are of Central or Eastern European origin. Most Ashkenazic Jews traditionally spoke Yiddish which is a mixture of High German, Hebrew, Slavonic and Aramaic languages, although this language is dying out today. Many of the traditional customs or rituals that are associated with Jews in the United States and many parts of Europe are Ashkenazic in origin. Sephardic Jews descended from the Jewish communities of Spain, Africa and the Middle East. Sephardic Jews do not speak Yiddish, but they may speak Ladino, a mixture of Spanish, Arabic and Hebrew. Today Sephardic communities can be seen all over the world, although their customs may not be as familiar as those of the Ashkenazic Jews. Ashkenazic and Sephardic burial and bereavement customs differ, and these differences will be discussed when applicable.

There are varying differences around the world as to how Jewish traditions are still kept. Ever since the destruction of the Great Temple in Jerusalem in 463 BCE (Before the Common Era, equivalent to the term BC), Jews have been dispersed to all areas of the world. As they moved to other areas, the Jews began to assimilate into the local cultures. This assimilation was mostly done out of necessity, for in many cultures those who are different are viewed as evil, or bringers of bad luck. As the Jews assimilated, many customs and traditions were discarded or were blended in with traditions of the country in which they lived.

Over the years, Judaism split into several denominations, the most common of which are Orthodox, Conservative and Reform. Discussion of these denominations is beyond the scope of this chapter. However, some of the differences in regard to burial and mourning practices will be mentioned. Jewish assimilation is especially pronounced in many areas of Europe, United States and Canada. As a consequence, many Jews in Europe and North America do not observe all of the customs and traditions discussed in this chapter, and may in fact not know of their existence. The experience of the death of Anna, the woman who will be mentioned throughout this chapter, reflects the traditions of Ashkenazic Jews living in the United States.

Anna was an 88-year old woman who died of breast cancer while her family was in another state celebrating the graduation of her niece. She had been born in Russia, and had come to the United States as a young girl. She had grown up in a small town in New York State where her parents were dairy farmers, had married a local boy, and raised two children. She had been a widow for many years before her death. While she had remained in the small town for most of her life, the other family members, with the exception of one brother, had moved to other parts of the USA. At the time of her death, only the brother, his wife, and Anna's daughter and son-in-law were living in the same town as Anna.

After Anna's surgery, her physicians felt that she would recover. So her family decided to attend the graduation ceremony of Anna's niece.

However, after the graduation was over, they received a phone call from the hospital in New York. Anna was failing, and her physicians felt that she would soon die. Upon hearing this news, the family members who could arrange to do so rushed to the small town where she lived. They took turns staying with Anna in the hospital. Some family members took care of the shopping. While Anna kept a kosher home (in accordance with Jewish dietary laws), many of the family members did not. Thus one of her nieces who also kept a kosher home volunteered to purchase groceries and keep Anna's house clean. Anna's brother notified their rabbi that she was dying. The rabbi helped the brother make arrangements with the *Chevrah Kadisha* (burial society) in the town to prepare her body for burial when the time came.

According to Jewish tradition, our lives are measured by our deeds and by whether we have lived up to our full potential. Therefore, the time before death is usually spent in a review of one's life. When a person is aware that he or she is dying, he or she begins to look back on his or her life, wondering, 'Did I do all that I could have done to make this world a better place?', 'Was I helpful to others?', 'Did I live up to my potential?', etc. Death is only meaningful if one's life was meaningful as well. This reflection has resulted in an interesting tradition in Judaism, that of the ethical will. Ethical wills are documents in which the person who is dying states his or her legacy to the family. It is a statement of the individual's hopes and dreams for his or her family, the values which he or she would like to pass on, and any other thoughts or messages which the individual would like his or her family to remember. Ethical wills are usually warmly and lovingly written, and can be a great comfort to the family once the individual has died. Anna did not leave such an ethical will, and it is doubtful that she knew of this concept. But before she died, she spoke with several members of her family, including her son and daughter, and told them what she thought would happen to her after she died. She also spoke of her hopes for her children and grandchildren.

The concept of an afterlife, of a world-to-come is fundamental in Judaism. Life after death is referred to as *olam ha-ba*, or the world-to-come. This concept refers to the belief that at death the soul returns to G-d. It also refers to the time of the coming of the Messiah or Messianic Age, when the dead will be reborn and G-d will reign supreme. Suffering on earth will be vindicated, and the righteous will live in eternal peace and harmony, while the wicked will remain in the dust. It is taught that *olam ha-ba* will be experienced by each person as a direct result of that person's life, and the good works that he or she has performed. For it is said: 'Whoever fails to take account of his deeds in this world will not have time to take account of them in the next world. Whoever has not acquired wisdom in this world will not acquire it in the grave' (Moses Hayyim Luzzatto).

Death is seen as a natural ending to life, part of the cycle of life and all living things. Death is not only the great equalizer, it allows us to value life. In the *Pirke Avot* (Ethics of the Fathers) it is said that 'The world is like a vestibule before the world-to-come, prepare yourself in the vestibule, so that you will be able to enter the banquet hall' (*Pirke Avot* 4:21). G-d created death. Death is not meant as a punishment, but something that is natural. The knowledge that life is not forever, and that life is only given to us by G-d for a finite time, assists us in living a life full of meaning. When death approaches, we are filled with anxiety, not about dying, but about how we will be judged after we die. This is demonstrated in the story of Zusia which opened this chapter.

'Better is one period of repentance and good deeds in this world than all of life in the world-to-come, and better is one period of spiritual bliss in the world-to-come than all of life of this world' (*Pirke Avot* 4:22). While the spiritual bliss in the world-to-come is unlike any pleasure to be found in this world, this world is also important. Life is not measured by its length, but by whether we have fulfilled our potential. It is our deeds which bring a fulfilment which is not matched in the world-to-come. Thus this world is important, and should not be given up readily.

In Jewish tradition, when an individual dies, his or her soul returns to G-d. The soul is immortal, and has consciousness and awareness. It is thought that at the time of death the soul hovers near the body and observes the funeral. Then the soul goes through a purification process to cleanse it of the sins which it committed during life. Every soul goes through purification, but the length of the process varies. For a truly righteous soul, the process may take only a moment. For the very wicked, the process may take over a year. Once the purification process is completed, the soul 'lives' in the presence of G-d, in a world of peace and contentment, without pain and suffering. Maimonides, a Sephardic Jewish physician and one of the greatest of the Jewish scholars during the Middle Ages believed that the world-to-come is a world of pure spirit, where the soul lives on for eternity without the body. Other theories say that the soul sleeps, waiting for the final judgement which will occur when the Messiah arrives, at which time the soul and body will be rejoined in the world-to-come. One who believed in the latter theory was the prophet Ezekiel, who had a vision of a valley of dry bones. These bones represented the Jewish people. One by one the bones arose, and were reattached into bodies. The souls of the dead were joined with the bodies. Ezekiel believed that he was seeing the time of resurrection in the world-to-come. 'Thus said the Lord G-d: I am going to open your graves and lift you out of the graves . . . and bring you to the land of Israel. I will put My breath into you and you shall live again' (Ezekiel 37:12–14).

Among many modern Jews, immortality is viewed as not coming from the immortality of the soul, but through our descendants, our deeds and achievements, and through the continuance of the Jewish people on Earth. Thus Jewish customs surrounding death and dying are intended to accompany the dying and the bereaved, to dispel the loneliness that comes with death and bereavement, and to embrace the dying and bereaved within the Jewish community.

As with many societies, care of the individual before death is seen as important. Jewish tradition values life. Judaism is a faith that embraces all of life. It is written in the Bible: 'I put before you, life and death, blessing and curse. Choose life' (Deuteronomy 30:19). Death is seen as a transition from the life that is to the life that is yet to come. Jewish tradition holds that every life, even as it ebbs, is to be respected and revered. Therefore, one of the most important obligations in Judaism is visiting the sick. However, the rabbis also realized the reality and inevitability of death. Thus one should not only visit the ill, one should also do whatever one can to aid the dying person's peace of mind. This may involve assisting in the preparation of a will, making funeral arrangements, disposition of property, etc. Anna's family visited her in the hospital, and took care of her house and her pets. Her son and daughter talked with her of her hopes and fears, and her wishes for her children. Her son also made sure that her will was up to date and legally in order. Her brother contacted the rabbi to make arrangements for the funeral.

When the time came for Anna to die, the family members gathered around her bed in the hospital to say good-bye to her. Anna and her family had agreed beforehand that no heroic efforts should be taken to continue to keep her alive, but that she wanted to be as alert as possible in order to say good-bye to her loved ones. These decisions were discussed with Anna's physicians, who agreed to make her as comfortable as possible. While Judaism emphasizes the importance of life, it also accepts the reality of death. For centuries there has been controversy over both prolonging and hastening death. The Talmud, the source of Jewish law. states that one should not hasten death. 'Rabbi

Meir used to compare a dying man to a flickering lamp; the moment one touches it he puts it out. So, too whoever closes the eyes of a dying man is accounted as though he has snuffed out life' (Talmud, Tractate Mourning, chapter 1, p. 4). However, the dying must be made as comfortable as possible, and nothing must keep the soul from leaving the body. It is stated that one must remove any hindrances, such as noise, so that the person may die in peace. In modern times this also means that the patient or family may ask for a 'do not resuscitate' order, or for the withdrawal of life support systems.

Since one cannot hasten death, it has been asked if one can pray for the death of another as a release from insufferable pain. Jewish law states that it is permissible to pray for mercy for a very sick person, so that his or her soul may rest easily. As it says in Ecclesiastes 'There is a time for dying' (3:2). When a person's time to die comes, the soul should be able to depart from the body in peace, and those around him or her must let the soul depart without heroic efforts to retrieve it, and without wailing. However, the issue of artificial life supports (including feeding tubes, hydration and other methods of giving medication) is currently being debated among rabbis. Therefore, the patient and/or family may want to consult a rabbi concerning these issues.

Before Anna died, the rabbi came for one last visit in order to help her recite the *Vidui*, or deathbed confessional prayer. The *Vidui* emphasizes the reality of death. It can be very comforting to the patient and/or the family. As Anna read the prayer, she affirmed her awareness of the reality and imminence of her death. After she read the *Vidui* she then recited the *Shema*. This is the fundamental prayer in Judaism, which affirms our faith in the one G-d, the G-d of Israel. The prayer also reflects the fact that although we die alone, we are not totally alone, for G-d is with us, and that we have faith that when we die, our soul will rise up to be with G-d.

Over the centuries, rabbis and sages have developed rituals for death and mourning which emphasize the reality of death, and help the bereaved to face that reality and acknowledge their grief. These customs and rituals enable the bereaved to grieve, to recover emotionally, to continue their lives, pay respect to the dead and to honour the dead by perpetuating their memory. There are two basic principles of Jewish law which relate to death and dying. The first law is that humans were created in the image of G-d, therefore the body must not be altered in any way. The second law is a corollary to the first. Since we are created in the image of G-d, we must show respect for the whole person, both the body and the soul. Therefore, the principle governing the care of the body immediately after death is that of the sacredness of the person. The preparations for Anna's burial were carried out in respect for the sacredness of her as a person created in the image of G-d.

Jewish customs at the time of death are numerous. Although many of these customs may not be possible if the individual dies in a hospital, Anna's family performed or participated in several of the customs.

During the last moments of Anna's life, no one left her room. (It is permitted to leave the room if one cannot control one's emotions or is physically ill.) All of her family and friends who could attend were there, from her 80-year old brother, to her nephew's nine-month old daughter. It is considered an act of great respect to watch over a person as their soul leaves this world to be with G-d. After Anna died, the windows in the room were opened so that the soul could leave the body at the time of death and begin its journey to G-d.

Family members closed Anna's eyes, and straightened her body so that her feet pointed towards the door. Her body was covered with a sheet. These are gestures of respect, and of honouring the body. Some Orthodox Jews keep the old custom of placing the body on the floor after twenty minutes, then pouring water outside the home as a sign to friends and neighbours that a death has occurred (the hospital did not allow this for safety reasons). This is actually a custom that was adopted during the Middle Ages from non-Jewish cultures who thought that ghosts and spirits cannot cross water. Among some Jews it is also customary to place ashes on the eyelids of the deceased, symbolizing the phrase 'For dust you are, and to dust you shall return' (Genesis 3:19). A candle is sometimes placed near the head of the deceased – however, again the hospital did not allow this for safety reasons.

Anna's relatives and friends asked her for forgiveness for any harm or discomfort they may have caused her during her lifetime. (This may be done at the time of death or at the burial.)

Back at Anna's house, her mirrors were covered. This custom dates back to a superstition that the soul could see the reflection of loved ones in the mirror, and may try to 'snatch' them. The rabbis reinterpreted this custom as a method of discouraging vanity and the emphasis of beauty in a time of grief and despair. Another explanation given is that the image of G-d that is reflected in the mirror has been diminished by the recent death.

From the moment of death until the burial, Anna's body was not left alone. This custom may have originated from the need to protect the body from animals in the night. However, as Judaism considers an individual to have been created in G-d's image, and that the body is the receptacle of the soul, the body is to be honoured, respected, and guarded. A *shomer* (watcher or guard), preferably a family member or friend, stays with the body at all times. It is considered an honour to be a *shomer*. Anna's son and grandsons took turns guarding her body from her death until the burial.

Anna died on a Tuesday. However, if she had died on the Sabbath (from sundown on Friday to sundown on Saturday), the Sabbath candles would not have been lit near her. Only minimal arrangements for the funeral may be made during the Sabbath, as it is a day of rest. The arrangements are made only out of respect for the dead. The body may not be moved on the Sabbath.

At the time of Anna's death, her rabbi was notified. He in turn notified the mortuary as well as the *Chevrah Kadisha* (burial society) who are in charge of washing and preparing Anna's body for burial.

PREPARATION OF THE REMAINS

An absolute requirement of Jewish law is that the body must be cleansed and made pure. This is usually performed by the *Chevrah Kadisha* (burial society) through the religious ritual known as *Taharah* (purification). If there is no *Chevrah Kadisha*, a rabbi should be consulted, as non-Jews are not allowed to perform the *Taharah*. Members of the family do not participate in the *Taharah*, as it is considered too painful for them to bear.

Jewish tradition recognizes that everyone must die, rich and poor, and that everyone is equal before G-d. In Judaism, it is not a person's possessions, but their soul which is of supreme importance. Therefore, Anna was washed by the female members of the *Chevrah Kadisha* (male members were not allowed, in order to honour her and preserve her dignity). She was then dressed in simple, handmade, perfectly clean, white garments, which symbolize purity, simplicity and dignity. During the cleansing and preparation for burial, the women recited prayers asking G-d for forgiveness for any sins that she may have committed, and that she may be granted eternal peace.

If the deceased is a man, after he is clothed, he is wrapped in his *tallit* (prayer shawl). At least one of the four fringes of the *tallit* is cut off. The fringes serve as reminders of G-d's commandments, and as the individual is dead, there is no need for a reminder, since the individual's soul is with G-d. If the man has never worn a *tallit*, one may be purchased for the burial, if the family so desires. Many Conservative and Reform Jewish women also wear a *tallit*. A rabbi should be consulted as to whether a woman may be buried with the *tallit* wrapped around her. Anna was raised in an Orthodox family, and did not wear a prayer shawl.

A tradition among some Spanish Jews is that of the final blessing. When a parent dies, the surviving children gather in the presence of the rabbi. The rabbi asks the children to ask for forgiveness from the parent. The children kiss the hand of the parent, then the rabbi places the hand of the parent on each child's head and recites the Priestly Benediction (the blessing that the parent gives to the child every Sabbath), symbolically marking the final blessing children receive from their parents.

In general, Jewish tradition objects to post-mortem examinations. The body is a reflection of the image of G-d, and must not be mutilated. Post-mortems are generally permitted in cases where causes of death must be ascertained for medical or legal reasons (e.g. in cases of murder, suicide or accidental death). When in doubt over whether or not a post-mortem can be performed, a rabbi should be consulted. If the deceased was found with bloody clothes, severed limbs, or had a previous amputation, the limbs and bloody clothes must be buried with the person. Jewish law considers blood and any body parts to be part of the individual, and thus they must be buried with an individual.

Similar issues surround organ or tissue donation. However, this is another area which is currently debated by many rabbis. As organ donation may help to save the life of another, some rabbis consider it a very important and positive act. Other rabbis argue that the body must not be mutilated, since it is thought that when the Messiah comes the physical body will be resurrected, so therefore the body must be kept intact.

BURIAL

Anna's funeral was held the day after her death, in accordance with Jewish law which states that the burial should take place as soon after death as possible, preferably within twenty-four hours of the death. Historically, Jews have always buried their dead. This tradition dates back to biblical times. The law reflects the Jewish notion of reverence for the dead, but not worship of the dead, which was common among many ancient societies. A man or woman, created in the image of G-d should be accorded the greatest respect. It would be disrespectful to have the body untended after the soul has returned to G-d. Also, by having the burial take place immediately, the bereaved will be able to start the mourning process without the pain of a delay. However, if the death took place immediately before or on the Sabbath or a major Jewish holiday or festival, then the burial is postponed until after the Sabbath or the first two days of the holiday or festival. On these occasions one should consult a rabbi.

Jewish law states that the dead must be buried in the earth. This law is based on the commandment in Genesis 3:19 'For dust you are, and to dust you shall return.' While the soul of a person rises to be with G-d, the body must return to the earth from which it was created. This is the guiding principle for burials. So Anna's coffin was made of wood, with wooden nails. This allows both the body and the coffin to return to dust at the same rate. Sometimes holes are drilled into the bottom of the coffin, so that the deceased may return to dust quickly. Metal is not used in the making of a coffin as metal does not decompose at the same rate as the human body. Another reason given for not using metal is that instruments of war are made of metal, and thus the deceased would not be able to 'rest in peace' if metal was used.

As with her shroud, Anna's coffin was plain and unostentatious. It is thought that the custom of a simple shroud and casket can be traced back to the time when the ancient Israelites lived in Egypt (around 1600 BCE). The simplicity of the Jewish burial was in contrast to the lavishness of the Egyptian burial chambers and pyramids. The interior of the coffin was also unlined and plain. In some countries (e.g., Israel, Morocco and some parts of Europe), the dead are sometimes buried on a bed of intertwined reeds instead of in a coffin, as a way of returning the body to the dust of the earth. In Jewish tradition, it is preferable to give money to charity than to spend it on lavish coffins.

Earth from the Holy Land was placed in the coffin next to Anna's body. It is thought that soil from the Holy Land has atoning power, and may help the deceased spiritually. Another reason for adding the soil comes from the belief that when the Messiah comes, the dead buried in the Land of Israel will be the first to be resurrected. Among some Moroccan Jews, four coins are thrown in different directions or placed in the coffin. This custom was thought to ward off evil spirits.

It is against Jewish law for the deceased to be interred in a mausoleum, as this is not returning the body to the dust from whence it came. However, some Conservative and Reform rabbis will allow interment in a mausoleum. There is also a prohibition both on cremation (destroying the body) and on embalming (altering the body). These prohibitions also stem from the commandment of honouring the body. We are created in G-d's image, and the human body once housed the spirit of G-d. To alter or destroy a body is considered a desecration of G-d's creation. Additionally, embalming also creates an illusion of life, and may hinder the bereaved from acknowledging the death of their loved one. Some Conservative and Reform rabbis will perform services for those who are cremated. Disinterment is also prohibited by Jewish law. In situations where a body must be exhumed, a rabbi should be consulted.

THE FUNERAL

Anna's funeral was simple, and consisted of prayers, psalms and a eulogy honouring her memory. In Jewish tradition, it is at the funeral that the reality of the loss becomes clear. The funeral service is designed to honour the deceased and to allow the bereaved to confront the reality of death, and thus begin the grieving process. Jewish funeral services are simple but full of meaning, respect, dignity and honour for the deceased. This tribute to the deceased is usually conducted at the funeral chapel, not at the synagogue. The service is composed of a eulogy, recitation of psalms or selections from the Book of Proverbs, and the Memorial Prayer.

The tradition of reciting a eulogy dates back to Abraham, who recited a eulogy when his wife, Sarah died. The purpose of the eulogy is to praise the deceased for his or her worthy qualities and to express the grief experienced by the mourners and the entire Jewish community at the loss of the person. Tradition expects that the eulogy be appropriate and simple. Jewish tradition frowns upon exaggeration or invention of the qualities of the deceased, viewing this as mockery and disrespect rather than a tribute. The most common psalm used at funerals is Psalm 23. The Memorial Prayer has been chanted at Jewish funerals for many years. It is a prayer on behalf of the dead, and is also recited at *Yizkor* (memorial) services which are conducted on certain Jewish holidays and festivals.

After the prayers were recited, Anna's coffin was taken from the chapel to the hearse by her nephews and Jewish male friends. Gentiles (non-Jews) are welcome to attend but cannot take part in this part of the service, and are not allowed to handle the coffin at any time. Males wear a hat or *yarmulke* or *kippah* (black skull cap) throughout the service. Among Ashkenazic Jews sons do not carry the coffin, therefore Anna's son did not participate in this part of the funeral. However, among Sephardic Jews, sons may carry the coffin.

Anna's coffin was followed to the burial site, where her family and friends paid homage to her. Among Ashkenazic Jews the entire family accompanies the deceased to the cemetery. Among Sephardic Jews different customs prevail. For example, among Syrian Jews the sons may go to the cemetery for the burial of a mother but not for the burial of a father. Syrian men and women are buried in separate sections of the cemetery. In Morocco, and among some Jews of Spain, Portugal, the Balkans, Greece and Turkey, women do not go to the cemetery, although Moroccan Jewish women in America often do so.

Anna's coffin was carried to the grave, and placed in it. This custom dates back to the Bible, where Jacob's children carried him from Egypt to Israel to be buried. Carrying the coffin is considered a great honour. In the USA, many cemeteries have a custom of holding the family cars back from the hearse at the cemetery, so that the cemetery gravediggers may carry the coffin to the grave. This rule may be due to insurance regulations, but it is against Jewish tradition, and arrangements must be made before the funeral to allow family and friends to carry the coffin from the hearse to and into the grave.

All of Anna's family and friends followed her coffin to the gravesite where Anna's husband already lay, and where she would soon join him. During the procession, several pauses were made. This reflects the hesitation of family and friends to end the service and leave the deceased. According to Jewish writings, these pauses also give time for the mourners to reflect upon death and re-assess their own existence and meaning of life. How many stops are made is dependent upon local custom, although seven pauses are customary in most places.

Following the coffin to the cemetery is considered one of the symbols of respect. The sages of the Talmud (the books of Jewish law) stated that one who sees a funeral procession should stop whatever it is that they are doing and follow the procession for at least six feet as a sign of respect to the deceased.

Respect and honour for the dead are so important in Jewish tradition, that when no other Jews are available to care for the deceased, the obligation for burial falls upon the first Jew who finds the body. Even a *Kohen*, a member of the priestly clan of Israel who is traditionally barred from handling corpses or going to funerals is obliged to bury a Jew if there are no other Jews around.

During the procession to Anna's gravesite, the rabbi recited Psalm 91. This psalm is referred to as the 'Psalm of the Spirit' and was thought to be written by Moses or a poet who was influenced by Moses, and was recited at the building of the Tabernacle in the desert. Others believe that the psalm was a dialogue between King David and King Solomon or recited by them at the dedication of Jerusalem and the

Temple. The psalm asks G-d to guard us against the evil that surrounds us. In this psalm we state our confidence that G-d will watch over us.

At the gravesite, the rabbi recited the *Tzidduk Ha'din* (justification of the divine decree). This prayer is recited immediately before or after the body is interred, at the time when the reality of the grave confronts the mourners. This prayer has three main themes: (1) we acknowledge that for reasons we may not understand, G-d ordained this end to life, and His decree is justified; (2) we pray that G-d be merciful to the survivors and for all of humanity; (3) we accept G-d's decree, and thank the Lord for the years that He has given us. This prayer is not recited if the funeral is on the day before or during one of the Jewish holidays or festivals, as it is thought that the solemnity of the prayer would be contrary to the joyous nature of the festival or holiday.

After the *Tzidduk Ha'din* was recited, Anna's family and friends took turns shovelling earth into her grave, while asking her forgiveness and saying a final good-bye to her. Shovelling earth into the grave is a very important custom in Jewish tradition, and is not left to anonymous gravediggers. While this custom may seem cruel, as the mourners are already filled with grief, shovelling earth emphasizes the finality of death and the reality of the loss. It is considered an honour to help cover the grave with earth.

The rabbis also recognized that healing cannot be completed when there are feelings of guilt over 'unfinished business' with the deceased. Therefore, Jewish tradition includes asking the deceased for forgiveness at the funeral. The rabbis were aware that the deceased would probably not hear, and thus it was emphasized that the mourner was actually asking for forgiveness from themselves, and for a release from feelings of guilt. There is an Israeli custom in which the mourners place a stone on the covered grave and ask for forgiveness for any injustice that they might have committed against the deceased. Iranian Jews may sprinkle rosewater on the grave. Traditionally, family members and friends take turns saying 'good-bye' by shovelling three shovels of earth into the grave. Once a person has shovelled earth into the grave, the shovel is placed back into the earth. The shovel is not passed from hand to hand, in a symbolic gesture showing that the tragedy of death is not passed on. It is thought that this tradition is Sephardic in origin. Among the Orthodox, the grave is completely filled in. Among other denominations, the grave may be only partially filled.

After Anna's grave was completely filled with earth, the burial *Kaddish* was recited. Among some Sephardic Jews a *shofar* (ram's horn) is sounded before the *Kaddish* is recited. The *Kaddish* is a form of prayer used in synagogue and burial services. It is a declaration of faith, and is one of the most beautiful prayers in the Jewish liturgy. The burial *Kaddish* is a prayer affirming our faith in G-d, that at the proper time He will create the world anew, and that the deceased will be raised up to everlasting life. Through this prayer Anna's family and friends were given hope that there was a future for them and for Anna. The *Kaddish* prayer can only be recited when there is a *minyan* present (a *minyan* is a quorum of ten Jewish men in traditional congregations, although in less traditional congregations women are counted as well). As with the *Tzidduk Ha'din*, the burial *Kaddish* is not recited during festivals and holidays.

After the recitation of the burial *Kaddish*, Anna's friends formed two parallel lines, and her family members walked between the lines away from her grave. This recessional redirects the sympathies and concerns of those at the funeral from the deceased to the mourners. The traditional words of comfort, 'May the Lord comfort you among the other mourners of Zion and Jerusalem' (or 'May Heaven comfort you' for Sephardic Jews) were recited as the mourners passed. This phrase was also repeated by those who came to visit Anna's family after the funeral. It is used as an expression of consolation and comfort, acknowledging the grief of the mourners. It also refers to the notion that all Jews are mourners since the destruction of the Holy Temple in Jerusalem in the year 69 CE (Common Era, equivalent to the term AD).

There were no flowers at Anna's funeral; flowers are viewed as instruments of joy and celebration, thus would be out of place in a funeral. Instead of sending flowers, Anna's friends and family donated money in her memory. Money was donated to cancer research societies (since Anna died of breast cancer), to Anna's favourite charities, to her synagogue, to the hospital where she died and to other institutions in which the donor was active. Donation to charities is an ancient Jewish custom, and is a very important part of Jewish life.

After the funeral, many of Anna's friends joined the family at Anna's house for the beginning of *shiva*. Either at the cemetery or before entering the home, those who attended the funeral performed the ritual of washing the hands, in which water is poured from a cup first on the right hand, then the left. This ritual follows the ancient custom of purification, which is performed after contact with the dead. By the washing of hands, one symbolically leaves the death at the cemetery. It also symbolizes the Jewish concern with life, rather than worship of the dead. As with the shovel at the grave, the cup of water is not passed from hand to hand.

Many of Anna's friends banded together to provide the *se'uddat havra'ah*, the Meal of Consolation for her family. They brought the traditional foods, including wine, hard-boiled eggs, and round rolls. The roundness of the egg and the rolls symbolizes the cycles of life and death, as well as birth and new life. Among Sephardic Jews olives are also eaten. Providing food for the mourners is an ancient custom intended as a way of showing comfort and helping the mourner eat in order to keep up his or her strength. Often mourners do not want to eat, as they may feel too depressed, or may feel that they want to die and join the deceased. For these reasons, they may also not want to prepare food. Thus it becomes the responsibility of friends to prepare food for them.

MOURNING OBSERVANCES

Jewish tradition separates out six graduated periods of mourning, during which the mourner can gradually express feelings of grief. The periods are very structured, and allow for expression of grief at times when it is most keenly felt. These phases should not, however, be interpreted as marking a 'right' way to grieve. Jewish tradition recognizes that each person will grieve in his or her own way and time.

1 *Aninut*: the period between death and burial

This is the time when the individual is in shock over the loss. It is also a time when despair may be at its most intense point. From the moment of Anna's death (or the moment he or she had learned of her death), each immediate family member of Anna's family (in Anna's case her brother, son and daughter) would have been referred to as an *onen* – a person in deep distress. According to Jewish law, one is obliged to mourn for the seven people who are considered immediate family members (father, mother, brother, sister, son, daughter and spouse). However, if the person is not able to participate in the funeral arrangements, either because he or she lives too far away or is so ill (physically or mentally) that he or she cannot participate, or if the body is not in the possession of the relatives (if the person has drowned, is missing in action, etc.), then he or she is not considered an *onen*. There is no obligation to mourn for adoptive relatives, or relatives who are not Jewish. As all of Anna's immediate family members were present when she died, they all were considered *onen*.

The *onen* is a person who has been pulled away from normal life. He or she is in shock, is numb, disoriented and emotionally fragile. The sages said that at this time the deceased is before the mourner, and the mourner is constantly reliving the life and death of the deceased. Even though psychologically the mourner has not assimilated or accepted the death, he or she must still make arrangements for the funeral, contact other family members, etc. The numbness and shock of this time is adaptive in that it enables the *onen* to be able to make funeral arrangements, notify others, etc. The rabbis recognized that it is not possible to comfort the mourner at this time, as he/she is in shock over the loss. Jewish tradition believes that it is useless to try to comfort a mourner before the burial, while the deceased 'lays before them'. The time of comforting is after the funeral, when the reality of the loss has set in. Therefore, following Jewish tradition, Anna's friends offered condolences and comfort after the burial, during the time of *shiva* (which will be described later). As an acknowledgement of the shock and disbelief at this time, the rabbis developed rules of behaviour for an *onen*. Anna's immediate relatives, as *onen*, could not attend parties or festive occasions, bathe for pleasure, shave, cut their hair, adorn themselves for pleasure, or indulge in any conjugal relations during the period of mourning. In addition, they could not conduct normal business during this time. It is expected that the *onen*'s time is spent making funeral arrangements, and the *onen* is too distressed to take part in social activities or attend to a job.

On the Sabbath or holidays, these rules are cancelled. Anna's relatives were allowed to attend religious services, but they could not serve as a reader or cantor, or recite the *Kaddish* (prayer for the dead). There are specific rules for specific holidays, and it is best to consult a rabbi.

Just prior to the funeral service, or at the cemetery (or, among some Sephardic Jews, after the mourners return home) Anna's family members tore their outer clothing while standing, as an expression of grief. This custom comes from instances in the Bible where a bereaved person tore his or her clothes upon hearing of the death of a loved one. For example, David tore his clothes when he heard about the death of King Saul. And when Jacob saw the blood-stained coat he had given to his son Joseph, and thought that Joseph was dead, he tore his clothes in his grief. Tearing the clothes is seen as an expression both of anger and of grief at the death of a loved one. When the deceased is a parent, the clothing is torn over the heart, fulfilling the Jewish law of 'exposing the heart' and indicating that the heart of the *onen* is torn or broken with grief. For other relatives, the tear is made on the right side, and need not show. The torn garments should be worn throughout *shiva*, if the deceased was a parent. Some Conservative and Reform Jews do not follow the custom of tearing the clothes, although they may wear a black ribbon which is torn.

2 The first three days following the funeral

The first three days after the funeral are seen as a time for weeping and lamentation. Anna's family stayed at home and engaged in private mourning. Visiting the bereaved is discouraged at this time, for it is considered that the wound of bereavement is too fresh, and he or she cannot respond to others at this time.

3 *Shiva*, the seven days following the burial

For a period of seven days after the funeral, Anna's family 'sat *shiva*'. *Shiva* is usually observed in the home of the closest relative of the deceased and in this case it was held in the home of Anna's brother. During *shiva*, Anna's family remained at home, sitting on low chairs or stools. (Not all Jews follow this custom. Sephardic Jews may sit *shiva* on the floor, as the original custom was to sit on the ground.) The low chair or stool represents a departure from normal life. This does not mean that the mourner has to remain sitting. He or she may stand and walk as much as he or she wishes. The family were not expected to be able to perform daily tasks, as they were so wrapped up in their grief. Therefore, during *shiva*, Anna's family did not go to work. Traditionally *onen* do not go to work during this period, unless the individual's livelihood is at stake, or if there is a public need for the individual's services (for example, a rabbi, policeman, physician, etc.). For example, one of Anna's grandsons was a policeman, and as there was a public need for his services, he returned to a limited work schedule after the first three days of mourning.

The period of seven days of *shiva* may have come from passages in the Bible such as Genesis 50:10, where Joseph mourned for seven days for his father Jacob. The period of *shiva* includes the first three days after the funeral, described above. While Anna's family observed the entire period of *shiva* (with the exception of her grandson), some Jews do not observe the full seven days of *shiva*, returning to work and other activities after the first three days. However, the seven days of *shiva* are thought to be very important psychologically. During this time, the mourner gradually emerges from the feelings of intense grief to a state in which he or she feels able to talk to and accept comfort from others.

During *shiva* the mourners are not obliged to greet people when they come, nor to act as hosts. During *shiva* the roles are reversed. Anna's friends acted as hosts and took care of the needs of the family. The friends brought food and supplies so that Anna's family did not need to leave the house or focus on worldly issues. They could focus their time and energy on the grief process, knowing that friends would take care of them.

While they sat *shiva* Anna's family wore the garments that were torn at the funeral. They also wore slippers instead of shoes. Leather shoes are not worn, since leather, an expensive item in biblical days, was considered an object of luxury and vanity. The mourners did not shave, bath, groom or use cosmetics, except for hygiene purposes. One should be neat and presentable, but not enhance one's appearance for the sake of vanity. The mirrors in both Anna's home and her brother's home were covered. By covering the mirror and prohibiting the wearing of makeup, or grooming other than required for health and sanitary reasons, the rabbis acknowledged that during the time of mourning one should not be concerned with vanity and pressures to 'dress up'. Also, Jewish law states that worship must not take place before a mirror, or with a mirror behind one, so that it does not appear as if one is worshipping an image in a mirror. So Anna's friends covered the mirrors with a cloth or turned them to face the wall.

The family also lit a memorial lamp or candle and kept it burning during the week of *shiva*. Candles are very important in Jewish tradition and are lit on important days in one's life. Candles also represent the human being: the wick symbolizes the body, while the flame symbolizes the soul, striving upwards and bringing light into darkness.

Death and bereavement are lonely processes. After the death of a spouse or a parent, the bereaved often fear being left alone to fend for themselves. Jewish tradition acknowledges these fears by surrounding the bereaved with the community. Friends and acquaintances come to the home in order to comfort the mourner, see to the mourner's needs, and to join with the family and the rabbi in order help make up a *minyan* so that the daily prayer services and the mourner's *Kaddish* may be said. Anna had many friends, and there was no trouble enlisting enough volunteers to bring food and participate in the daily morning and evening *minyan* with Anna's family and her rabbi. However, in some communities it may not be possible to gather sufficient people for prayers to be said daily. In this case, the mourner's *Kaddish* may not be said at home, and the mourner may have to wait until services are held in the synagogue. The mourner's *Kaddish* may not be said alone or without a *minyan*, as it is the presence of the community during the recitation of the mourner's *Kaddish*, as well as the prayer itself, that is comforting to the mourner.

The laws and traditions surrounding behaviour in a house of mourning are designed to allow the mourner to express his or her grief. When one visits a house of mourning, traditionally no greeting is given. Visitors wait for the mourner to speak, and do not engage in idle chatter. Jewish law concerning condolence calls recognizes that true compassion involves being present and being silent, and thus the law states that one should remain silent and allow the mourner to speak first, enabling the mourner to focus on his or her grief, and not on social etiquette. The visitor should be sensitive to what the mourner needs. Crying should not be discouraged.

The condolence calls Anna's friends made to her family provided comfort and companionship and helped to reduce the feelings of loneliness that ensue when a beloved person dies. Anna's friends shared stories and memories of living in the small town with her over the years. These stories were very comforting to the family, especially those who lived far away and had not spent as much time with Anna. The condolence calls were usually short visits. When Anna's friends were preparing to leave the house they spoke the traditional words to her family: 'May the Lord comfort you among the other mourners of Zion and Jerusalem' (for Sephardic Jews the phrase is: 'May Heaven comfort you'). Anna's friends did not bring gifts when they visited, but instead donated to charities in her honour and memory. An interesting custom among some Syrian Jews is to make either one or three condolence calls. Visiting only twice symbolizes the possibility that death could return to the house.

At the end of seven days, Anna's family took a walk outside to symbolize the end of *shiva*, and a return to normal life. In Jewish tradition, the day starts at sundown, and part of a day is equal to a full day. *Shiva* ends on the morning of the seventh day. Thus if a person begins to sit *shiva* for as little as an hour before dark, that hour is considered as the first full day of the mourning period. Similarly, a few minutes on the seventh day count as an entire day. The Sabbath does not count as a day of *shiva*, as it is seen as a day of joy, and so the mourning rites are not observed on this day. Similarly, on festivals and other holidays the mourning rites are not observed, as they are in conflict with the joyous nature of the holiday. If one is sitting *shiva* and one of the major holidays (Rosh Hashana, Yom Kippur, Passover, Sukkot or Shavuot) occurs during the seven-day period, *shiva* is automatically ended at the start of the holiday. This is true even if one has only mourned for a few hours or minutes before the holiday. Among Moroccan Jews, at the end of *shiva* a special meal and study session is held. Iranian Jews may hold a special study session in honour of the deceased at the synagogue, during the week of *shiva*. The mourners are allowed to come to the synagogue where they are joined by many friends and relatives for the special service. Anna's family, as Russian Jews, did not observe these customs, although they attended Sabbath services on the Friday night after *shiva* ended.

4 *Sheloshim*, the thirty days following the burial

After *shiva*, Anna's family returned to their homes and slowly began to return to their normal lives and rejoin society. The period of *sheloshim* includes the period of *shiva*, discussed above. During this time Anna's family felt lonely and sad, but their grief slowly lessened. The mourners were now able to leave the house and conduct their usual business. However, Jewish tradition realizes that the grief has not yet abated. Even though Anna's son and daughter returned to work, they still wore the torn clothing and did not shave or cut their hair. The family members who were considered *onen* (Anna's brother, son and daughter) did not wear new clothes or attend parties or other joyous celebrations. Among the Orthodox, television is not watched, nor radio listened to. These rules are designed to keep the mourner from participating in activities which they may find hard to cope with.

Why does *sheloshim* last for thirty days? The tradition may stem from the mourning periods for Aaron and Moses when the Israelites mourned for thirty days (Numbers 20:29, Deuteronomy 34:8). As with *shiva*, *sheloshim* ends on the morning of the thirtieth day. When one of the major holidays occurs during *sheloshim*, if *shiva* was completed prior to the onset of the holiday, the remainder of *sheloshim* is cancelled. Otherwise the days of the holiday count toward the thirty days of *sheloshim*. As Anna died less than one month before Rosh Hashana, once the holiday began, the rest of *sheloshim* was cancelled. The regulations surrounding holidays are complex, and a rabbi should be consulted. (Among Moroccan Jews, as at the end of *shiva*, at the end of *sheloshim* a special meal and study session is held).

If a mourner hears of the death within thirty days of the funeral, or is unable to arrive in time for the funeral, the garment is torn, and the mourner joins the rest of the family in sitting *shiva* or observing *sheloshim*. If the news was received after thirty days have passed, the garment is not torn, and the mourner need not sit *shiva* nor observe *sheloshim*. However, if the deceased was the person's mother or father, the mourner is obliged to tear their garment, and observe both *shiva* and *sheloshim*, no matter when the news was heard. In this way the mourner is observing the commandment to 'honour your father and your mother'.

5 The eleven-month period following burial

During the ten-month period after *sheloshim*, the lives of Anna's family slowly began to return to normal. However, Anna's brother, who was Orthodox, did not cut his hair or wear new clothes during this period. Anna's brother attended daily services at the synagogue. During *sheloshim* he recited the mourner's *Kaddish* during these daily services. Anna's children also recited the mourner's *Kaddish* at their synagogue's Sabbath services during the rest of the eleven-month mourning period. In Jewish law there is a requirement to recite the mourner's *Kaddish* at Sabbath services every week during the eleven-month period when one is mourning the death of a parent. The other members of Anna's family were not required to recite the mourner's *Kaddish* after the end of *sheloshim*, since this requirement is only for a parent. However, Anna's niece continued to recite the mourner's *Kaddish*, as she had felt very close to her aunt. In addition, the mourner's *Kaddish* is recited every year by children and other close relatives on the *Yahrzeit* or anniversary of the death.

The mourner's *Kaddish* is an affirmation of the beauty of life and of faith in G-d as redeemer. This prayer helps to heal the psychological wounds of grief at the same time as it teaches lessons about life and death. As with the burial *Kaddish*, the mourner's *Kaddish* is only recited in the presence of a *minyan*. Thus the mourner's *Kaddish* also provides a sense of social support, which is vitally important when one is grieving. Traditionally only men say the mourner's *Kaddish*. However, today many non-Orthodox women also say the mourner's *Kaddish* for their loved ones, as Anna's daughter did for her mother.

The mourner's *Kaddish* is recited for only eleven months for a parent. The reason for this tradition is that it is thought that at least a year is required for purification of the souls of the very wicked. Thus, if a person says *Kaddish* for the entire twelve months, it implies that he or she viewed his or her parents as wicked and in need of extra help.

This eleven-month period encompasses the periods of *shiva* and *sheloshim*. At the end of eleven months, the mourner is not expected to continue mourning, with the exception of the periods throughout the year when memorial prayers are said (during the festivals of Passover, Sukkot, Shavuot, as well as Yom Kippur).

At the end of one year, Anna's family unveiled her tombstone. The custom of erecting tombstones is an ancient one. The custom is mentioned in the book of Genesis, when Jacob erected a tombstone for his wife Rachel. The purpose of the tombstone is to mark the area where the grave is, so that the area is not defiled, so that others can find it and to show honour to the dead. Anna's family, in keeping with Russian Ashkenazic tradition, erected her tombstone upright. (Sephardic cemeteries have flat tombstones.) The tombstone had a picture of Anna on it as well as her name in English and Hebrew: *Anna bat Yitzchak v' Miriam* (Anna daughter of Isaac and Miriam). A person's Hebrew name is traditionally listed in Hebrew as the person's name, son or daughter of (parents' names). In addition the date of her death, and words of affection, praise, and remembrance were also carved on the tombstone. A custom has arisen that the tombstone is not erected until the twelve months of mourning have passed. However, there are no laws regulating this, and a tombstone may be erected at any time. When visitors come to the grave, they usually place small stones on top of the tombstone as a remembrance, a sign that someone has visited and that the deceased is still loved and has been remembered.

Although this was not the case when Anna died, sometimes the deceased may not wish for a funeral to be conducted, or may want changes to be made in the tradition which are contrary to Jewish law. These wishes must not be followed, since the funeral and mourning periods of *shiva* and *sheloshim* (described above) are for the benefit of the mourners, as a way for them to express and work through their grief. However, if the deceased specifically requests that the eulogy should not be given, then those wishes are adhered to. This is because the eulogy is intended to honour the deceased, rather than for the survivors.

6 Rituals following the year of mourning

Although Jewish tradition recognizes that people's grief heals at varying rates, it does not emphasize continual mourning, as the religion is focused on life, not on death. Therefore, mourning beyond the eleven-month period is discouraged. However, the dead are not forgotten. There are specific periods throughout the year when Anna's family gathered at their synagogues to remember her and recited prayers for her.

Yahrzeit (the anniversary of the day of death) is observed for any of the seven relatives for whom one is obliged to mourn. The word *Yahrzeit* is of German origin; Sephardic Jews call the anniversary of a death *nahala meldado* or *annos*. Some traditional Jews observe *Yahrzeit* according to the day of death on the Hebrew calendar, whereas others observe the day according to the Georgian (Christian) calendar. The tradition commemorates the date of death and not the date of birth because a person's life is judged by their deeds, and thus can be best assessed at the end of his or her life. Therefore, this is a day to recall the deceased and to remember their deeds and teachings. A *Yahrzeit* is generally a private observance.

On Anna's *Yahzreit*, her brother fasted and did not shave. Anna's relatives who lived nearby visited her gravesite. They lit a twenty-four-hour memorial, or *Yahrzeit*, candle. They recited the mourner's *Kaddish* in the synagogue. Her family and friends also honoured her memory on that day by donating money to charity in her memory.

The *Yizkor* memorial service is a part of four of the major Jewish holidays: Yom Kippur, Passover, Shavuot and Sukkot. At this time the congregation recalls all of their deceased family and friends. The mourner's *Kaddish* and other memorial prayers are read at this time. The service is based on the belief in Judaism that the deeds of the living can help to redeem and bring honour to the dead. Thus at this time prayers are said, and money is often given to charity in memory of the deceased. Traditionally, at this time a *Yahrzeit* candle is also lit.

SPECIAL CIRCUMSTANCES

Minor children

Minors (children under the age of thirteen) are not viewed as *onen*, as they are not seen to be mature enough fully to understand the loss of the relative. Anna's grandniece and nephew did not go to the funeral, nor did they observe *shiva* or *sheloshim*, nor follow the observances of mourning, since they were under the age of thirteen. Her grandchildren who were all over the age of thirteen participated fully in the ceremonies and ritual. Jewish tradition does realize that children should be allowed to grieve. They should not be discouraged from attending the funeral or participating in the mourning observances. While minor children are not considered as *onen*, a symbolic cut in their garment may be made so that they do not feel left out.

Bride and groom

As the time of marriage is seen as one of joy, and mourning is incompatible with joy, a bride and groom are not obliged to observe the laws of mourning during the first seven days of their marriage. They are not required to attend a funeral during the first seven days of marriage, except if a parent has died.

After the first seven days of marriage have ended, the bride and groom immediately follow the rituals of *shiva* and *sheloshim*. If the death occurred before the wedding, the full *shiva* and *sheloshim* are observed. If the death occurred during the seven days after the wedding, at the end of the week of rejoicing the mourner joins the family in observing *shiva*, and completes the observance with them. Other rules apply to the bride and groom, and a rabbi should be consulted.

Miscarriages and children under 30 days

If a child dies before it has attained thirty days of life, it is considered to not have lived at all. Therefore no mourning practices are observed. This tradition dates back to the Middle Ages when many infants did not survive birth. The rabbis of the time felt that by not mourning an infant who died shortly after birth, the parents were freed of the burden of mourning. Therefore, according to Jewish tradition, attendants for the funeral procession are not required, and a minimum of three people at the cemetery is sufficient (a *minyan* is not required). The *Tzidduk Ha'din* prayer is not recited. However, some sources say that tombstones must be erected to mark the graves of stillborns and children under thirty days of age.

Many Jews today are working to change this custom of not mourning a child under thirty days of age. The Conservative movement has established new legal responses for burial and mourning of infants and miscarriages. New customs are being developed among the Reform and Conservative movements for mourning infants and miscarriages or still-births. In general, for infants under thirty days, the Conservative movement allows for the body to be buried according to standard Jewish practice. Parents may sit *shiva* for the baby. In the case of a miscarriage, both parents are considered as ill (the father is ill from the psychological trauma), and prayers for their recovery are recited in the synagogue. The commandment of visiting the sick is encouraged.

Apostates

One who denounces Judaism and adopts another religion is not permitted burial in a Jewish cemetery. As he or she has left Judaism, he or she is not honoured or mourned. However, a person who publicly disowns the ways of Judaism but does not embrace another religion may have the *taharah* performed, may wear a shroud and may be buried in a Jewish cemetery (although they are usually buried in a distant part of the cemetery). There is no formal mourning.

Cremations or interment in crypts and mausoleums

Anna was buried in a grave next to her husband. According to Jewish law, cremations or interment in a crypt or mausoleum are not permitted. There are several reasons given for the prohibition of cremation. One is that the body is a reflection of G-d, and destroying not only what G-d has created, but what He has created in His own image is an insult to G-d. Another reason is that in ancient times cremation was seen as a pagan practice. Also, cremation or interment in a crypt or mausoleum does not allow the body to return naturally to the dust from which it was formed (Genesis 3:19). Even if the deceased wished to be cremated or interred, his or her wishes must be ignored in order to follow the law. Cremated ashes may not be buried in a Jewish cemetery, although they may be buried as close as possible to a Jewish cemetery (e.g. in the area of a non-Jewish cemetery next to the Jewish area of the cemetery). Jewish law also requires that there be no mourning for those who are cremated or interred, as they are considered as rejecting Jewish law, and have therefore surrendered their rights to an honourable burial. Some Jews will observe mourning if the ashes have been buried in the earth. However, some Conservative and Reform rabbis will conduct a funeral if there is a cremation or interment in a crypt or mausoleum.

Suicides

Death is seen as an end to the opportunity to do good on this earth. Suicide is therefore seen as a sacrilege, an unspeakable crime, as the individual is not only willingly giving up the opportunity to do more, to right wrongs, to help others, to heal the earth, but is also destroying his or her own soul. Thus suicides are not mourned, and if they are buried in a Jewish cemetery, they cannot be buried within at least six feet of other graves. Honour is not given to the deceased, as suicide is seen as a dishonourable act. However, the mourners are entitled to comfort, since they are the victims and sufferers, not the perpetrator of the suicide.

Suicide has a strict, legal definition in Judaism, in which the rabbis distinguish between someone who intentionally kills him/herself and one who commits suicide when not fully aware of his or her actions. If the person is considered not to be fully aware of his or her actions at the time of death, then all of the customs and rituals of burial and mourning may be followed. For purposes of Jewish burial and mourning, the decision of whether or not the deceased was fully aware of his or her actions can be made only by a rabbi, not by the police or a doctor. Most rabbis consider suicide a result of uncontrollable depression, in which case the deceased was not responsible for his or her actions; thus they may be buried according to Jewish customs and rituals.

Missing persons

If a person is missing and presumed dead, but if the remains are expected to be found (e.g. if the person drowned, or was murdered and it is anticipated that the body will be found), then the mourning period should begin after the body is found, or after an exhaustive search has been undertaken and all hope of finding the body has been abandoned. Mourning is not observed as long as there is hope that the body will be found.

If there is no expectation of finding the body (e.g. when someone is lost at sea or killed in an unknown place), and there are no witnesses to the death, then certain rules of mourning apply. For a wife, there should be no demonstrable mourning for fear that she will then be considered eligible to remarry. In reality she may not be eligible to remarry, as her husband may still be alive. If there is no wife, then mourning is begun as soon as the judgement of death is made. In both of these cases rabbinical guidance should be sought.

CONCLUSION: HELPING JEWS FACE DEATH OR BEREAVEMENT

Visiting the dying

Visiting the sick, giving comfort and aid is one of the most important obligations in the Jewish tradition. If you have patients who are Jewish, you may want to make sure that their family and friends are aware of customs surrounding the dying. According to Jewish law, nothing must be done that will decrease or diminish the hope of the person who is dying. Thus visits are encouraged as a comfort to the individual and the family. One exception to this law is that one should help the person arrange for the disposition of property. The healthcare worker may be involved in these decisions, and can help to see that property is taken care of without unduly stressing the patient.

It is common to ask the rabbi of the individual's or one's own synagogue to offer a prayer for healing. In Hebrew this is called a *Mi Sh'beirach*. In addition, many people who strictly observe the Sabbath may not know that when death is imminent it is permissible to violate the laws of the Sabbath in order to comfort the dying and his or her family.

After the death

Immediately following the death of a loved one, the healthcare worker can be invaluable in helping the family sort out what to do next. The healthcare worker may be able to arrange for the family rabbi, or, if there is no family rabbi, a local rabbi to come and advise the family in the correct ways, according to Jewish law, to conduct the funeral and interment. However, it is important that if there is no family rabbi, the rabbi who is selected is of the same denomination (e.g. Orthodox, Conservative, Reform, Reconstructionist) as the family. In the case of Anna, she had been brought up Orthodox: the rabbi of her synagogue was contacted, and he conducted the funeral, even though many members of Anna's family were not Orthodox. You may also become involved in recruiting friends to help with the funeral and *shiva* preparations (e.g. food for the Meal of Condolence), or to coordinate the arrival and placement of out-of-town family members.

The healthcare worker may also want to pay attention to any young children in the family circle. Often children feel left out when a loved one has died, and may not always get the chance to ask questions or express their grief or other emotions. In addition, arrangements may need to be made for someone to care for the children and take them to school, etc.

You may want to attend the funeral. Judaism is based on a sense of family and community. In this tradition, people are not to die alone or be buried alone. That is one reason why at least ten people are required to be at a Jewish funeral. The community shares in the life of the person and grieves as a community at his or her death. It is also important to 'be there' for the mourner, to be a source of comfort. To be at a funeral is a comfort to the mourners and an honour to the deceased.

Similarly, it is also appropriate to attend the *shiva*, if you were close to the deceased or a mourner, even if you are not Jewish. If you do want to make a *shiva* call, times will be announced at the funeral. If you want to visit at a time other than those announced, it is best to call ahead first. In many homes, the door will be left open during *shiva*, so that greeters do not have to ring the door bell. In many traditional homes during *shiva* the comforter does not speak until the mourner speaks first. It may be difficult for the mourner not to act as the host or hostess, especially if the *shiva* is being held in his or her home. During *shiva* the mourner is not expected to take on any obligations, but is expected to reserve all his or her energy for the work of grief. Often the mourner will not have the energy to talk, but will value silent company. Sometimes if the mourner feels like talking, sharing memories of the deceased can be a comfort. If a prayer service is conducted while you are there, participate to the extent that you are able. As you leave, you may want to give the traditional farewell (which is also given at the grave site) 'May G-d comfort you among all the mourners of Zion and Jerusalem' (for Ashkenazic Jews) or 'May Heaven comfort you' (for Sephardic Jews).

After *shiva*

As friends and the community go on with their lives, fewer people may visit the mourner as time goes by. For example, after the other members of Anna's family returned to their homes, Anna's brother was alone with his grief. The healthcare worker may want to continue to check on the mourner from time to time. You may want to check in with the mourner at the division points for mourning in Judaism, at the end of *shiva*, at the end of *sheloshim*, and at the one-year remembrance. If there is an unveiling of the tombstone at the end of the first year, it is considered an honour to the deceased and a comfort to the mourner for others to attend any ceremony surrounding the unveiling.

The time of the unveiling and the yearly *Yahrzeit* and *Yizkor* services may be times of great catharsis for the mourners. These may be times when the mourner is able to finish his or her grief work and re-enter life fully. These may also be times when 'unfinished business' or emotions arise. *Yizkor* services offer a time for the mourners to gather with other mourners in a community acknowledgement of grief. For some people this service can be very comforting and may be all that they need to deal with unresolved grief. Others may need further work on grief issues. It is important to 'be there' for the mourner at this time, to help him or her with any unfinished grief or emotions that may surface.

Using Jewish traditions to help with mourning

Teshuva, Tefilla and Tzedaka

During mourning, people may look back on their relations with the deceased and feel guilt over things that were said and done, or not said and done. Judaism sets aside one day each year, *Yom Kippur*, to look back on the year that has gone by and repent for things which one feels he or she has done wrong to others and to G-d. Repentance in Judaism is called *Teshuva*. *Teshuva* is a healing process by which the individual prays (*Tefilla*) for forgiveness. It involves recognizing and confessing any wrongdoing, genuinely expressing regret for any wrongdoing which we have caused, and taking steps not to repeat the wrongdoing. As most people have regrets over perceived wrongdoing which they may have caused to the deceased, they may feel even more upset and guilty over the fact that it is too late to apologize or make up for the misdeed to the person directly. The process of *Teshuva* can also help to heal a person in mourning, through the use of *Teshuva, Tefilla* and *Tzedaka* (charity).

Prayer

In Judaism, prayer is used to express emotions, praise G-d and make requests to G-d. Prayer can be very useful in expressing grief and other emotions. Many of the rituals and prayers surrounding the death and mourning process are designed for the expression of grief and other emotions. Prayer has been described as the 'cry of the heart'. When we pray, we bare our hearts and souls to G-d. However, praying is often a difficult thing for mourners to do. They may be angry with G-d, and blame Him for taking their loved one away. The healthcare worker may want to explore and confront doubts about the usefulness of prayer. He or she may also want to enlist the aid of a rabbi or spiritual friend of the mourner to help him or her learn to pray in a way which is comfortable and cathartic.

Memorials

Jewish tradition believes that the soul is immortal. In addition, it is believed that one lives on through good works. Many synagogues have memorial plaques. It is also common to give money to a charity in the name of the deceased, so that their memory lives on. One can also donate items such as the deceased's clothing to a charity so that others can benefit from the deceased's actions. Naming children after the deceased is also an important and enduring tradition among Ashkenazic Jews. Anna's niece, who was pregnant at the time Anna died, named her newly born daughter after her aunt. Such actions by the mourner can provide a release of emotions and grief and can be very therapeutic. You may want to help the mourner to create a plan to memorialize the deceased, such as regular donations to charity, purchasing a memorial plaque, making plans to attend synagogue to say the *Kaddish* prayer, continuing a favourite hobby of the deceased, etc.

Ethical wills

When working with the person who is dying, the healthcare worker may want to assist the person to write an ethical will. Ethical wills have been around for centuries in Judaism, and in fact the book of Deuteronomy has been described as the ethical will of Moses to the Jewish people. Ethical wills are documents (although nowadays they can be recordings, videos, etc.) in which the person who is dying transmits his or her wishes, hopes, values and instructions to family or friends. The ethical will is designed to pass on wisdom, spiritual wealth and inspiration to the next generation.

APPENDIX

One translation of the *Vidui* is as follows (Wolfson, 1993, p. 51):

> My G-d and G-d of my ancestors, accept my prayer. Do not ignore my supplication. Forgive me for all the sins which I have committed in my lifetime. I am abashed and ashamed of these deeds I have committed. Please accept my pain and suffering as atonement and forgive my wrongdoing, for against You alone have I sinned.

> May it be Your will, *Adonai* my G-d and G-d of my ancestors, that I sin no more. With your great mercy, cleanse me of my sins, but not through suffering and disease. Send a perfect healing to me and to all who are stricken.

> I acknowledge to You, *Adonai* my G-d and G-d of my ancestors, that my life and recovery depend on You. May it be Your will to heal me. Yet, if You have decreed that I shall die of this affliction, may my

death atone for all my sins and transgressions which I have committed before You. Shelter me in the shadow of Your wings. Grant me a share in the world to come.

Parent of orphans and Guardian of spouses left behind, protect my beloved family, with whose soul my own soul is bound.

Into Your hand I commit my soul. You have redeemed me, *Adonai*, G-d of truth.

Hear, O Israel: *Adonai* is our G-d, *Adonai* is One.

Adonai is our G-d. *Adonai* is our G-d.

SUMMARY

- [ ] There are many regional differences in Jewish customs at the time of death.
- [ ] Two of the most important commandments in Judaism are to honour the dead and comfort the mourner.
- [ ] The time before death is usually taken up with a review of one's life.
- [ ] Ethical wills are messages by the dying to their families. They express hopes, values and comfort to the bereaved.
- [ ] Three views are current: 1) At death the soul hovers near the body until after the funeral, when it goes through a process of purification of varying duration, to cleanse it of sin. After this some say that it returns. 2) The soul must await the Messianic Age when the righteous will be reborn to live in eternal peace and the wicked remain in the dust. 3) Immortality comes through one's descendants not through the immortality of the soul (this is believed by many modern Jews).
- [ ] Every life, even as it ebbs, is to be respected and revered. One should visit the dying and help them to find peace of mind. No 'heroic' efforts should be made to prolong life or hasten death. Those at hand should not wail or make a noise.
- [ ] The rabbi should be called at the approach of death to say a confessional prayer (the *Vidui*) and recite the fundamental affirmation of faith, the *Shema*.
- [ ] At the moment of death no one should leave the room.

☐ Since we are created in the image of G-d, the body must not be altered in any way and must be treated with respect. The family close the eyes, straighten and cover the body with a sheet, the feet are pointed to the door. Some Orthodox Jews lie the body on the floor for twenty minutes and pour water outside the door. Others place ashes on the eyes and a candle may be placed near the head. Mirrors in the house are covered.

☐ On death the rabbi is notified, he calls the undertaker and the *Chevrah Kadisha* who carry out the ritual washing of the body (*Taharah*) and clothe it and, if male, wrap it in a prayer shawl. Non-Jews should *not* wash the body.

☐ Among Spanish Jews the rabbi gives a final blessing in the presence of the children.

☐ Jewish tradition is opposed to embalmment, post-mortems and exhumation. Bloodied clothes or severed parts should be buried with the body without washing. Some Jews are opposed to organ donation.

☐ From death until burial the body is guarded. Mourners are not comforted at this time. They may not shave or socialize. The outer garment is torn.

☐ Funerals are simple and unostentatious, consisting of prayers, psalms and a eulogy. Gentiles may attend and men should wear a head covering. There are no flowers but donations are given to charity in memory of the deceased.

☐ Burial must be in the earth and should take place within twenty-four hours of death (unless the Sabbath intervenes). Soil from the Holy Land is placed in the coffin.

☐ Gentiles should not take part in the interment, at which the grave is filled in by family and friends followed by a ritual washing of hands.

☐ Traditional foods are brought as gifts for the gathering at the home of the deceased.

☐ *Shiva* starts after the funeral: the first three days are for weeping and lamentation in private. There is no visiting. The next four days the family sit *Shiva* on low stools, friends visit, bring food and give comfort. No greeting is given, and visitors wait for the bereaved to speak first. Candles are burned. The prayer of *Kaddish* is said daily. Gentiles are welcome.

☐ *Sheloshim*: for thirty days following burial the family do not shave or cut their hair but may return to work. *Kaddish* is recited daily.

☐ For the next ten months *Kaddish* is recited weekly primarily by men (in some congregations, women as well) on the Sabbath. Thereafter mourners are encouraged to stop mourning.

☐ At the end of one year the tombstone is unveiled. Visitors to the grave often place a small stone on it.

☐ *Yahrzeit*: this is the family meeting on the anniversary of death.

☐ *Yizkor*: this is the annual Jewish holiday at which the congregation recalls their dead in memorial service, and lights candles.

☐ No mourning is carried out if a baby dies within thirty days of birth, for a Jew who has adopted another religion, been cremated, committed suicide or whose body is missing (unless irrecoverable). However, a rabbi should be consulted in the case of a suicide as mourning may be permissible.

☐ *Teshuva* – prayers for forgiveness are helpful to mourners who blame themselves.

Chapter 7

Christianity

Harold Ter Blanche and Colin Murray Parkes

On the assumption that most of our readers will be familiar with the basic tenets of Christianity we shall not dwell on these here. This account of things as they are is not intended as criticism of Christianity as such. It does, however, raise important questions about where Christianity is going.

George Jones had not thought much about death. He knew it happened and at 73 he should, perhaps, have been prepared; but the topic is not one that people talk much about in Britain and, after his first heart attack, the doctor had been so optimistic that he had tried to dismiss the possibility from his mind. His second attack occurred a few weeks later.

George had been pottering about the garden, a cigarette in his mouth. He had bent over to pull up a weed when the worst pain he had ever had hit him. It was like a vice around his chest and took his breath away. He collapsed on the ground and his wife, who saw it happen from the kitchen window, came rushing, with a neighbour, to help him back to the house. 'I've had it, love', he said, as they waited for the ambulance to arrive.

Phyllis had been half expecting this to happen. She had nagged him to stop smoking but he would not listen. She had prayed to God to keep him safe but did not have much confidence that her prayer had been heard.

Phyllis was an Anglican; she believed in God and went to the local Church of England regularly. She had learned her religion from her parents and saw the godhead very much as a Holy Family. She loved Jesus, whom she knew to be the Son of God and regarded as a personal friend. She particularly enjoyed the pictures of Mary and the baby Jesus which reminded her of her relationship with her own children. She had grown accustomed to the horrific picture of Jesus on the cross and took comfort in the thought that he had been rescued from the jaws of death by a loving father. She had confidence that, when her time came, Jesus would find a place for George and herself in heaven. She sometimes worried about his refusal to go to church.

George thought religion was 'nonsense' but he explained to his friends that that did not mean that he was an atheist. He went to weddings and funerals and reprimanded his grandchildren when they swore.

George survived in hospital for less than a day. He was in intensive care and every beat of his heart was monitored. Surrounded by a bank of machines and with tubes injecting fluids into his veins, he no longer seemed to belong to his family. They were intimidated by the atmosphere of the Intensive Care Unit whose staff seemed very nice but were far too busy saving lives to sit and talk. The doctor told Phyllis that George's chances of pulling through were poor, although he said no such thing to George. To George he was optimistic: 'Don't you worry', he said, 'we'll get you through'.

'Of course you will', said George. It would have been impolite to contradict the doctor.

The chaplain came around, said a few words of encouragement and, when he asked George if he could say a prayer, George had no objection. He was feeling very ill by this time and was not in a mood to argue. He asked if these were 'the last rites' and the chaplain explained that nowadays we don't have 'last rites'. Anyone who is seriously ill can be prayed for; it didn't mean that anyone was going to die. 'He don't fool me', said George to his wife, but she was very upset and told him not to be silly; then she burst into tears and George wished he had not said it. He did his best to cheer her up but found it hard to make the effort and it was a relief when she left the ward for a cup of tea in the canteen. 'I think I'll have a little sleep' he told the nurse, and closed his eyes. When Phyllis got back there was a crowd of doctors round the bed trying to resuscitate him, but it was soon apparent that he was dead.

'I'm sorry, love, he's gone', said the ward sister, and sent for a nurse who put her arm round Phyllis and sat with her in the sister's office until the family arrived. Somehow Phyllis had expected that they would then return to the bedside but, by this time, 'the body' had been removed on a covered trolley to the hospital mortuary. The family saw none of this and were not told that George's toes had been tied together and his cheeks and nostrils padded with cotton wool. Had they chosen to view his body they might have been surprised how much better he looked now he was dead than when he was alive. But although the nurse had told them that they could see him if they wished, his son had said firmly, 'I'd rather remember him the way he was', and this had swayed the decision not to view him in the mortuary.

The doctor explained to Phyllis that, as George had died so soon after being admitted to hospital, his death would have to be reported to the Coroner. It would be for the Coroner to issue the death certificate and no funeral arrangements could be made until the body had been 'released' for burial. When Phyllis said, 'They won't cut him open, will they?' she was told that this was for the Coroner to decide. Although Phyllis did not like the idea, she did not argue. She had, after all, relinquished George to the care of the experts when she sent for the ambulance and she saw the Coroner as an extension of the same impersonal but necessary system of control.

For Phyllis the next few days passed in a blur. Friends came and went, expressing their sympathy and telling her to contact them if she needed anything, but Phyllis did not know what she needed and did not ask for help. She would have liked it if they had stayed longer to keep her company but her friends had seemed embarrassed by her grief. Her brother too had been upset when she cried and told her to pull herself together, advice which she found unhelpful.

The Coroner's Officer was a gentle policeman who was soon able to reassure her that the Coroner was satisfied that no post-mortem examination would be needed and that she could make arrangements for the funeral. She went, with her brother, to a local funeral director who showed her pictures of coffins and promised to make all the arrangements. Her brother agreed to notify the family and his wife said she would look after the catering for the reception afterwards. Phyllis began to feel that she was redundant, a feeling that was to recur frequently during the next few months.

George, in a closed coffin, was cremated after a service in the local crematorium. This was conducted by a duty clergyman whom none of the family had met. This was his fifth funeral service that day and he had switched into automatic – the words came out right, but the meaning had somehow got lost. Phyllis wished she had asked for a proper service in her local church, but she had been overruled by her brother and the funeral director who had persuaded her that she wanted 'something quiet'. The worst moment was when the clergyman pressed a button and the coffin unexpectedly went down through the plinth. Phyllis had a mental picture of flames licking up from a fire beneath and had to check herself from shouting for them to stop. She embarrassed herself by bursting into tears and had to lean on her brother as they left the chapel. There was a great number of bunches of flowers, each bearing a tag with the name of the donor and a few words of remembrance. Phyllis was trying to look at each one of them when the funeral director gently reminded her that another funeral was due and she would have to move on.

After the funeral thirty people came home to eat sandwiches and sip sherry. Most of them were distant members of the family who now only met at funerals and weddings. They were delighted to see each other, and soon forgot that this was a solemn occasion. They laughed and talked about their grandchildren and the cricket score and George was seldom mentioned in Phyllis's presence in case she got upset again. Phyllis found the whole occasion unreal and an ordeal. She was greatly relieved when the guests departed with the usual injunctions to her, to keep her chin up.

When the funeral was over Phyllis found herself on her own for the first time. At first this was a relief but she could not get over the feeling that something was about to happen. She sat waiting to be told what to do, but nobody came and, after a while, it began to dawn on her that this was how it was going to be from now on. She prayed to God but he too seemed to have gone away. This was the true beginning of her grief, the pain of which she had never experienced or imagined before.

Phyllis and George are typical of mid-twentieth-century British people, who will give their religious persuasion as 'C of E' (Church of England) but whose faith is very different from that of their forebears and of many other Christian denominations across the world. We live in a world in which religion and the fundamental ideas with which it deals – birth, death and the meaning of life – have been taken over by professionals and quietly downgraded in personal significance. Even those who continue to go to church often do so out of habit or a sense of duty rather than an enthusiastic commitment.

When, in the course of time, we suffer a bereavement or develop a terminal illness, as we all must sooner or later, we feel let down by God; 'If there were a good God he wouldn't let this kind of thing happen'. The 'last rites', which formerly provided reassurance and comfort to the dying, and the funeral and mourning, which provided the bereaved with social sanction for grieving, social support and a set of beliefs that gave meaning to death, are now too often empty ordeals, of doubtful help to the dying or the bereaved. These problems are not confined to the Church of England and, as we shall see in Chapter 9, they are found to some degree in most countries of the Western World.

Likewise, we should not assume that all members of the Church of England or of other Christian churches find their faith and the rituals which accompany death and bereavement to be meaningless. For some they can be inspiring and deeply significant. The variation is large.

THE ROOTS OF CHRISTIANITY

Christianity began as a Jewish sect. Only after its adoption by the Emperor Constantine, in AD 313, did it make a wide impact among Gentiles and it then spread rapidly throughout the Roman Empire while dying out among Jews. Christianity is based on the teachings of Jesus of Nazareth who began his mission about AD 30 and was crucified by the Roman occupying power at the request of the Jewish priesthood about two years later. He obtained a following at the time as a preacher and healer and, after his crucifixion, was seen and believed to have returned from the dead, by a number of his disciples.

His teachings were first written down in the Gospels and the Acts of the Apostles at least thirty years after his death. These were added to by other followers in a series of books which, after protracted debate, were assembled as the New Testament and added to the Jewish Bible. The last, and most controversial book, the Revelation of St John the Divine, was finally accepted by the Council of Carthage in AD 367 (for a detailed and well researched account of this history see Johnson, 1976).

Central to Christian faith is the belief that Jesus was the Son of God who was sent by his Father to save mankind from sin and that he chose to die on the cross as a demonstration of his love for mankind. Since that time those who repent of their sins and turn to him will be forgiven and will join him in heaven after death. Attempts to reconcile the divinity of Christ with monotheism (the doctrine that there is only one God) led to considerable controversy in the early church and to the formulation of the doctrine of the Trinity, three persons (God the Father, Son and Holy Spirit) in one God.

Despite further attempts to produce uniformity of belief by consolidating the Bible and making it the final authority on all matters of faith, the Christian Church soon split into a number of subdivisions.

The main splits were the Great Schism of AD 1054 when the Eastern churches severed their links with Rome, to form the Eastern Orthodox Churches, and the Protestant Reformation which followed in the sixteenth century and affected many churches in northern Europe.

Roman Catholicism

The Roman Catholic church remains the predominant Christian sect in most of southern Europe, the whole of South America, South Africa and much of the southern, eastern and northern parts of North America.

Jesus Christ, as intermediary between God and humankind, is the central figure of the Catholic faith and his mother, Mary, is also revered. This female element is missing from the other major world religions. At the head of a male, celibate, priesthood is the Pope, whose status derives from St Peter, the founder of the Christian Church. Thanks to the influence of the Pope (the Vicar of Christ) it shows a much greater uniformity of belief than other Christian sects. When speaking with full authority (*ex cathedra*) his word is thought to be infallible and binding upon all Catholics. Aspects of Catholic faith that are relevant to medical care are the prohibition of abortion and contraception. Most Catholics will not eat any food before taking Mass.

Sacraments

The Mass is the most important sacrament and can be said at the bedside of Catholics who are too sick to go to a church. It is a part of the funeral service. Non-Catholics may attend but should not take Communion (i.e. receive the bread and wine; these are the body and blood of Christ, and not a symbol, in Catholic, though not in other Christian faiths).

Baptism is important, and a child who remains unbaptized may not receive eternal life. This makes it essential that babies whose lives are in danger be baptized immediately. A priest should be called at once in this event.

Confession (and reconciliation) are also important, and absolution (forgiveness for those who confess and repent their sins) can only be given by a priest. This makes it most important that Catholics who are approaching death be seen by a priest and in conditions of *absolute privacy*. Absolution can be given up to three hours after death.

Anointing the sick, formerly *Extreme Unction*, is also only administered by a priest and should not be left to the last moments of life. This cannot be given after death and adds further emphasis to the importance of ensuring that calling a priest be given high priority for Catholics who are close to death.

The Act of Contrition is said by all Catholics and takes on special importance at the approach of death: 'O My God, I am sorry for my sins because I have offended you. I know I should love you above all things. Forgive me my sins. Help me to do penance to do better, and to avoid anything that might lead me to sin. AMEN.'

Requiem Masses are commemorative services which are often attended by the bereaved some time after a death has occurred. They can be deeply moving and some of the greatest music ever composed was written for them.

Eastern Orthodox churches

These remain the predominant Christian churches in the former USSR and, in similar form (the Greek Orthodox), in Greece and its areas of influence. Although Orthodoxy is still relatively uncommon in the West it is likely that the increase in contact which has begun in recent years will lead to greater diffusion of populations and beliefs across the former 'Iron Curtain'. They arose as a reaction against domination by the Pope, and the Orthodox churches are administered by a central Ecumenical Council and each nation has its Patriarch (who is the 'first among equals').

Unlike Catholic and Protestant churches the Eastern church still gives priority to God the Father rather than to his Son. Each church and chapel contains icons (gilded images of sacred personages) which are treated with great reverence. The regular services are long and include a great deal of singing and chanting. Those who are able to do so remain standing throughout the service, though there are a few chairs for the elderly and disabled. People come and go at will and only the most devout are likely to attend the complete service.

Because the Eastern Orthodox church is less inclined to adopt strict rules than the Roman Catholic, there is more individual variation in practice. Those who are most devout will not eat animal products on a Friday and will fast for three days before taking Communion and at other major festivals.

Sacraments

When someone is very sick they will appreciate visits from their priest, who will chant the *Office for the Sick* at their bedside. Obviously this is less likely to disturb other hospital patients if carried out in a single room. A hospital chapel that contains an icon is appreciated.

A priest should always be called when death approaches. He will chant the *Office for the Parting of the Soul* and anoint the patient with oil. If no priest is available a suitable prayer from that service is

> Receive thou in peace the soul of this thy servant, [N], Lord give it rest in the everlasting mansions of thy Saints; through the grace of thine only begotten Son, Our Lord, and God and Saviour, Jesus Christ: with whom also thou art blessed, together with thine all-holy, and good, and life-giving Spirit, now, and ever, unto all ages. AMEN.

After death the body is washed and clothed in new clothes. The family members may wish to do this. The body is often then returned home where it is laid out in a coffin whose top is open to reveal the head and shoulders of the dead person, whose hands hold an icon.

Several days before the funeral the body is taken to the church where it is displayed before the altar. A cross is placed on the coffin lid. On the night preceding the funeral an all-night *Vigil* is often kept during which close family and friends will chant the psalms and read from the Gospels.

The Funeral is one of the shortest Orthodox services. It only lasts about forty-five minutes but may be considerably longer if there is a large congregation because many of those present will prostrate themselves before the dead person (in recognition that the body is a temple) and then kiss the cross. Non-Orthodox are welcome to attend but need not prostrate themselves.

Burial or cremation is permitted. If there is a burial, a *Service of Interment* takes place at the graveside following which family and friends drop earth on the coffin while moving their hands to make the sign of the cross.

Three, eight and forty days after the funeral, memorial services (*Panikhidi*) are held at which psalms are chanted along with short anthems (*Contakion* and *Trepanion*). These mark the passage of the soul on its journey. Some believe that, during the first three days the souls of the dead grieve for the loss of their life and roam the earth. They are then relieved of their grief and escorted by their Guardian

Angel to appear before God. They spend the next five days viewing the souls of the elect who are in heaven; after a second appearance before God the next month is spent viewing the torments of the damned. Only then do the souls appear for their own judgement.

At the *Panikhidi* those present pray: 'With the Saints give rest, O Christ, to the soul of thy servant, where there is neither sickness, nor sorrow, but life-everlasting.'

Members of the Eastern Orthodox church tend to be more committed in their devotions than those in the West. Under Communist rule many rejected religion altogether and became atheists rather than dilute Christians. The current decline in faith in Communism is accompanied by a resurgence of interest in the Eastern church. It remains to be seen if the increased tolerance of dissent will lead to dilution.

Protestantism

Whereas the Catholic and Eastern churches lay emphasis on obedience and membership of the church community, which is more important than the individual, Protestants emphasize each person's personal and unique relationship with God. Salvation is achieved by our own efforts alone and there is a tendency for deeds to count more than prayers. Prayers for the souls of the dead are heretical because the dead are in the hands of God and will be judged on their own merits alone. This does not prevent some Protestant churches holding Memorial Services.

Protestant churches vary greatly in the extent to which their services and beliefs resemble those of the church of Rome. Even within the Anglican Communion there is great variation between the 'high' and the 'low' church, with members of the 'high' church confessing their sins to a priest. Their services are formal, incense is burned and there is much singing and chanting. By contrast the 'low' churches are less formal, the laity share with the priest more responsibility for running the church and services are simpler. This does not mean that members of the 'low' church are less devout and there are many who adopt fundamentalist beliefs (taking the Bible as literally true on all matters). Some disbelieve the theory of evolution and come into conflict with educational authorities where this is taught in schools.

The descendants of immigrant groups, whose forebears were converted to Christianity, such as those from the Caribbean, often belong to these 'low' churches. In South Wales, where people can often attend either 'church' or 'chapel', the multiplicity of chapels reflects the ethnic origins of the immigrant miners as well as the faiths of the diverse preachers who competed for the souls of the faithful in Victorian times. Recent attempts at ecumenical union tend to blur the distinction between these sects.

Similarly, members of the former slave cultures were converted from their former African religions by preachers from many denominations. Those from the English-speaking world tend to be Baptists, Pentecostals and Unitarians while those from the French-speaking world are most often Catholics. Echoes of their pre-Christian religions linger on in Voodoo and other beliefs in witchcraft and spirit healing. Despite the number of sects there is a surprising degree of uniformity in the ways in which black people grieve and the public expression of emotion at funerals.

Burgoine, who used the same questionnaires to compare the reaction of Bahamian widows to bereavement with that of London widows who had been studied by Parkes, found that Bahamian widows, who express their grief more fully, suffered less lasting depression than London widows. She also found that widows from higher social class groups, whose grieving approximates to that of the London widows, suffered more lasting depression than Bahamian widows of lower socio-economic status (Burgoine, 1988, and Parkes, 1970).

The Anglican Communion

This includes the churches of England, Scotland, Ireland and Wales with their sister churches in Commonwealth countries, the USA and elsewhere. Variants include the Protestant Episcopal Church of the United States and the Nippon Sei Ko Kwai in Japan.

Sacraments

Baptism is the formal recognition of membership of the church. It is normally conducted in infancy and newborn babies at risk of death can be baptized as an emergency if their parents wish. In that event the chaplain should be called without delay. Adults may also choose to be baptized at home or in a hospital if they are too sick to attend a church.

Prayers for the sick have replaced the former Extreme Unction and should not be assumed to indicate that a person is about to die. Those who wish to be anointed by a priest can be.

A *commendatory prayer* can be said at the moment of death or soon afterwards. This is of comfort to Christians and may be said by anyone who is at hand.

> Into Your Hands, O Merciful Saviour, we commend your servant, acknowledge, we humbly beseech You, a sheep of your own fold, a lamb of your own flock, a sinner of your own redeeming. Receive him/her into your arms of mercy, into the blessed rest of your everlasting peace, and into the glorious company of the saints in light. AMEN.

Holy Communion is the equivalent of the Catholic Mass and the principal sacrament of the Anglican Church. It includes a general confession of sin which is said by the congregation after which the priest pronounces absolution. In most branches of the church this has replaced individual confession. Communion can be administered at the bedside of a sick patient and many members of the church will welcome this, particularly if they are close to death.

Funeral services usually take place about a week after death. They often include a eulogy or tribute to the dead person which may be spoken by a clergyman or by a friend of the dead person. The family should be consulted about the choice of prayers, readings and hymns but many prefer to leave this entirely in the hands of the 'experts'. Funeral directors have largely taken over from the church the planning of funerals. Because cremation is now preferred to burial in Britain, most funerals are now carried out in crematorium chapels by a priest who knows nothing of the family or the dead person. The ashes are then placed in an urn to await interment in hallowed ground or scattering. This is often carried out without ceremony.

We have given a rather depressing view of the Anglican funeral because this is how it often is. On the other hand it can be a deeply moving and fitting tribute to round off the life of a loved person. The words of the ritual have a poetic significance which can even reach non-believers. Uttered by someone who knew the dead person and has consulted the family to design a service that is personally meaningful to them, it can leave memories to be recalled with pride instead of being an ordeal to be forgotten.

Although memorial services are unusual, they are sometimes held, particularly if the funeral was held overseas or many people were unable to attend. It is common for the names of those parishioners who have died to be read out in church on the Sunday morning after the anniversary of their funeral in thanksgiving for the life of the departed.

Free churches (including Methodists, United Reform, Congregational, etc.)

These resemble the 'low' churches of the Anglican Communion in many respects. They tend to favour simple services, good works and the teachings of Jesus as found in the Gospels. Some of them are fundamentalist, adopting a literal interpretation of the Bible. Members of these churches who are dying or bereaved will often wish to hear readings from the scriptures.

Methodists have introduced two rituals which are uncommon in other sects. These are the Vigil, an ancient custom of service which is held in the presence of the dead body on the evening before the funeral, and an Office of Commendation for children who have been stillborn.

Baptists attach importance to adult baptism by total immersion. They do not baptize children.

Quakers have no priesthood. At their meetings, including funerals, people sit in silence until moved spontaneously to speak whatever is within their hearts. Non-Quakers are welcome to attend and to speak if they wish.

Pentecostals emphasize the work of the Holy Spirit. Their services, including funerals, are often emotional occasions and may include 'speaking with tongues' when members of the congregation cry out or speak in an incomprehensible language. Prophecy and healing also take place.

Jehovah's Witnesses see it as their duty to convert others to the faith before the imminent end of the world. They emphasize service rather than ritual. Witnesses are forbidden to consume blood in any form and this has led to refusal of blood transfusion or other blood products (but not plasma volume expanders). Those who hold to this will accept full responsibility for the consequences of their decisions and will release those treating them from any adverse consequences. Problems arise when they refuse life-saving treatment for their children and this has led to Courts ordering children to be taken into care. Witnesses also forbid organ donation and abortion.

Christian Science (Church of Christ, Scientist) was founded in 1879 by Mary Baker Eddy. The adherents to this faith believe that death is the last enemy and that disease must be treated by prayer alone. Like the Jehovah's Witnesses they will often refuse blood transfusions and other treatments. Alcohol and smoking are also prohibited. They tend to ignore the fact of death, they hold no funeral or other ritual when it takes place and give no support to bereaved members of the church. Post-mortem examinations will be resisted unless required by law. Only women should touch the body of a dead woman.

Mormons (Church of the Latter-Day Saints) believe in a spirit world before birth and after death. Only those who have been baptized can enter the kingdom of heaven. Children cannot be baptized but baptism of adults can be carried out after death. This has led to the collection of genealogical information and mass baptisms of all the dead persons whose names can be elicited throughout the world.

All worthy male Mormons enter the priesthood at the age of twelve. Mormons who have undergone a special ceremony wear a *sacred undergarment* throughout their lives. This *should not be removed after death*. Because death is only a brief separation from loved ones no rituals are observed. Burial is the preferred method of disposal of the dead.

Spiritualists believe in the Communion of Saints (the spiritual union of each and every Christian, whether in heaven, purgatory or earth) and the Ministry of Angels (who care for us both before and after our death). The dead occupy a spirit world and remain available to help the living who can communicate with them, usually through a medium. This is done in simple services at which a medium will go into a state of trance and deliver messages form the dead for members of the congregation. These usually take the form of comforting reassurance that the dead are happy and at peace. Spirits of dead doctors and other healers are also called upon to heal the sick.

Many bereaved people attend services of the Spiritualist church in the hope of regaining contact with a lost person. While many of them receive such messages, few return more than once or twice and some are upset by conflicting messages. The practice is strongly opposed by most denominations of Christians who quote Deuteronomy 18:11 in prohibition ('There shall not be found with thee . . . a consulter with a familiar spirit, or a wizard or a necromancer. For whosoever doeth these things is an abomination unto the Lord').

Indigenous variants of Christianity

There is a tendency for indigenous groups who have been conquered or superseded by Christians to become converted to Christianity but to retain aspects of former pre-Christian faiths. This occurs among native Americans, Africans, New Zealanders and Australians. It is not possible here to describe all of these customs and beliefs (there are over 350 tribal variants in North America alone). Instead we shall describe one interesting example which has particular relevance to New Zealand.

The Maori Tangi has been retained, virtually unchanged, in a society that has been a Christian community since the nineteenth century. It enables Maoris to commemorate their dead in a traditional way, before performing a Christian burial.

When a Maori dies the body is brought back to the communal meeting house where it will rest for three days and two nights. Family members and close friends will remain with the body during this time and are not permitted to cook or do anything except mourn. Mourning includes chanting and singing to the dead person whose spirit is present. All forms of non-violent emotional expression are permitted including criticism of the dead who is often taken to task for sins or omissions. More distant relatives and friends including non-Maoris (*Pakeha*) bring small gifts of food or money to the mourners. They should greet the dead person first and then every other person in the room, in the traditional Maori way, by touching their nose to each side of the other person's nose.

When the three days are over the Tangi comes to an end and the Christian priest will conduct a funeral and inter the body in a Maori cemetery. Graves are marked in the usual Christian way but the fence around the cemetery is carved with traditional Maori symbols.

In recent years there has been a tendency across the world for young people to take an interest in their ancestral customs and this has led to a revival of many rituals which would probably otherwise have been forgotten. It is not unreasonable to hope that this kind of activity will help to redress the balance away from the uniformity and loss of personal identity which threatens to emerge in the modern 'global village'. From the point of view of members of the caring professions who come from other faiths the important thing is to respect such views and take the trouble to find out how one can be of help.

SUMMARY

☐ Westerners live in a world in which religion and the fundamental ideas with which it deals – birth, death and the meaning of life –

have been taken over by professionals and quietly downgraded in personal significance.

☐ The 'last rites' which formerly provided reassurance and comfort to dying Christians, and the funeral and mourning which provided the bereaved with social sanction for grieving, social support and a set of beliefs that gave meaning to death, are now too often empty ordeals, of doubtful help to the dying or the bereaved.

☐ Christians hold that those who repent of their sins and turn to Jesus Christ will be forgiven and will join him in heaven after death.

☐ Roman Catholicism shows a much greater uniformity of belief than other Christian sects.

☐ A priest should be called whenever people are dying, to anoint the sick and take their confession. Privacy should be provided. Babies whose lives are in danger must be baptized immediately.

☐ The Mass is a part of the funeral service. Non-Catholics should not take Communion.

☐ When someone of Eastern Orthodox faith is very sick they will appreciate visits from their priest, who will chant the Office for the Sick and, later, the Office for the Parting of the Soul, at their bedside.

☐ The open coffin is displayed in the church on the night before burial and a vigil kept.

☐ At the funeral friends view the dead person and may prostrate themselves.

☐ The souls of the dead are assisted on their journey by chanting of psalms and anthems on the third, eighth and fortieth days after the funeral (*Panikhidi*).

☐ Whereas the Catholic and Eastern churches lay emphasis on obedience and membership of the church community, which is more important than the individual, Protestants emphasize each person's personal and unique relationship with God. Salvation is achieved by our own efforts alone and there is a tendency for deeds to count more than prayers.

☐ Protestant churches vary greatly in the extent to which their services and beliefs resemble those of the church of Rome. Some expect and others discourage emotional expression at funerals and other occasions.

☐ Bahamian widows who express their grief more fully, suffer less lasting depression than London widows.

☐ Within the Anglican Communion there is great variation. Clergy are glad to visit the dying. Prayers for the sick, Holy Communion and anointing are optional and have replaced Extreme Unction.

☐ The Anglican funeral service allows for personal commemoration and eulogy but is too often impersonal and routine. Cremation is replacing burial as the preferred method of disposal and further increases mechanization of the ritual.

☐ A summary account of the principal Free Churches is given above.

☐ There is a tendency for indigenous groups who have been conquered or superseded by Christians to become converted to Christianity but to retain aspects of former pre-Christian faiths. An example, the Maori Tangi, is described.

☐ In recent years there has been a tendency across the world for young people to take an interest in their ancestral customs and this has led to a revival of many rituals which would probably otherwise have been forgotten.

Chapter 8

The many facets of Islam
Death, dying and disposal between orthodox rule and historical convention[1]

Gerdien Jonker

INTRODUCTION

Islam has many faces. Since its origins more than thirteen hundred years ago the Islamic religion has mingled many people and nationalities and adapted to a great many social surroundings, geographical conditions and historical backgrounds. The religion based on the Quran and the life of its prophet has rooted in republics and nomadic societies, in kingdoms and under Communist rule. From Morocco to Indonesia, from Kazakhstan to the USA, Islamic religious rule has given direction to the religious behaviour of minorities and majorities, of private believers and communities. Among other things it has determined the way the believers interpreted death and has led to conventional schemes for how to handle the body.

Religious rule continues to hold sway in the matter of death in today's changing world, where Turks and Moroccans might find themselves in Holland, Pakistanis and Bangladeshis in England, Bosnians and Lebanese in Germany, Algerians in France and Egyptians in the USA. To explain exactly how all these different groups react to Orthodoxy, how they perceive death within their own surroundings old or new, and how they translate religious rule into fitting actions is the purpose of this chapter. It intends to make clear that the burial practices of Muhammad's time have allowed for many forms and interpretations since. It will explain that religious rule, although global in its directions on how to interpret death and how to handle the corpse accordingly, leaves space for local expressions of loss and mourning. This will be

1 This chapter could not have been written without the Muslim men and women who told me their stories: also the Turkish undertaker Vatan in Berlin who took me on as an apprentice. I thank them all for their trust.

illustrated by two examples. The first is the earliest reported burial in the Islamic era, the second, a description of a recent double funeral in the Islamic community in Berlin. The different ritual stages, of dying, handling the corpse, saying farewell and the burial proper will be explained step by step. The examples used here are taken from the Mediterranean world, the Maghreb, the Middle East, Turkey and Bosnia. Differences between these people and those presently living on the European continent are explained. The question of how death and burial are differently perceived by men, women and children will form an undercurrent throughout.

MECCA, 8 JUNE AD 632

It was on a Monday that the prophet Muhammad died. He had felt ill for a long time. He had sought the nearness of death, had been seen going to the graves at night, in order to talk with the dead and pray for them. When he had finally lain down for what was to be his last illness, he indicated that his uncle should lead the congregation in prayer during his absence: he had prepared himself. When the prophet died, his head rested in Aisha's lap. Aisha was his beloved wife, who had taken care of him in his last moments. As soon as she realized that he had gone, she laid his head on a pillow and stood up to beat her breast and slap her face, together with the other women, as a sign of mourning.

They decided to bury him on Tuesday and the men came to prepare the body. Here a difficulty arose. Out of respect for the body these men, all sons and intimate friends of the deceased, would not strip him bare, so they washed the corpse with his clothes on. When Aisha heard this, she is reported to have said, 'We should have done it ourselves.' The body then was wrapped three times and covered with a coat and laid upon the bed. Men, women and children appeared in separate groups to say their farewell and pray. Nobody intervened or took the lead in prayer.

Discussion arose about the proper place of burial and it was decided to bury the prophet in the place where he had died, right under his bed. The women, not having been consulted about this, only knew what was going on when they heard 'the pick-axes ringing' under their roof. Thus the grave was dug, with a niche in the bottom of it, in which to rest the body. When his sons and friends finally laid the prophet in his last resting place, some threw an object in after him, a garment or a ring, so as to touch him for the very last time. After the burial a great many mourning songs were composed after the literary fashion of the period.

By these the prophet was mourned as no one before him. A poem by one of his followers, Hassan b. Thabit, puts it thus:

The night they laid him unpillowed in the dust
And went away in sorrow without him
Their arms and backs of strength devoid
They mourned him whom the heavens mourned
The earth did too – yet men grieve more
Can any day a death is mourned
Equal the mourning of the day Mohammed died?

BERLIN, 16 JANUARY 1995

8.30 a.m. The deserted forecourt of the Islamic cemetery is steeped in a grey winter light. The first visitors arrive. Hands are shaken and inquiries made where the funeral is to take place. Nobody knows. We wait.

8.45 a.m. Two cars drive up, transporting two men and three women. The elder woman wears a small white scarf loosely tied around her hair. The younger one has a bloated face and swollen eyes. They all remain standing outside the building awaiting instructions from the undertaker. A couple of men appear behind the glass doors leading to the washing quarters. One of them identifies himself as a representative of the funeral institute. 'The first one is the Lebanese child, the man from Bosnia comes after that', he says. Behind the doors of the washing room one can hear water running. The young woman has followed the others into the building and asks whether she can see her baby now. She is gently led away to the waiting area.

9.00 a.m. A Turkish woman comes out of the washing room. On outstretched arms she is carrying the small white coffin into the anteroom. She is an elderly woman and is covered from head to foot in plastic. She wears a white plastic apron, transparent plastic gloves, rubber boots, and a plastic cap, which she has slipped over the brown kerchief covering her hair. Over her mouth she wears a white mouth protection. She puts the coffin on a low black podium, which stands crossways in the anteroom. Behind her, one can look through the opened doors of the brightly lit washing room. All around, the walls and floors are tiled in white. The water taps, the metallic table, the water basin, even the drain in the middle of the floor, are sparkling and glittering under the light.

9.05 a.m. The family is beckoned to enter. The white cloth covering the child is carefully pushed aside, so that everybody can have a view of her. All take a short look only. Nobody speaks, nobody is seen crying. Immediately afterwards, the coffin is screwed tight, and covered with a green cloth. Then the men position themselves in two small rows. Their faces are directed towards the coffin, their feet stand a little apart, their arms hang down loosely. The women retreat into the washing room.

The Imam, an elderly man with a kind face, quietly speaks, almost whispers, a few words. Then he begins intoning the Prayer for the Dead. All others, almost inaudibly, join in his prayer. They perform the movements of devotion simultaneously: thumbs behind the ears, the palms touch the face, and are then briefly turned towards the sky. Only the regularly returning praise *allahu akbar* (God is Great) is audible.

9.15 a.m. The prayer is finished. Two men lift the coffin, the family make their way through the glass door into the open. Here, the funeral manager halts the group, and tells them that they cannot continue yet. The priest still has to 'prepare' the Bosnian man before they can proceed. The family will have to wait for another half an hour. So the little coffin is carried back into the anteroom. Outside a little crowd has already gathered. I count seventy men and two women. Photos are being taken. One man even has a video camera.

The young Lebanese woman stands forlorn, crying to herself. She tells me that the child was only three months old, when, one morning, it had suddenly died. She, the mother, had not noticed anything, had slept. Her mourning is mingled with guilt. Had she given the child too little too eat? After its sudden death the child had been brought to hospital for post-mortem, and she had not seen it again since. Did I notice any scars on the child's body? How big were the cuts? Only with some effort can I explain that I did not do the washing.

9.30 a.m. The second corpse has been washed and wrapped up, the coffin stands ready on the podium. The visitors receive instructions. They line up in a row, and speedily are being led past the uncovered face of the departed. An old man with a sunken face and dishevelled, still wet hair lies between the shrouds. Nobody cries. The video camera is running.

In the adjacent room, the baby coffin is unscrewed again, in order to allow a late visitor a last view. The old woman leans against the wall, she is crying behind her hand. The priest has changed into rubber boots and a large white rubber apron. He is standing at a water basin at a corner of the room, soaping his hands up to his elbows.

9.35 a.m. The old man's coffin is screwed up, carried outside the washing quarters, and placed out in the open. The men form a line, the women observe the scene, the camera is still running, photos are being taken, the Bosnian priest steps in front. He gives a short speech, then starts the prayer. The forecourt is filled by the indiscernible whispers of the mourners.

9.45 a.m. The old man's coffin is presently shouldered by six men, all the other men lining up behind, the women taking the rear. As the coffin is speedily walked to the grave, it wanders from shoulder to shoulder till every man present has had his share in the burden. The women do not participate in this ritual. The grave is at the rear edge of a new field. Ten flattened mounds of sand already form a row there. Green boards inscribed with chalk are placed at their head ends.

9.50 a.m. While the men lower the old man's coffin with long straps of material, the Lebanese mourners, coming from the other side of the field, advance. The father carries the coffin in front of them. For the child a grave has been dug at the other corner of the field, about 50 m from the first. On both burial places the earth is being shovelled back into the holes. One can hear the thudding noise as long as it hits the coffin. Most of the men participate and silently pass the shovels among them. While the work continues the religious leader recites from the Quran. To my Western ears, the melody sounds melancholy, and strangely soothing. At the same time a thin melody coming from the other burial site can be heard. The child's grave is filled much quicker than the adult's grave. There the Lebanese mourners have already put flowers on the small mound. Presently their Imam can be observed squatting down in front of the grave, lifting his palms towards the sky. The others remain standing, and also lift their palms. They appear to be praying.

10.00 a.m. The Lebanese group breaks up. The men walk across the field, towards the path they have come from. They do not look back. Only the young woman lingers, puts something on the mound, tugs the flowers. The three other women slowly walk towards the mourning hall, occasionally looking back. One of them stops, and calls something to where the young woman remains standing. She follows hesitantly.

10.05 a.m. The old man's grave has been filled with earth and finished with a flattened mound. Two huge wreaths, decorated with bows, are positioned on top. Everyone present lowers themselves onto their haunches. The Bosnian priest is heard intoning a new melody. Around him one sees a squatting audience, palms turned up in prayer, and many lips are moving silently. Now another man takes over the recitation, raising his voice a little. The recitation moves along the squatting rows, intoned by both strong and quavering voices.

10.15 a.m. It is over. Palms touch faces to indicate the end of the prayer. The mourners rise, shake hands with each other. A little sheet of paper is handed down the rows and given to the religious leader. While the mourners turn and start towards the road in silence, he positions himself once more at the head of the mound and starts another recitation.

DYING

What these two stories have in common is the care with which the dead body is surrounded. In all three funerals the corpse is washed and wrapped, looked at, cried over and prayed for, and eventually carefully laid in a dug-out cavity in the ground.

This behaviour springs from the presumption that although life on earth is finished, life after death will continue in a form to which the preservation of the body is absolutely essential. And in fact cremation is forbidden by Islamic law. Islamic believers prepare themselves for the continuation of a bodily existence after death. Death as such is seen as the fulfilment of life, as the ending of a fixed term only known by God, and some say that this term stands written between a person's brows. And even when during life religion has hardly played any role, when the person dying and those surrounding him or her have lived secularized lives, in the face of death they will prepare themselves, presuming that 'it will go on somehow'.

Most people consider it important that when death approaches the dying are helped to sit up or at least turn their faces towards Mecca, in the direction of prayer, this being the last time they can pronounce the confession of faith. More often those present will say the prayer instead, soaking a little piece of cottonwool with water and laying it in the mouth of the dying one, reciting the words softly near their faces and the dying, too weak to repeat the words, will lift their index finger as a sign of presence.

This little ritual is important for both parties present, the dying and those witnessing the death. It will consolidate the dying person's expectation that death is not the end, that he or she is now entering the world of the divine with the proper attitude. For the survivors it means defying the definiteness of death by taking a first step towards continuation.

HANDLING THE BODY

As soon as death has occurred the body is laid out on a hard surface, on the floor of the room or on a board placed on the bed. The feet are put together, the arms straightened along the sides, the eyes closed and the chin wrapped up with a piece of cloth.

It is now that the body is washed. Sometimes the ablution is performed by close family members of the deceased but more often the washers, who usually act in pairs, are from a specialized trade. As a rule only men wash a man's body as only women will wash a woman's. They are paid for their services, although in some Arabic countries this is considered a modern abuse, as the service of washing a corpse counts as a pious deed. Migrant communities often find it difficult to explain to the social services of their guest country that the costs for washing the corpse should be found, since such institutions tend to see it as simply a routine washing which could be performed by anybody present. But this is not the case.

The act of cleansing a corpse fulfils two aims. Dead bodies should be cleaned to ensure that no impurity, urine, blood or excrement, will stick to them. At the same time the washers perform the ritual ablutions before prayer so as to prepare the deceased for what awaits them. This is why a Quran reader often accompanies them and chants from the holy book during the ablution.

All washers follow a fixed pattern. They will first clean themselves three times over. The water for the ablution might be mixed with perfume, herbs, rosewater, lotus or camphor. They then will clean the corpse's nose, ears and neck, twice repeat the washing of the right forearm and hand, and follow the same procedure for the left one. Then the body will be cleaned, the feet always coming last. All this is done gently and with the utmost care; the water used should not be too cold, loud talking is avoided. This is because although the deceased undeniably is dead, a little life is supposed to linger in or around the corpse through which the dead still can feel and hear. This awareness also means that corpses never will be denuded totally, the flesh being laid bare only in parts. In this way the body will not be exposed to others' eyes, and saved from the shame against which the deceased can no longer defend him- or herself.

When somebody has died at home, the washers will come early in the morning and perform their trade there. But if that is not the case, ablutions can be performed elsewhere, in the morgue of a hospital or in the specially equipped washing rooms attached to Muslim cemeteries.

This done, the deceased are considered ritually clean and ready to face whatever awaits them. But before they can go on their journey they are shrouded from head to toe in clean white cloth, rough linen for some, cotton or even damask for others. At least three pieces of textile of 240 to 250 cm in length (which should not contain any knots or sewing since these could obstruct the liberation of the soul) are spread out for this purpose, and the corpse is wrapped up in such a way that the head can be freed later on.

Some people, mostly older people from a traditional background, keep their shrouds at hand long before they are needed. But others, among them Muslims from former Communist countries, consider it more appropriate to clothe their dead in a suit or dress and some personal attire. As long as people remained in their homelands, no difficulty ever arose out of this difference. However, if they find themselves in a third country, where an international Muslim community is providing only one undertaker, and where religious leaders of one nationality look after Islamic believers of another, then differences in custom can lead to explosive encounters. These unerringly lead to the question of what is lawful, and consequently who is the better Muslim.

EXPRESSING THE LOSS

Should one cry? Should one let go? Is it permitted to express emotions on losing a husband, a child or one's own parents? And if so, what is appropriate? These questions might sound strange in a Western and secularized world where people are socialized into expressing their own feelings. But many Muslim mourners grapple with such questions.

In a Muslim context reactions to loss differ widely, and not only from one country to the other. A wide gap yawns between law and custom, between rural customs and those of the big city, and on a social level between men and women, husbands and wives. Basically one can discern two classic reactions to loss, both backed up by a long history and many local variations. The first consists of extreme crying, accompanied by breast beating and scratching of the face, which is gradually moulded into a longwinded dirge, halfway between singing and crying. In this song all the details of the departed's life are recalled, together with the way they died and an expression of the mourner's difficulty in accepting the loss. The second response is one of constraint. It is a fierce attempt to 'let go', to separate one's life from that of the deceased, and strive towards the 'point of no return', where the survivors face the fact that they will go on living and have to leave their dead behind. The attainment of this inner attitude is encouraged by Quran recitation. The latter reaction is generally considered a male preserve, while the first is considered a woman's duty.

It is not always the case that the two are practised on an amiable, equal level, where one party witnesses the performance of the other. Some men abhor the women's reaction to their loss, and try to suppress any overtly expressed emotion by keeping the women apart, or forbidding them to attend the funeral for fear of crying or tumultuous scenes. However, one cannot deny that there is an inner coherence and link between the two attitudes. The first generally works as a catharsis for the men and women who are witnesses. And it allows for an attitude of serene stoicism to be built upon it.

There are many regions within the Islamic world where men and women have found complementary roles, and developed a cultural capacity to give vent to their innermost emotions through song. Here the Shi'ites from the Lebanon should be mentioned, the Palestinians, the peasants from the Syrian desert, the Roma Muslims of the Balkans, and the Turkish people. These groups, like many other regional groups, consider it their duty to honour the deceased with improvised couplets, which should be sung in such a way as to make others cry.

Usually one or two professional singers are engaged to perform. As a rule they are women. In some Lebanese villages a professional male singer will come to sing with the men outside the house of the deceased, while the women are crowding inside around the bier, where they cry and clap to the rhythm of a female singer.

When a mother has lost her child she herself will compose the song. No fixed time is set for such an intimate expression of grief. Sometimes she will start singing immediately upon death, holding on to the child with her hands. Sometimes she will wait till the burial is over, then go into her garden, or to the grave and spread out a piece of the deceased child's clothing. In Turkey some of these songs are remembered for a long time. A beautiful song is repeated on other occasions and can even be taken into the official repertoire of a popular singer and broadcast on the radio.

But even in a country like Turkey, where the practice of composing dirges is held in high esteem, you will find elderly people, especially men, who question the custom, asking, 'Why cry? It is not right. He or she has now gone to another world, is finally united with God, has found a new life. Maybe one can laugh there, maybe not. At least life goes on, so why cry?' Other people feel that the soul of the departed might be offended by the crying and the singing. They believe they could restrain the soul on its journey, and could even call it back from where it has gone. They prefer a quiet shedding of tears, and concentrate on the organization of Quran recitation.

Such recitation can take different forms. When the mother of King Hussein of Jordan died in 1994, Quran recitation was broadcast on radio and television for three successive days, in which period the whole of the Quran was recited and the broadcasting of news or entertainment strictly forbidden. In a big city like Cairo a family will erect a striped tent in the middle of the street, starting in front of their house and stretching as far as necessary, depending on how many guests are expected. Quran recitation usually starts here when dusk has fallen and is performed with the use of amplifiers so that the neighbouring streets of the quarter too can benefit from the drone of the on-going recitation.

Islamic minorities in secularized countries do not organize such public manifestations. Instead they will go to the house of the bereaved family. The men might gather at the mosque and leave the women at home. In these foreign parts the singing of dirges is often omitted all together. Confronted with the differing opinions of their brothers and sisters in faith, though strangers to them in custom and mentality, people sometimes even start to doubt whether it is really Islamic at all to express their feelings. Added to this is the increasing antagonism between the 'modern' secularized European majorities and their Islamic minorities. In their new surroundings the latter are perceived as 'backward' and some try to cut out all signs of their recently discovered 'backwardness' in response, including the genuine expression of loss, so as not to become a target or to 'act differently'.

SAYING GOODBYE

The greatest service one can render to the dead is to bury them immediately – if possible on the same day. Due to circumstances this period might have to be extended to twenty-four hours. Immigrants alone have to wait till any resting periods prescribed by the laws of their guest country are over.

Shortly before burial the one and only ceremony for the dead takes place. It consists of a short period during which all who wish to do so make their last private farewell, followed by the prayer for the dead. During this ceremony the deceased is forgiven his or her sins by the whole congregation. The ceremony can take place almost anywhere: inside the mosque or outside on the village square, at the graveside, in the antiseptic rooms of a mortuary or in the drab courtyard of a German funeral institute. Although theological disputes continue there, the exact spot does not really matter in circumstances of migration, the main thing being that the ceremony takes place. As it begins, the cloth covering the head is folded to the side, allowing the face to become visible. It is an extremely emotional moment and accordingly occasions extremes of attitude.

Those opting for constraint will now gather all the aloofness they possess, look at the dead face in silence, utter a silent prayer and withdraw immediately. Perhaps the women will approach the body first, shedding discreet tears, but they will signal dignity to their menfolk through their upright heads and rigid body language. In a way their attitude makes easier the task of the waiting men who still have to go through the movements of wrapping up the remains and burying them. It is forbidden for these people to touch the body as touches and tears could undo its purity.

If on the contrary people have found a way to express and channel their innermost feelings in song, this is the moment emotions will reach a climax. The women, sustained by their men, will go singing and shouting to the bier, and men can be seen to break down in tears. All present will crowd around the body touching and kissing the face and the lips. They will hold on to the corpse as if they will never let it go. But within minutes this outburst of emotion too is controlled. The women withdraw and the men now form three disciplined rows facing the bier.

Theologically speaking this is the most important moment of all. It is here that the deceased is forgiven every single deed which has hurt or disadvantaged others. 'Was it a good man, was it a good woman?' the Imam will ask, and all present will answer: 'good!' even if this was not so. (In rural surroundings it might be a good moment to arrange outstanding debts since the whole community is present and can witness this.) Then the congregation will proceed to utter the Prayer for the Dead, which consists of four short praises to God, four times interrupted by *allahu akbar* (God is Great). After this, the body is ready for burial.

THE BURIAL

The burial is a men's affair. Only female next of kin might decide (or be allowed) to attend, depending on their status or independent position. They are ordered to walk at the back of the procession, lest the crying should continue. Six men, preferably next of kin or close friends of the deceased, will carry the bier and often the bier is handed on through the rows of mourners until every single man, from young to old, has helped to carry the dead to his last resting place.

The body can be seen lying on the bier in its white wrappings. No coffin is needed or wanted. On reaching the graveside it will be lowered down with shawls or lengths of cloth. It rests in a small cavity dug into the bottom of the grave and positioned as if sleeping. The corpse is turned a little on its right, the dead eyes facing Mecca, the feet pointing south. A stone or a handful of mud is used to support the head. This done, wooden boards are placed on top of the body slanting in such a way that it leaves some space for the head to move. Then the grave is quickly filled with earth.

Filling the grave is a task where all men present join in. Six or seven shovels have usually been placed at hand for this purpose and the next of kin will start to pile big heaps of earth onto the boards, followed by others who are impatiently waiting their turn. Some will even scratch the earth with their bare hands. A grave of a grown-up person is filled within minutes and during this shovelling the Quran is read. The work being done, silence settles and all present crouch on the earth, turning their hands towards heaven to receive the blessing. The religious leader chants a particularly beautiful passage; others might take over and sing words of praise. The mourners will then wipe off their faces with their hands, stand up and leave in silence. Only the Imam will stay at his post at the head of the gravemound, in order to have a final word with the departed.

RETRIBUTION

As soon as the last foot has resounded on the grave, as soon as silence has settled, the deceased will wake up and receive a visit, or so most people think. This is the visit for which the body has been prepared all along.

The story goes that two angels – some call them devils because their fear shows the angels in a bad light – enter the grave and ask the deceased to answer the five final questions.[2] Here the story takes a

2 The five final questions every believer has to be able to answer after death are:

- Who is your God? [My God is Allah.]
- Who is your prophet? [My prophet is Muhammad.]
- Which is your book? [My book is the Quran.]
- Who is your Imam? [My Imam is ——.]
- Which is your qibla (prayer direction)? [My qibla is Mecca.]

dramatic turn since the dead is irretrievably dead and cannot make use of his mouth or hands anymore to make his intentions clear, even (and this is stressed a thousand times) if he knows all the answers. However, the religious leader is still at the head of the gravemound: he is there to help, and loudly calls the dead by name. He also expects an answer.

After they have left in silence, the mourners are supposed to go home straight away, but many linger within earshot. Soon they hear their Imam calling the deceased. The dead is supposed to react by hitting his head with a bump against the wooden board. When the Imam only calls once everbody will say: 'This is a good believer; he or she is not afraid to answer the final questions!' However, when the dead is called time and again, and his name is boomed out over the village ten, fifteen, or even twenty times, people will know for sure what they knew all along in their hearts: 'No good'.

It is a story often told with glee and remembered satisfaction. The many variants make clear that really two verdicts are being pronounced in this moment. One is the imagined *mise-en-scène* under the ground to which the Imam is prompting the right answers. The other forms the final judgement of the community; here it is decided whether or not this person has been 'good' after all. This story of course belongs to the rich repertoire of rural stories, but citizens from big cities have also found ways to make their judgement. In Cairo, Tunis or Amman people will watch the funeral procession. When it proceeds quickly, when it looks as if the mourners have 'wheels in their legs', then the departing is judged to have been 'all right', since no fear of the grave is shown. But whenever they proceed slowly it will make people think, 'What is going on there? What has he or she done?'

This 'anguish of the grave', as it is called, decides the future of the dead. That last day when the trumpet will sound and all the dead will rise is still far off. In fact, one has no way of knowing how long it will be until then. So the dead are judged right away and the rightness of their answers decides whether they will land in a private hell (their corpse being beaten to pieces by their visitors, not to mention the streams of little animals, worms and beetles which soon will follow) or, what one hopes for, in a private paradise, or rather a window that will be opened on the right side of the grave. This will afford of paradise from which refreshing winds blow over one's head, letting one sleep in peace.

Whatever the judgement, those surviving the dead are very much aware of the body's presence in the grave. This awareness counts for the many ghost stories in rural settlements, but also for the various exchanges people have with the 'good' dead. It explains the belief that holy persons go on exuding 'blessedness' from their graves. The surrounding earth can be used for medicine and sick persons visiting those graves might be healed. Those who can afford it buy burial places near a holy grave. This determines the topography of cemeteries like those in Istanbul, Algiers or Marrakesh.

MOURNING

In North Africa women will wear white. In the Middle East they wear black. In the Lebanon women cover their heads with little white wrappings and in Turkey they will choose subdued colours. Just as the expression of sorrow is seen as women's duty, the task of mourning the deceased is also carried out by women. First and foremost they express it with their clothing, appearance and food restrictions. In doing so they represent their family, particularly their men, and function as a constant reminder for all to see.

Second, women prepare special food for special days, for which the third, the seventh and the fortieth days after burial are seen as especially fitting. On these days the men gather at the mosque, but the women stay at home and receive visitors, serve special sugary dishes and are consoled. Sweets and little bread rolls are handed out to the neighbours and everyone who eats them is supposed to send up prayers and 'sweet thoughts' for the departed. For some the fortieth day is the most important of all. On this day the story of the prophet's birth is read aloud and all present will shed many tears, since it is considered full of consolation. Some even hold that the deceased returns to the house in order to listen to the recitation.

Young women wear their mourning attire for three successive months, but older women will wear it the whole year round. When the anniversary of the day of burial has been reached, a stone will be placed on the mound, accompanied by a little celebration.

CHILDREN: A VIEW FROM THE FRINGES

Where are the children? Do they play a role in the proceedings? Are they present at all? Children are not supposed to know anything. They are sent to the neighbours almost immediately. They are not allowed to take part in the farewell ceremony nor indeed to participate in the funeral procession. They are not encouraged to ask any questions. On the contrary children are expected to forget whatever they noticed as quickly as possible.

For young adults the memory of the death of a close relative ranges among the most striking pictures of their youth. What they encapsulate in their minds are glimpses from the fringe. Children see many things; a funeral procession, for instance, glimpsed from behind the closed curtains of the family apartment. And they listen intently, for instance to the comments of the women, who are not allowed to join in. And occasionally they have little roles on the edge of the main events.

Take the announcement as an example. In many rural settlements the news of a death is made public for all to hear. In rural Bosnia the news was announced early in the morning together with the call for prayer from the village minaret. Many children remember vividly having run to the mosque before breakfast to collect the details for their waiting parents.

One young Egyptian woman remembered that every new death in the village was announced by a loudspeaker van slowly moving through the streets just before dawn. Then people would stop whatever they were doing and listen intently. Their reactions invariably were loud and spontaneous. As a child these moments never failed to frighten her. The solemn sing-song voice of the announcer, the shocked comments of her grandmother, and her parents' bland faces whenever she asked for an explanation formed an inexplicable pattern she brooded over for a long time.

Others keep pictures in their minds of endlessly boring days on which they were sent to the deserted apartments of the neighbours. There they heard the drone of the recitation and wondered what was going on. No explanation was ever given afterwards. A grandparent had gone 'for travel' and never returned.

For children born in the countries their parents have migrated to, the blanket of silence and exclusion seems to have lifted a little. Many parents want their children to have a modern education and all the benefits of the country they can get. Also, parents hear and learn more through their children about the world they live in than they would have on their own. Some still depend on them for translation. A noticeable changing of roles is the result. Parents lose their secretiveness towards their offspring and sometimes even adopt 'modern' behaviour. As one Turkish undertaker put it, when he himself came to die, he would now prefer his children to attend to the ceremony, even recite the Quran, so as to give them a chance to realize what had happened.

THE TOPOGRAPHY OF DEATH

We have seen how the dying are assisted, how the loss is expressed, how the ceremony of farewell, the burial, and the mourning are performed, and how all this forms a meaningful pattern together. For the survivors every single step helps to domesticate the irrevocable loss. The dying leave with the certainty that their physical presence will be replaced by lasting memory. Ways have been found to express despair collectively. It helps to move towards the crossroads, where the living go on living, and leave their dead behind. Many paths have been trodden to continue communication across death. A continuing stream of recollection, a collective memory of all those who have gone, has found its eternal source here. Remembrance is expressed through poetry, memorials, genealogies. Also, the family will regularly invite others to take meals by the graveside, which is considered another way of communicating with the dead.

In this tight social fabric the places where the remains are buried occupy a vital position. In Muslim countries they form the secret source from which social life and collective memory take their point of departure. Keeping all this in mind, it may not come as a surprise then that the bodies of 89 per cent of those who die on the European continent are transported back to where they come from. The above description of the Islamic cemetery in Berlin is typical. Those who rest in foreign earth form a community of siblings and refugees. All others are re-collected by their extended family and brought back 'home'.

A sort of 'voyage of the dead' is the result. It is a controversial journey. The bodies are sealed in aluminium caskets, covered with wood, signed and paid for, packed in airport terminals, and eventually transported as goods. The procedure can take days or even weeks, and is a very expensive affair. Also the journey makes it difficult to go through the movements of saying farewell. The emotional expression of singing and crying is inhibited all together, where no corpse is found at hand. The weight of the procedure rests on the men, who now feel forced to show their sorrow. The oblong form of the casket complicates the proper burial, and inhibits accompanying thoughts about 'sleeping' in the earth. Doubt even sometimes creeps into the minds of the receiving party whether it really is their own dead whom they are burying. But no doubt has arisen as yet about the rightness of the decision to take the bodies away from their family 'in exile'.

Lastly, those who stay behind feel all the more 'foreign' in their foreign surroundings, since no collective memory can accompany them, and no common past can be construed from generations of bodies mingling with the new earth. Indeed, it seems to be the growing problem of the European Islamic community that they are bound together only by religion. As a consequence religion is given a weight which it was never meant to carry.

Death forms the starting point for the awareness of a common past. Death could also function as a basis for solidarity in the present. Tending the dead might even be a business which generates life. Exactly because this quality seems to have gone missing in the newly built Muslim communities on the European continent, this is what one can learn from the Islamic example.

APPENDIX

Some 'practice points' for hospital workers to keep in mind when tending dying patients of Islamic faith

When a Muslim patient is dying, and he or she is alone, it would be good to warn the family, or, if that is not possible, a close friend. When you do, tell them to bring an Imam with them, so they will know what to expect and are able to take steps to prepare the dying person.

More often, you will find a number of persons (family, friends and neighbours), sometimes as many as fifteen or twenty, already assembled by the bedside of the dying patient. To the Muslim mind, it is not good to leave the dying alone. Also, many people come to forgive the dying for their sins and in return want to be given forgiveness. Accounts, both spiritual and financial, are thus balanced before death. This is an extremely important ceremony in the life of every Muslim. Hospitals should allow space for it, even when it means a disturbance of the hospital routine.

Once the patient has died, one should keep in mind that the body will always be viewed at a later stage. So close the eyes and the mouth and place a pillow under the head, lest the mouth should fall open again.

When you are laying out the dead, never cross the dead person's hands on his or her breast. Once the corpse has stiffened, the arms will stand off the body, which makes shrouding almost impossible. It is therefore advisable to straighten the arms and hands along the sides.

Those who wish to study these issues in more detail are recommended to read papers by Garnett (1909), Guillaume (1956), Smith and Hadad (1981), Racy (1985, 1986), and Munson (1984); also the articles on *Marthiya* (mourning songs) and *Mawt* (death) in *The Encyclopedia of Islam*.

SUMMARY

☐ Among Muslims, religious rule continues to preside over death. There is, however, much local variation in expression of loss and mourning within Islam.

☐ When death approaches most Muslims consider it important to sit up and face towards Mecca.

☐ The family should always be warned of approaching death and advised to bring an Imam. Islamic believers prepare themselves for existence beyond death by confession of faith. Those at the bedside moisten the mouth and will repeat the words over the dying patient who, if unable to speak, will lift an index finger in acknowledgement.

☐ Life after death will continue in a form that makes the preservation of the body essential.

☐ Immediately after death the body is laid on a flat board, feet together, arms to the side, eyes closed and chin wrapped in a cloth to prevent the mouth opening. If no Muslims are present this should be done by healthcare staff.

☐ The body is washed in a special way by the family or by specialized washers of the same sex as the deceased. It should *not* be washed by non-Muslims. It is then shrouded in white linen made without knots.

☐ Some Muslim sects lament loudly, scratch their faces and cry a long dirge for the dead. Others attempt to accept and contain grief, while reciting from the Quran. They aim for a serene stoicism. Those from Mediterranean countries often express emotion in couplets of song which aim to make others cry. On the whole women mourn more vocally than men. Professional female singers may be employed.

☐ Immigrants to secularized countries seldom lament loudly. Men go to the mosque to pray and friends visit the women at home.

☐ The dead must be buried as soon as possible, and preferably within twenty-four hours.

☐ Shortly before burial, a short ritual enables friends and family to say farewell, pray for the deceased and join in ceremonial forgiving of sin. This can be held anywhere. The cloth covering the face is folded aside.

☐ Among those sects that permit it, emotional expression peaks at this time. In this case people may crowd the body to touch and kiss the face before burial. In other sects the men must contain emotions while wrapping and burying the body without touching it directly. Women are permitted to shed discreet tears.

- [ ] The Imam asks 'Was this a good or bad man/woman?' and all present answer 'Good', then recite the prayers for the dead.
- [ ] The burial is done only by men, who lay out the body with eyes towards Mecca and head covered with a board. They then leave and the Imam remains to pray, while the soul of the dead person is answering five questions.
- [ ] The dead are believed to remain in the grave to await the judgement on their fate but their state of bodily and mental peace will be affected by their sins. The good have a view of paradise and remain bodily and sensorily intact.
- [ ] Graves remain the secret source from which social life and collective memory take their point of departure.
- [ ] North African women mourn in white, Middle Eastern in black and Turkish in subdued colours. Young women mourn for three months, older women for a year.
- [ ] On the third, seventh and fortieth days after death men gather at the mosque and women prepare sugary dishes for visitors who pray together for the dead. The story of the prophet's birth is read aloud and tears are shed.
- [ ] On the first anniversary a ceremony is held, when a stone is placed on the grave.
- [ ] Children are not permitted to attend these rituals, are discouraged from asking questions and expected to forget the death as soon as possible.
- [ ] Most Muslims who die overseas want their body returned to their 'home'. In doing so they leave their family 'in exile'. As a consequence, those left behind feel all the more foreign, bound only by their religion, which may therefore take on particular importance.

Chapter 9

Secularization[1]

Tony Walter

> To hear others publicly proclaim their love, respect and admiration
> for my husband made the funeral an uplifting experience. After-
> wards so many who had attended told me that it was the most
> interesting, most moving, most relevant and best funeral that they
> had ever been to. Their remarks gave me a great deal of comfort and
> I knew that I had treated my husband's atheism with the respect and
> dignity that it deserved.
>
> (Wynne Willson, 1989)

Though the business of dying in the West has been profoundly
influenced by Christianity, it is today very largely a secular affair. The
reference point in death, as in life, is no longer God but man; death is
seen as the end of the person's life rather than the beginning of a life in
heaven. Christians are free to believe otherwise, but their beliefs are
held privately and are no longer the basis – except in the funeral – of
public institutions. Modern death is therefore characterized by tension
and accommodation between Christian ideas and secular, rational
processes. To understand how death has been and is being secularized,
we must look at both the philosophy of humanism and the sociological
processes of secularization and humanization.

HUMANISM: A PHILOSOPHY

In the Middle Ages, religious persons tended to devalue human affairs,
in favour of prayer and meditation on God and the life to come. From
the fourteenth century, however, intellectuals and artists began to show

---

1 I am indebted to Nigel Collins and Jane Wynne Willson for their very helpful
comments on a draft of this chapter.

more interest in human achievement and fulfilment in this life. These 'humanists' rediscovered the classical writings of the ancient world ('the humanities') and, while still believing in the Christian God, began to explore human possibilities, especially the human ability to control the natural world. This humanistic movement started in Italy with writers such as Petrarch, but spread north of the Alps particularly through the writings of Erasmus and aided by the newly invented printing press. This freeing of the human mind also helped religious reformers such as Luther and Calvin to challenge the previously unchallengeable authority of the Catholic church. Although the French humanist Montaigne saw no reason why ethics should depend on religious principles, most humanists in this period were also Christians. Perhaps the last major humanist of this golden age was Shakespeare, whose plays celebrate both human greatness and human frailty. Classical humanism may be summed up thus: man is the measure of all things.

The modern Humanist movement has its roots in the ethical and secular societies of the nineteenth century. Twentieth-century Humanists have no belief in a god or an afterlife, and believe that human beings have sole responsibility for bettering and fulfilling their life in this world. If death is the end, we are forced to attend to putting all our energies into this life. (For this overtly non-theist life stance of modern Humanism, setting itself up against anti-religion, I use a capital 'H'. For any more general celebration of human potential – a stance which might be termed 'humanistic', 'humanizing' or 'human-centred' and which is shared by many Christians and non-believers – I use a small 'h'.)

About three Britons in ten do not believe in God and many of these subscribe to the basic tenets of Humanism, but very few actually call themselves Humanists or join a Humanist organization. This may be, as Humanists argue, because Humanism is not taught in school as an alternative to religion; or it may be that the pragmatic and non-ideological British feel no need to find a label for their non-belief.

Humanism in the first half of the twentieth century was optimistic about human possibilities. Two world wars, the bomb, the Cold War, famine in much of the world, looming possibilities of ecological disaster, and the ongoing difficulties governments face in controlling their economies have made most of us, including Humanists, less adventurous in our claims of what human beings can achieve. Human potential seems all too destructive; technology so often seems not to liberate but to enslave the human being. In response, Humanism over the past generation has lost some of its classical optimism and turned more to the task of recovering humane values from the impersonality of bureaucratic and technological systems. At the same time, the churches in most European societies have become more secular. These two trends together mean that there is now, in practice if not in theory, less distance between many Christians and Humanists. They may well find themselves allies on certain issues.

The extent to which Humanists today are self-consciously anti-religious is therefore declining, but still varies from one modern Western country to another. A key factor here seems to be whether or not the society has an established church, as in England. In England, Humanists are very aware of the privileges of the Church of England, the requirement that the head of state should be Christian, the presence of religious education in schools and the privileged position of Christianity in the British Broadcasting Corporation. In Eire, the Catholic church has an even more privileged position. Humanists therefore fight hard for equal recognition for secular philosophies.

In the USA, by contrast, there is a constitutional separation of church and state – the state is not constitutionally bound to any particular religious belief. Anyone may explore human possibilities without church or state having any formal power to stop them, so Humanists are free to be non-religious without needing to be anti-religious. The same is effectively true of Australia. And in the Netherlands, the state gives formal equality to all religions and to Humanists.

All this affects the form of funerals. In England and in France, Humanist funerals are non-religious, always recognizing and sometimes celebrating the deceased's atheism or agnosticism (as in the quotation with which this chapter began). This is not so in Australia and the USA, as we will see. But before looking at the funeral, I will ask whether there is a specifically Humanist approach to dying and bereavement.

Dying

The implications of Humanism for death are simple. Since death equals extinction it is not to be feared. Since there is nothing after death – no possibility of hell – there is nothing to fear. Or at the very least, because we can never know about any life beyond the grave, there is no point in worrying about it now. Humanists like to quote the ancient Greek, Epicurus:

A right understanding that death is nothing to us makes the mortality of life enjoyable not by adding to life an illimitable time, but by taking away the yearning after immortality. For life has no terrors for him who has thoroughly apprehended that there are no terrors for him in ceasing to live.

A good deal of research has been done on the relation between fear of death and religious belief (summarized in Kalish, 1980, pp. 114–16), and it shows that those with a firm belief – either a firm belief in God *or* a firm belief that there is no God and no life after death – fear death the least. The most anxious about death are those with a less than secure religious faith. It seems then that belief that death is the end does indeed have a positive effect on how people approach their own death.

Most Humanists support voluntary euthanasia. Christians see a person's life on earth as originating in God and leading to everlasting life, which means that human beings are not the lords of their own destiny. Humanists, by contrast, believe that individuals are responsible for themselves and have the right to die with dignity at the time of their choosing – assuming safeguards against exploitation of the vulnerable. Humanists likewise have no concept of suicide as a sin with eternal consequences, as has been the traditional Christian view.

Beyond this, Humanists have rather little to say about dying. Humanist accounts of good deaths tend to come from the classical world, such as the death of Epicurus, and Humanists have nothing like the last rites of Christians or Hindus. The main implications of death for Humanists are to be found in how they live, not how they die.

Bereavement

Humanists argue that the dead live on – not in an immortal soul but as an influence still at work in the lives they shared. Humanist funerals sometimes include the following passage from Boris Pasternak's *Doctor Zhivago*, in which Yura is speaking to Anna on her death bed:

You are anxious about whether you will rise from the dead, but you have risen already – you rose from the dead when you were born, and you didn't notice it. . . . However far back you go in your memory, it is always in some external, active manifestation of your self that you come across your identity – in the work of your hands, in your family, in other people. . . . This is what you are. This is what your consciousness has breathed and lived on and enjoyed throughout your life. Your soul, your immortality, your life in others.

And what now? You have always been in others and you will remain in others. And what does it matter to you if later on it is called your memory? This will be part of you – the real you that enters the future and becomes a part of it.

This is the comfort for Humanists who grieve. The implication is that ceremonials should be minimized, and an acceptance reached of the on-going influence of the deceased. One book on humanism speaks of the funeral as follows: 'This is a harvest ritual, not a tomb ritual, not a process of mourning but of fulfilment, a realisation of value not a recognition of pointlessness, of achievement and permanence not of futility and ephemerality' (Blackham, 1968, p. 152).

Beyond this, however, there is little that specifically characterizes a Humanist approach to grief. Apart from providing information about euthanasia (The Voluntary Euthanasia Society), the British Humanist Association fact sheet on bereavement is indistinguishable from those widely available from funeral directors and bereavement organizations.

Funerals

If there is very little written about a specifically Humanist way to die or to grieve, I would argue that this is because modern society is essentially secular in its institutions, including those that process the dying, the dead and the grieving. These are described in the second half of this chapter. The funeral – by which I mean not the complex business of funeral directing and the management of cemeteries and crematoria, but the twenty- or thirty-minute service – is the one exception. It is overwhelmingly still in the hands of the church.

Figures are difficult to find, but my guess is that – depending on the country – between 50 per cent and 99 per cent of funerals are religious, conducted by a priest or minister according to a religious liturgy. Religious funerals remain the norm even in countries where baptisms and church weddings are in decline. It is in the funeral that we can most clearly distinguish the Humanist from the religious. And it is in the funeral that in some countries, like England, we find Humanists still fighting a church monopoly or near monopoly.

The reasons for the growth of secular, or Humanist, funerals are twofold. First, there are an increasing number of people who feel that if the deceased was not religious then the funeral should not be religious. It does not reflect the person he or she was, and therefore lacks integrity. Related to this is the second reason: many religious funerals are nowadays felt to be impersonal. Traditionally, the Christian funeral commended the soul to God and was not usually concerned with celebrating the life of the departed. Indeed, such personal celebration would contradict the view of the departed as a sinner needing the prayers of the living and/or the grace of God. In the rubric of the 1662 Prayer Book, for example, a funeral could be conducted without even mentioning the name of the departed – he or she appears not as a person mourned by the living but as a sinful creature about to meet the Creator. This was no problem in small-scale communities in which priest and people clearly all knew one another: personal familiarity was presumed, not stated. But in a large-scale urban society, where priest or funeral director may have personal knowledge of neither the deceased nor the congregation, the lack of personality in the traditional Christian liturgy can become intolerable. The deceased is despatched by an impersonal routine that as a last statement about human worth is truly appalling (Walter, 1990, ch.6).

The Humanist funeral is a response to these two problems of hypocrisy and impersonality. It is a celebration of a life lived, not a commendation to a life to come – in Australia, the term 'life-centred funeral' is used in preference to 'humanist funeral'. It is a celebration of human goodness, not a ritual concerned with the eternal effects of human sin. One Australian celebrant observes:

> There is good in everyone. There are very few people who have not contributed to human-kind in some way. The paradox is this. Sometimes the seemingly ordinary and humble have done a great deal for humanity and/or their family. I have rarely found it difficult to talk about a person in good terms without exaggeration, excessive praise or presenting an unbalanced picture.
>
> (Messenger, 1979, p. 111)

(In Britain, those who conduct Humanist funerals prefer to be called 'officiants' rather than 'celebrants', not because they do not believe in celebrating the life lived, but because they do not want to give offence in circumstances, such as a funeral for a stillborn or very young infant, where the focus is on comforting the living rather than on recounting the all too short life lived (Wynne Willson, 1989, pp. 56–7).)

The Humanist funeral

What then does a Humanist funeral ceremony consist of? It usually starts with the officiant introducing the reason for their coming together, followed by some general thoughts on death. A funeral in Britain for someone who died after a long and full life began:

> We are meeting here today to honour the life of Anne Smith and to bring consolation to those of her family and friends who are here. Our ceremony will be a short and simple one, which will be in keeping with what she would have liked.
>
> The world is a community, and Anne has been a part of that community. We are all involved in the life and death of each of us. Human life is built on caring.
>
> It is natural that we should be sad today, because in a practical sense Anne is no longer part of our lives. But we should not grieve – to live a good and fulfilling life for ninety years, with only the last year seriously marred by failing health, and then to die in one's sleep, is something to be thankful for. . . .
>
> (Wynne Willson, 1989, p. 23)

The funeral continued with quotes about death from Pasternak and Bertrand Russell, and a reading from one of Anne's favourite poets. The centrepiece of the ceremony was a tribute by one of her grandsons, recounting her life and what she meant to those present. The ceremony ended, as it began, with music – two items taped, one sung by a grand-daughter.

This format is common in Britain, the USA and Australia where an experienced officiant is hired to conduct the ceremony. But the account above does not reveal what had gone on behind the scenes. How does an officiant who does not know the deceased put together a tailor-made and uniquely personal funeral? When in 1987 I was researching the Australian life-centred funeral, I accompanied Brian McInerny – one of thirteen celebrants in the city of Melbourne – on a pre-funeral visit to the home of Pete and Jenny. (The following appears in Walter, 1990, pp. 218–19.) Pete's father had died. We sat around the kitchen table, and Brian explained that at the funeral he wanted to give a clear picture of Pete's dad and that the picture could come only from them: 'We've only got one shot at it, and we've got to get it right.' Stories, a few tears and a few more smiles flowed easily for an hour or so. Their two little children sat and drew quietly. Their drawings came to be part of the conversation as it became clear that they represented the children's own feelings about their grandad.

Brian then found a quiet corner of the house, and wrote what was to be the centrepiece of the funeral – a thousand-word, ten-minute eulogy capturing Pete's dad and his life. He returned to the kitchen to read it to

Pete and Jenny for them to edit, stressing that it was *their* eulogy, and he was simply their servant. The aim was to create a shared picture of Pete's dad, to include all his significant relationships especially with those who would be at the funeral. They then discussed the possibility of poems, readings, songs, prayers or other items for the funeral, and whether anyone in addition to Brian was to participate in reading any of this material.

A couple of days later, the funeral was held in a nearby funeral parlour. It took about fifteen minutes, with just a short introduction before and after the eulogy. One might think that with no reference to a continuing soul, there is nothing a humanist ceremony can do for the deceased. Nothing could be further from the truth. What Brian was doing was enabling Pete and the other mourners to *pay their respects* to a father and friend, affirming what his life meant to himself, his family and his friends. The life-centred funeral rounds off the life. If in the Humanist view, we have to make of life what we will, then the final act is a public statement of what that was. This final statement can be made only after death, and it is what the life-centred funeral achieves.

Officiants often take care to talk to at least one friend outside the family, from whom a whole new picture may emerge. Likewise good officiants, while celebrating the person's life, love and achievements, will not omit their failings and peccadilloes. It is surely true that it is often a person's weaknesses that make them especially lovable, and an account of the life that is only praise will fail to capture the life. It will not be recognized by the mourners, and they will be unable to say goodbye to the person they actually knew.

Humanist and Christian funerals deal with 'unfinished business' in rather different ways. Without needing to name specific failings, Christian funeral liturgy routinely acknowledges sin and asks for forgiveness – for the living and for the dead (Walter, 1990, ch.22). Humanists do not believe in sin, but can confront complex relationships and contorted feelings by recourse to appropriate readings, though since the Humanist funeral is by definition tailor-made, this may require great sensitivity on the part of the officiant.

Trends

I have mentioned above the explicitly non-religious ethos of many secular funerals – and of Humanism in general – in Britain and much of Europe, contrasted with the life-centred funerals of Australia and the USA, and related this to the institutional power, including a near monopoly on funerals, held by the churches in places such as England and Scandinavia.[2] This has, until now, tended to limit life-centred funerals to those with no religious faith. At the time of writing (1994), funerals conducted by officiants from the British Humanist Association and similar organizations account for less than 1 in 200 funerals. But the mounting dissatisfaction with impersonal, 'production line' funerals, together with the considerable publicity given to Humanist funerals in national newspapers like the *Independent* and the *Guardian* is expanding demand rapidly. I therefore anticipate increasing demand for funerals that are truly personal but not necessarily non-religious – perhaps with the *Lord's Prayer* or *The Lord Is My Shepherd* included to keep one or two members of the congregation happy. The number of Humanist officiants is growing in response to increased demand, and I have met at least one whose willingness to include such religious items would scandalize the older generation of Humanist officiants. Humanist funerals in Britain are expanding fast and may in time come more to resemble the life-centred funerals of Australia and the USA where, for example, a secular celebrant may provide the eulogy and a priest perform the final committal to earth or flames. (In Australia, one main promoter of the life-centred funeral has been Des Tobin, a *Catholic* funeral director.)

Given the shortage of Humanist officiants in Britain, another increasing trend is the non-religious funeral conducted by someone other than an official Humanist. Though the number of funerals conducted by an officiant provided by the British Humanist Association is less than half of one per cent, the manager of a crematorium in East Anglia told me in 1991 that he estimated as many as 10 per cent of funerals in his crematorium to have been conducted without a priest. Few of these were conducted by a BHA officiant (though rather more may have had some BHA input via the BHA telephone help-line[3] or via Wynne Willson's booklet *Funerals Without God – A Practical Guide to Non-Religious Funerals*, which currently is selling very well). Most of these funerals took place in silence, or just listening to music; in others, friends or family spoke of the deceased without an 'official' master of ceremonies (a style common in the Netherlands). A funeral director in

2 The Lutheran Church in Finland holds an even more effective monopoly on funerals, yet atheists seem willing to go along with this. I recall attending one such funeral with a Communist and atheist friend who was singing the hymns lustily, something his British counterparts would be unlikely to do. The church in Finland, however, has a special role in carrying the precarious Finnish national identity, a role hinging on its guardianship of the war dead, and is a special case (see Walter, 1996, ch. 7).
3 From the UK 0990 168122. From outside the UK 44 171 430 0908.

south London told me in 1994 that about 3 per cent of his customers do not want a religious funeral; he knows a range of people locally who will conduct such funerals, including a Macmillan Cancer Relief nurse and a member of The Compassionate Friends (an organization for those who have lost a child). A funeral director on the south coast, who is also a practising Christian, will conduct secular funerals for his clients. Some non-conformist, especially Unitarian, clergy will do the same. At the same time, clergy are under pressure to make their religious funerals more personal. The result is that the clear distinction between the impersonal religious funeral and the personal Humanist funeral is blurring. In the funeral, as in dying and in grieving, the Humanist focus on the person is gaining ground over the Christian focus on God.

THE PROCESS OF SECULARIZATION[4]

Humanism is a philosophy, a set of ideas about the nature and purpose of human life. I have outlined how this philosophy has affected the modern way of death. But people do not live – or die – through ideas alone. Irrespective of what Humanist or religious ideas you or I hold, the manner of our dying is affected by the social institutions that process our dying. These institutions are undergoing the twin processes of secularization and humanization. These sociological processes are not caused simply by the advance of humanist philosophy – indeed, the reverse is in part true, that humanist philosophy advances with ease in a secular society. (We have already seen that the demand for more personal funerals derives as much from the impersonality of modern institutions as from humanist philosophy.) In this section I unpack the process of secularization; in the final section I turn to the process of humanization.

1 The disenchantment of death

One of the curious things about Judaism and Christianity, especially Protestant Christianity, is that – in contrast to, say, Hinduism or animism – there is an inbuilt potential for secularization. One reason for this is that the Bible radically separates God from humankind, and humankind from the natural world. Humans are clearly in a pecking

4 For further discussion of the issues covered in this section, see Walter (1996). On secularization in general, not specifically in relation to death, see Martin (1978) and Wilson (1966).

order, lower than God and lower than the angels, but with authority to dominate nature. Although created by God, the natural world is not God – it is not imbued with spiritual life. As the sociologist Max Weber graphically put it, the radical biblical religion of Protestantism disenchants, or de-spiritualizes, the world. Whereas in the enchanted world of animism believers routinely use magic to produce rain or cure illness, in biblical religion this is not possible. It is a short step from this view that nature may not be influenced by spiritual forces[5] to the view of modern science that nature proceeds according to orderly laws and that repeatable observations of nature may be made and compared. Modern science, though originating in Islam, grew vigorously in the soil of post-Reformation Europe.

One inevitable consequence of this scientific view was a changed attitude to illness and death. Death ceased to be capricious – symbolized by the skeleton who could tap you or me on the shoulder at any time – and came to be seen by doctors and statisticians as caused by specific diseases of the body whose course could, in time, be known and predicted by medical research. Death, like the rest of nature, became disenchanted. The medical historian Roy Porter (1989) has shown how in eighteenth-century England death came to be seen as a natural process, instead of – or in addition to – a spiritual passage, and people were as keen to have at their bedside a doctor administering opiates as a priest administering prayer. By the twentieth century, this 'medicalization' of death is virtually complete – death is no longer the human condition, but a medical problem.

Doctors, nurses and paramedics did not launch a frontal assault on a religious view of sickness and death; indeed many members of the healing professions have been and are practising Christians. Rather, medicine has simply come to eclipse the idea of death as a spiritual transition – the achievements of, and belief in, medicine for the body have simply grown to such an extent that we now barely see the need for the cure of souls. The centre stage is now occupied by a throng of doctors and hospital administrators and life-support machines, and the priest and the humbly praying family who once had the stage almost to themselves have retreated to the wings and are barely visible. They are still there, but we don't notice them much these days. In Britain, seven out of ten still believe in God and four out of ten still believe in an afterlife (Ashford and Timms, 1992, Table 4.4), but these beliefs no

5 Miracles in the Christian tradition are exceptional, and presume that orderly laws normally govern nature – very different from routine magic.

longer mould the social institutions which process the dying and the bereaved. In Ireland and the USA, where many more believe, the relevant institutions are still largely secular.

2 The church's loss of control

If the advance of science and medicine is one side of the coin of secularization, the other is the decline of religion – both in terms of belief and in terms of institutional power. I will look in this section and the next at the loss of power.

The churches' loss of institutional power in Europe has been well documented by historians. In Protestant countries, the Reformation transferred widespread powers and property (land, monasteries, hospitals, colleges) from church to state or to private hands; in Catholic countries the transfer has been slower. One key area that the church once controlled, institutionally as well as ideologically, was death. The priest was present at the deathbed and the church ran hospices for the dying; the church owned and managed the burial grounds; and the church controlled post-death rites.

The modern secular hospital is where two thirds of Britons now die. Though the secular hospital in Britain employs chaplains, they are peripheral to the operation of the hospital and arguably their main function is symbolic – they reassure us that there is something more to life and death than germ-free stainless steel equipment and efficient nurses, but what that something is remains elusive. Patients are not obliged to see the chaplain in the way they are obliged to see doctors and nurses: from the patient's point of view, the chaplain is an optional extra.

The church has lost control not only of the dying but also of the dead. The corpse resting in the soil of the churchyard was a clear sign of the soul awaiting the day of resurrection. With the exception of Scandinavia and some of the Mediterranean societies, that is all changed. In Britain, the church abandoned its responsibility for burial of the dead to the urban municipality in the 1850s in a series of Burial Acts, so that burial in the local churchyard is now an option only in villages and small market towns where there is still space in the churchyard. Seventy per cent of the British are now cremated – most of the crematoria being owned by local authorities, a few by private companies, and none by the church. Unlike traditional burial, it is difficult to see the secular crematorium's high-tech reduction of the corpse to ashes as a sign of any kind of Christian understanding of resurrection (Davies, 1990). Though in Britain the churches still control the vast majority of funerals, they do not control what happens to the body before and after the funeral – except in the now rare case of burial in a churchyard. In any society what happens to the corpse tends to mirror and affirm what is believed to happen to the soul, so it is hardly surprising that in a society in which secular technology now controls the destruction of the corpse, belief in an afterlife has become at best optional.

In France, municipalities wrested control of the corpse from the church in the period of the Revolution and pioneered the modern rational cemetery (McManners, 1981), though the Catholic church regained considerable control over the funeral service in the nineteenth century (Kselman, 1993). In the USA, the burial ground was from the beginning likely to belong to the community rather than to a church, so the development of commercial cemeteries in the nineteenth century (Sloane, 1991) entailed no break with the churches. In the twentieth century, burial in a commercial cemetery has emerged as the norm in the USA, very different from the British norm of cremation in a municipal crematorium.

Protestant churches have given up control of their dead rather readily, perhaps because Protestants believe that the eternal destiny of the soul cannot be affected post-mortem by the prayers of the living. If there is nothing we can do now to help the soul, there is no religious purpose in retaining religious control of the body. The major exception to this is the Scandinavian countries, where the choice is between burial in the ground of the local Lutheran church and incineration in a crematorium owned by the Lutheran church. In these countries, formal membership of the Lutheran church is high but personally meaningful belief in God is low.

But whether burial or cremation is organized by church, private enterprise or the municipality, the basic framework has shifted from that of religion to public health. What determines the layout of the modern cemetery is not religious considerations such as closeness to the sacrament (as in medieval Europe) or orientation of the body to Mecca (as in Muslim graves) but considerations of public health. The spacing and depth of graves and the temperature of the cremator in no way assist the passage of the soul but are carefully designed to protect the physical health of the living. We find this obsession in the Burial Laws of Victorian England, in the environmental legislation of the 1990s that will lead to cleaner emissions from crematoria chimneys, and even in recent 'green' proposals for woodland burial. Whether the church is still formally in charge of burial and cremation is perhaps beside the point, for it is environmentalists and public health officials who dictate the terms of operation.

3 The privatisation of faith

Secularization entails a separation of religion from other institutions, not least the institutions that handle the dying, the dead and the bereaved. This means that religious belief ceases to be part and parcel of what it means to belong to society and becomes something the individual is free to accept or reject. American social surveys therefore ask their respondents, 'What is your religious preference?' (a question that would make no sense to members of an Islamic nation, a tribal society or indeed medieval Europe). The reason why so many people in modern secular countries are disturbed by Islam is that it rejects this idea of faith as a private choice that most Christian churches have so readily embraced. For many Muslims, if Islam is true then it should become part of the warp and woof of society. For this reason, many Muslims see Christians as hopelessly sold out to secularism; a faith that has relevance only to personal life and cannot be embedded in social institutions is hardly worth having.

It is this secular/Christian idea of religion as private faith that governs the modern way of death. The institutions that deal with death (excepting the funeral service) are secular, but individuals are free to inject into the process whatever personal religious meaning they choose. This means that clergy visiting those who are dying or bereaved cannot presume to know what the person believes: pastoral care becomes, in the first instance, the task of enabling the person to articulate, or perhaps discover, what it is they believe. The reason the Christian funeral is so problematic is that it necessarily involves public proclamation of a faith that some of those present may not share.

4 The decline of hell

When we turn from institutional power to belief, the most striking change is that somewhere over the last two or three centuries hell has disappeared. From the twelfth century the church emphasized the terrors of hell, but starting in the late seventeenth century we find evidence of clergy and philosophers doubting that hell is compatible with a God of love; by the early nineteenth century the penal system's shift from retributive justice toward punishments that aimed to reform the criminal made a retributive hell look archaic and obscene. By the late nineteenth century many clergy were, to say the least, sceptical about the hell they were preaching, and by the twentieth century many lay people frankly did not believe in it either. The First World War was a key event here: few field padres could so much as hint that the young man they were burying and who had fought bravely for king and country was going to the wrong place. After the Great War, the Church of England virtually stopped mentioning hell.

The Catholic hell has taken longer to disappear, but the Catholic hierarchy's disapproval of the contraceptive pill since the 1960s has helped precipitate its eventual decline. Catholics who took the pill could scarcely believe that it really was a sin they would go to hell for, so, unwilling to give up the pill, they had to give up belief in hell instead. Evangelical Protestants went largely silent about hell from much the same period, even though they theoretically still believe in it.

Without hell, death poses no spiritual risk, and the traditional purpose behind much Christian ritual at and around death vanishes. God as judge is replaced by God as love, and it is this emphasis on a loving God which underlies the Christian input into the modern hospice movement. Whether this is sufficient to distinguish a Christian hospice from a secular hospice, however, is open to question – many Humanists and others who would not call themselves Christians would dispute that love is a virtue to which only Christians can lay claim. Moreover, a hospice founded by Christians must in the second generation seek staff of the very highest expertise rather than of the highest religious devotion; and increasingly funds come from secular government (James and Field, 1992). The God of love may prove easier to secularise than was the God of vengeance and wrath.

5 Bereavement

In many religions, survivors engage in ritual and prayer in order to assist the ongoing passage of the soul. In the folk religion of Britain in times past and in many traditional African societies, another task has been to prevent the soul of the deceased from returning to haunt the living – hence the heavy stone deposited upon the grave, or the offerings of food and drink left by the grave in much of Africa: keep the deceased happy, fed, watered and under ground.

But what if there is no soul? If I am no longer to care for the continuing soul of the deceased, what am I to care for? The answer is simple: I am to care about my loss and I am to care for others in their loss. If I have no continuing relationship with either the deceased or the God who is looking after them, then I become concerned solely with the loss of the relationship enjoyed with the person before they died. I may attend, without distraction, to my grief, and/or to the grief of others. Whether this abolition of the soul frees me to attend to what in reality has throughout history been the pain of loss, or whether this turning my back on religious ritual has stripped me of a psychologically healthy way of dealing with grief, is a matter of debate which I cannot go into here. The point I want to make, and it is a crucial one for a book with 'bereavement' in its title, is that the very concept of bereavement is a secular one.

I do not mean by this that religious people do not suffer grief. What I mean is that the idea that the real problem after death is the grief of survivors, rather than the journey of the soul of the departed, is a secular idea. If, as Christians have traditionally believed, the most important thing is our relationship to God, then the most important thing after death is the destination of the soul. If, as Humanists believe, the most important thing is our life on this earth and our relationships on it, then the most important thing after death is how survivors cope with the rupturing of those relationships.

Whereas once the emotions of the dying and bereaved were judged in terms of whether they demonstrated faith and assisted passage to heaven (the Puritans, for example, feared that certain emotional outbursts on the deathbed could damage your chances of getting to heaven), now religious beliefs are judged in terms of whether they assist 'the grief process'. Clergy find themselves justifying religious belief and practice as being psychologically healthy – when I ask theological students what they have studied about death they refer not to the doctrine of resurrection but to classes on bereavement counselling. Human loss has replaced spiritual destination as the touchstone by which even Christians justify their practices. The only exceptions are more traditional religions, such as Islam and Hinduism which, even in the West, justify their death practices in terms not of psychological health but of religious requirement.

Whether secularization inevitably accompanies the process of modernization and industrialization is open to question. From a European perspective, it seems so; the pockets that resist secularization – such as Ireland and Poland – can easily be seen as special cases. The evidence from North America is more complex. In the USA, where religion has no official tie-up with the state, churches are thriving and belief in God, heaven and even hell is substantially higher than in

Europe. Yet at the same time, it is in the USA that the psychologization of dying, the medicalization of death and the commercialization of the dead have gone the furthest. Even books on death by religious leaders such as Billy Graham (1987) make substantial use of these secular ideas. In the Muslim world, an official state religion and modern technology seem compatible. In Japan secularization is proceeding apace. So it is impossible to make long-term world-wide prognoses about secularization, but we can say it is a potent force in Europe and Japan, and a more subtle force in North America.

THE PROCESS OF HUMANIZATION[6]

I have said earlier that there has been a massive concern by Humanists, Christians and others to recover the human and the humane from the abstract technological and bureaucratic systems that characterize the modern way of life and of death. This project of humanization is seen nowhere more clearly than in the attempt over the past three decades to devise a more human way of dying. The hospice movement attempts to re-discover the person amid the tubes and drugs and ward routines of modern medicine. Hospices see death as a natural process, not a medical failure – though it is important to emphasize that the modern hospice has been created not by a consumer rebellion but by doctors and nurses who have sought a better way of dying for their patients. The hospice entails therefore medicine's attempt to humanize itself. The life-centred funeral likewise places the deceased person centre stage. Bereavement organizations and self-help groups affirm the right of the bereaved person to their own feelings.

This respect for the person, and his or her right to self-determination, dominates debates about the ethics of euthanasia. Though religious arguments, such as life being a gift from God, are still heard, most arguments – for and against – are now couched in terms of self-determination. Those who argue for euthanasia (many Humanists among them) usually argue that, just as individuals should take responsibility for their own lives, so they should have the right to choose the manner and timing of their death. Those who argue against euthanasia (many Christians among them) suggest that, if it were legalized, for every one who freely chooses to have their life ended there are many more vulnerable elderly people whom relatives or hospitals see as a financial burden – the decision to end their lives

6 For further discussion of the issues in this section, see Walter (1994).

would be made not by them but for them. In other words, legalizing euthanasia would erode, not foster, self-determination.

Dying

The good death, according to many textbooks today, is not one where I prepare for the next life, but one where I complete my one and only life. This perspective is partly secular, but even more is it humanistic, focusing on the dying person and their relationships on earth. It involves saying goodbye to those I love, leaving my affairs in good order so as not to inconvenience survivors and 'finishing the business' so that there are no loose ends left in my relationships with others. This humanistic death finds its most famous expression in Kübler-Ross's (1970) five stages – shock, denial, bargaining, depression, acceptance – which constitute the process, she believes, by which human beings come to terms with the fact that their life on earth is going to end. Hospitals must make space for this intensely personal business to be conducted.

The good death, of modern textbooks, involves not just a satisfactory rounding off of what has already happened in my life but also positive growth – of maturity, personality or relationships. As the title of another Kübler-Ross (1975) book puts it, death is 'the final stage of growth'. Though religious people may cherish personal growth in the dying person, few historic religions see death as the *final* stage of growth.[7]

This person-centred death is cherished nowadays by many Christians. Dame Cicely Saunders, for example, enjoys saying of a patient that 'he was himself', that to the end he displayed that fondness for whisky, that sense of humour, which made him himself. The patient who comes to her Christian hospice as an agnostic, making wry comments about God to the end, is treasured by her as much as the one who begins to see something of God (du Boulay, 1984). For Saunders, the good death is when you remain yourself to the end – very different from the good death of 150 years ago in which, far from displaying your individuality, you displayed piety and conformity to the dictates of religion as you prepared to meet your Maker.

This attempt to humanize death is a response to the modern hospital's medicalization of death. In reaffirming human values, this response can re-open a space for the spiritual. But at the same time it is also a secularizing trend: by insisting that the doctor be concerned with

7 Kübler-Ross (e.g. 1991) has since written widely on life after death.

the soul as well as the body it furthers death's medicalization (Arney and Bergen, 1984).

The changing profile of death

The attempt to humanize death, not to mention the euthanasia debate, is occurring in part because of the changing profile of death. The early diagnosis of life-threatening conditions such as cancer and HIV, along with the development of treatments that prolong life but do not necessarily cure, means that a significant proportion of the population now spend a long time dying, and almost everyone in middle age or older knows someone with a life-threatening condition. The old conspiracy of silence that pretended death did not exist, that pretended it was a medical condition rather than a condition of life, is much harder to fabricate than even a generation ago. Doctors and nurses are discovering that, if once it was easy to ignore the dying, it now makes life easier for everyone if they are told of their condition and treated as fully competent persons. This entails, not a return to a traditional religious conception in which God and eternal life were central, but the promotion of a new humanistic death in which the person is central. We might characterize the trend as follows:

Death	Traditional death	Modern death	Humanized death
Traveller	Soul	Body	Person
Transport	Church	Hospital	Hospice
Authority	Priest	Doctor	Myself

Like the process of secularization, this attempt to humanize the technological and bureaucratic modern way of death is profoundly changing the relevant social institutions; practices originally developed in hospices and bereavement self-help groups, for example, are beginning to be found in some hospitals. Whatever the beliefs of the individual, he or she now dies or grieves in settings that are secularized and in process of being humanized. This poses relatively little problem for Christians, who have long since accepted the secularization of modern institutions and who are in many instances leading advocates of a more humanized way of dying and grieving.

It can, however, pose problems for those from more traditional communities. Take the Hindu requirement to die on the floor surrounded by all your (usually distressed) relatives – this conflicts with the requirement of the modern secular hospital ward for order, quiet and respect for the feelings of other patients (Firth, 1993). Likewise the requirement for coffinless burial in some Muslim groups is not allowed by many British burial authorities for fear that non-Muslim visitors to the cemetery may be disturbed. Traditional Muslims and Hindus are at root concerned, like Christians of previous centuries, not with the feelings of the living but with the spiritual destination of the dead. Such traditional religious requirements can usually be incorporated by humanistic hospice or cemetery staff, but there is always the potential for conflict between two views of death which are profoundly at odds.

CONCLUSION

In this chapter I have looked both at the philosophy of Humanism and at the institutional processes of secularization and humanization which are taking place to some degree irrespective of the fortunes of the philosophy of Humanism. These processes affect everyone, whatever their personal religious belief.

On the whole, Christians have come to terms with secularization and are positively embracing humanization. The modern way of death in the West is a hybrid of Christianity and secularism, so both Christians and Humanists can usually find a way through the maze – though Humanists faced with an immovable cross in the crematorium chapel have just cause for complaint. But for adherents of non-Christian religions who reject both Christianity *and* secularism, dying and grieving in the secular post-Christian West may be altogether more problematic.

SUMMARY

☐ Dying in the West has become a largely secular affair with tension between Christian ideas and secular, rational beliefs.

☐ Classical humanism combined faith in personal freedom, responsibility and control of the world with Christian faith.

☐ Modern Humanism adopts no belief in God or an afterlife, believing that human beings have sole responsibility for bettering and fulfilling their life in this world. People live on in the minds of those who survive them.

☐ Thirty per cent of Britons adopt humanistic beliefs without calling themselves Humanists. But they seldom choose a Humanist funeral.

☐ In recent times humanists and Christians have found common cause in opposition to the dehumanizing effects of bureaucratic and technological systems. Antipathy to religion has declined although it is still marked in countries where church and state are most closely allied.

☐ Humanist funerals in England and France, but not Australia and the USA, are necessarily non-religious.

☐ In theory those who believe that there is nothing after death have nothing to worry about. Those with strongest beliefs for or against life after death are less anxious than the agnostics.

☐ Most Humanists support voluntary euthanasia and the right to suicide. Christians are less likely to.

☐ Humanists keep ceremonial to a minimum and emphasize the ongoing influence of the deceased.

☐ The Humanist funeral is a response to the hypocrisy and impersonality of contemporary Christian funerals, a celebration of a life lived, not a ritual concerned with the eternal effects of human sin. It is chosen by only one in 200 Britons.

☐ Humanist funerals are planned individually with the family of the deceased and include a eulogy, with readings of poetry and prose reflecting the life of the deceased.

☐ In the eighteenth century death came to be seen as a natural process instead of a spiritual passage; by the twentieth century it had become a medical problem. Doctors, hospital administrators, life support machines and bereavement counsellors have displaced the priest and the praying family.

☐ The church has lost control of the dying and the dead. Seventy per cent of Britons are now cremated. No crematoria are owned by the church. In the USA most burial grounds are commercial. Considerations of public health take priority over religious considerations.

☐ Clergy visiting the dying or bereaved cannot presume to know what people believe; pastoral care becomes the task of enabling the person to articulate or discover what they believe.

☐ The reason the Christian funeral is so problematic is that it necessarily involves public proclamation of a faith that some of those present may not share.

☐ Over the last two to three centuries hell has disappeared. Without hell, death poses no spiritual risk and the purpose of much ritual around death vanishes. The God of love may prove easier to secularize than a God of vengeance.

☐ The idea that the real problem after death is the grief of the survivors rather than the journey of the soul is a secular idea. Religious beliefs are judged according to whether they assist grieving rather than assisting the souls of the dead. Hence, the very concept of bereavement is a secular one.

- [ ] The hospice is medicine's attempt to humanize itself. This response can re-open a space for the spiritual. But at the same time it is also a secularizing trend: by insisting that the doctor be concerned with the soul as well as the body it furthers death's medicalization.
- [ ] Respect for the person, and his or her right to self-determination, dominates debates about the ethics of euthanasia.
- [ ] The modern way of death in the West is a hybrid of Christianity and secularism. Christians have long since accepted the secularization of modern institutions and are, in many instances, leading advocates of a more humanized way of dying and grieving. For those from more traditional communities who reject both Christianity *and* secularism, dying and grieving in the secular post-Christian West may be altogether more problematic.

Part III

Practical implications and conclusions

Chapter 10

Childhood death and bereavement across cultures

Bill Young and Danai Papadatou

INTRODUCTION

Whichever perspective one takes; evolutionary, social, psychological or biological, the bond between parent and child is usually considered to be the most significant, powerful and enduring of any human relationship. When either a parent or child dies, not only is the survivor's grief likely to be severe but the loss presents a unique challenge to their future well-being and development (Papadatou and Papadatos, 1991). While some aspects of the parent–child relationship may be pre-programmed from conception, each unfolds and develops within a specific family, social and cultural context. Indeed, it is these wider influences which not only shape the nature and status of each relationship but also the experience and meaning for each member. While there is a considerable amount of clinical and research literature on the psychological needs of bereaved parents and children, scant attention has usually been given to cultural differences (Irish, Lundquist and Nelson, 1993).

In this chapter, we wish to highlight the unique emotional impact of parental bereavement and to argue that all children, because of their developmental vulnerability, merit specific and separate attention when they are facing their own death or that of a parent or loved one. In addition, we hope to describe that while parents and children the world over experience grief, the way their grief is expressed and the way each culture accords value and meaning to these types of bereavement and accommodates the wishes and needs of both the deceased and surviving member vary widely across cultures.

CHILDHOOD DEATH

Each culture attributes a unique significance to the death of a child. Each holds various beliefs about where children come from before they are born, and where they go after they die. Furthermore, the child's age, gender, family position and cause of death may affect the meaning attributed to such loss and determine the rites of passage and norms for 'appropriate' grieving behaviours within a given culture.

Throughout most of the history of humankind, the deaths of infants and children were common events. In countries where rates of mortality are currently high, the death of a child is often perceived as inevitable, with mourning lasting no more than a few days. On the other hand, in developed countries and some developing countries, since the beginning of this century, changes in nutrition, sanitation and medical advances have contributed to a sharp decline in childhood mortality. As a result, childhood deaths have become a rarity, and are likely to be perceived as tragic, unfair and unnatural as they reverse the perceived order of nature. While many cultures designate the status of individuals suffering certain bereavements, such as 'widows' or 'widowers' for those losing spouses or 'orphans' for children losing parents, there are often no culturally accepted terms to describe the state of the bereaved parent (Schmidt, 1987).

Parental grief

During the past two decades, parental bereavement has received considerable attention in the literature and a growing number of descriptive studies have brought into light the unique features of the grief experienced by parents over the loss of a child (Rando, 1986). When compared to other forms of bereavement, the response to the death of a child in Western societies appears more complicated, intense and long-lasting in its effects. This leaves many bereaved parents looking 'atypical', even 'abnormal', in their mourning when, in fact, they are not. When a child dies, part of a parent's self dies too. The dreams, expectations and hopes that parents held for that specific child are lost. This is particularly threatening to most Western families in which children become a major source of meaning and purpose in the life of parents. Furthermore, when a child dies, parents are robbed of their identities as protectors and providers, and are left with an overwhelming sense of failure. The world that was once experienced as secure and ordered, is now perceived as unjust and out of control and parents search for answers to the burning question of 'why?' in their attempt to reconstruct a world with meaning. This inquiry can become a lifelong quest with many parents still grieving up to ten years after the death of their child (McClowry *et al.*, 1987). Some clinicians refer to 'shadow grief' to describe the chronic and overwhelming effect of maternal grief over the loss of a baby before or soon after birth and over the loss of older children. They claim that these mothers do not want to relinquish their grief; pain is an inherent part of the child's memory and continues to be very precious to them.

In Western societies, parents are expected to grieve in private and return to their work and other activities soon after the child's death. Grief reactions, however, differ widely in other societies and must therefore be understood within the cultural context they occur, otherwise we run the risk of evaluating them as pathological by our own cultural standards. For example, an Egyptian mother who remains withdrawn, mute and inactive seven years after the death of her child, is considered to behave normally by the standards of her culture, as is a Balinese mother who remains calm and cheerful after the death of her child; in her culture emotional upset is believed to make one vulnerable to illness and malevolent sorcery. Grief reactions and the duration of bereavement may also be affected in some cultures by the child's gender. The death of a male child, who perpetuates the name of the family in future generations, and who provides and protects both his family of origin and the one he creates, is experienced as more traumatic in certain cultures when compared to the death of female children.

Body disposal and funeral rites

The value a culture holds for children and the significance of their death are reflected in the disposal of the body and the funeral rites, which quite often differ from those performed in adult deaths. In several cultures children are considered innocent and their premature death affords them heavenly status. Thus Puerto Ricans dress their child in white, paint the face to look like an angel and place flowers inside and outside the coffin. Greeks, on the other hand, dress their dead children in wedding attire as they perceive death as particularly traumatic when it occurs prior to marriage, which is believed to be the consummation of earthly happiness. This is apparent in Greek funeral laments which bear a striking resemblance to the songs that are sung at weddings. The similarities between weddings and funerals, which both involve rites of passage and imply separation, is not only apparent in Greece but in other cultures of the Balkan area, and across the world. Although the death of children is socially recognized and funerals are well-attended in several cultures, in others, such as the Chinese, the death of a child is perceived as a 'bad death', as is any form of violent death. Parents and grandparents are not expected to go to the funeral and they avoid discussing the death, which is considered shameful to the family.

Certain types of childhood death, like suicide and homicide, are more likely to be stigmatized and considered 'shameful', which prevents families from grieving openly and receiving social support. These attitudes are increasingly relevant in many Western societies which are witnessing alarming increases in adolescent suicide and homicide. Catholics, Orthodox Christians, Protestants and Jews regard suicide as sinful and a moral stigma is attached not only to the individual who commits suicide, but to all those related to him or her. Interpretations vary from culture to culture since suicide may be regarded as sinful, as a criminal act, as a sign of weakness and madness, or under certain circumstances it may be viewed as an honourable act serving a higher cause.

The deaths of infants have a special status in most cultures. Anthropologists have observed in the history of humankind that infant deaths provide only abbreviated rites, and grief is almost immediately completed. This may be understandable in the light of the high rates of infant mortality which obliged parents to expect that not all of their pregnancies would come to fruition and that some of their babies would die. For instance, the Yoruba of Nigeria dispose of the dead body of their baby by throwing it into the bush. This apparently 'cruel' custom makes sense within this particular culture which asserts that, if buried, a dead baby would be considered as deeply offending the earth shrines which bring fertility and ward off death. In contrast, Hindu infants and young children are usually buried rather than cremated since they are expected to return to earthly life and enjoy a fuller experience of it. In other cultures, infants are buried in specially reserved parts of the cemetery or, as in Japan, may have their own cemeteries and family members may or may not be expected and encouraged to visit the grave thereafter.

Similarly, in some West African countries, perinatal deaths (which include miscarriage, stillbirth, sudden infant death or any other form of death occurring between the 20th week of gestation to the first year of life) are regarded as 'minor' losses or they are completely disregarded by society, and sometimes by parents themselves. This complicates acceptance and adjustment to the loss of an infant, and may lead to psychosomatic problems that occur during future pregnancies or may affect the psychosocial development of a 'replacement' child born after the infant's death. In some cases difficulties are perpetuated through the transmission of unresolved grief from one generation to another.

Finally, cultural and religious beliefs vary on their position on abortion and influence both the grieving process of those involved in the act of abortion, as well as the attitude of society towards them. Regardless of whether one engages in a wilful act of abortion or not, grieving is almost inevitable. For those who regard abortion as 'murder', grieving is accompanied by intense guilt which is further intensified by social stigma. But even in the case of elective abortion, recent studies support the evidence of grief reactions that are most usually initiated with the decision to terminate the pregnancy, and their intensity is related to the length of pregnancy (Pepper 1989).

DYING CHILDREN

Each culture provides its own explanations for the illness of children and determines the procedures and rituals for handling the transition of the dying, the setting in which they will be cared for and the persons likely to be present during this passage. Until the turn of this century the family and community was responsible for the care of dying children, which occurred within the home environment. This still happens in many societies. However, in those affected by modern medicine, dying has become increasingly centred in the hospital and care is delegated to highly skilled professionals who emphasise 'doing', and often try, by all available means, to delay the death. As a result, today, a significant number of dying children become patients in an acute, cure-oriented, technology based system. This has caused several new psychological, social and ethical problems for families who adopt the Western medical model, but even more so for families who have different cultural beliefs.

Quite often, within the hospital environment, professionals and parents assume a 'protective' approach towards children, and avoid informing them about their illness and imminent death. However, studies show that, even if children are not told openly about their illness, they accumulate information through a variety of means such as their contacts with other dying children, overhearing conversations about themselves and observing the non-verbal communications of their carers and attendants. Through these personal experiences, they progressively come to an understanding of the seriousness of their condition and express symbolically and indirectly the knowledge that they are dying (Bluebond-Langner, 1978). Other clinicians, however, suggest that, regardless of age, children possess an intuitive 'knowledge' of their condition and imminent death and express their awareness long before they are able to understand it cognitively. When people fail to respond to their questions and fears, and when they assume an attitude of 'pretence', children are left confused, emotionally isolated and unsupported in the face of impending death. Although the adoption of an 'open awareness' has been found to have several benefits, it still does not ensure more successful coping for some Western families. The display of 'congruency' between the beliefs and actions of those surrounding the child undoubtedly affects the care they receive. An ability to remain open to the child's queries and to respond with age-appropriate information and reassurance would appear to be the most helpful approach although, in practice, it is often very difficult to adopt consistently.

Sometimes the values, beliefs and practices of Western medicine may clash with those held by families with a different cultural background. A family may use traditional medicine for a long time before bringing the child to the hospital in a terminal condition, or may object to certain procedures and treatments, or may have difficulty in complying with recommendations. For example, permission for surgery can be very difficult to obtain from a Hmong family, since the culture's belief system holds that persons will live for eternity in the after life in the same state they are in at the time of death. Furthermore, they believe that souls inhabit various parts of the body and that removal of any part will result in a deprivation of some of the life force of that person. Physical explanations regarding the causes of the child's disease may be disregarded because supernatural explanations are in accord with the culture's belief system (Landis, 1991). Western health professionals may have great difficulty in understanding a worldview so vastly different from their own, and Hmong families may feel totally frustrated by the lack of understanding and communication with staff. Thus, the challenges for health professionals who help families face the crisis of the child's impending death are multiplied when dealing with a totally different belief system.

Whether children face their own death or that of a loved one, dying has increasingly become an 'offstage' event since hospitals and institutions assume the care of patients and replace the family and the community in one of their critical functions. In an effort to alleviate many of the problems caused by this institutionalization, programmes of home-care services have been developed in many countries across Europe, Australasia and Asia (Martinson and Papadatou, 1994). Research findings suggest that paediatric home-based care has several advantages over hospital care: the child is in their familiar home environment, family members are more involved in the child's care, parents experience reduced feelings of helplessness and guilt, while family communication and intimacy is increased. In addition, family adjustment following the death of the child has been observed to be more effective for families whose child dies at home when compared to those whose child dies in the hospital. However, not every family chooses home as an alternative to hospitalization, and many have stressed the importance of taking into consideration socio-cultural, psychological and medical factors that affect families in their decision to care for the child at home or in the hospital. In a recently published report, the International Work Group on Death, Dying and Bereavement has commented specifically on the principles for care of terminally ill children across cultures – 'families express their feelings and react within the context of their own cultural background. Cultural customs may enhance or inhibit their ability to accept illness and death' (International Work Group on Death, Dying and Bereavement, 1993).

BEREAVED CHILDREN

Bereaved children merit special attention for two important reasons. First, a number of controlled studies based on population samples have confirmed that children who lose a parent have a significantly increased risk of developing psychiatric disorders and may suffer considerable psychological and social difficulties throughout childhood and later in adult life (Black and Young, 1995). Other types of bereavement such as siblings, close friends and teachers may also result in significant and enduring effects. Second, major bereavement is not an uncommon event in the lives of children. Statistics from the USA indicate that up to 1.2 million children, about 4 per cent of the total child population, will lose a parent through death by the age of 15. This figure will be considerably higher in developing countries or in areas afflicted by natural disasters and wars. Unaccompanied and orphaned refugee children are increasingly being rehabilitated within developed nations.

Developmental influences on bereaved children

Mourning, in both adults and children, is frequently conceptualized as a sequence of psychological tasks which have to be 'worked through' before the individual can fully adjust to their loss (Worden, 1991). However, a brief synopsis of these tasks demonstrates that each one presents additional difficulties and risks for children in comparison with adults.

1 Adjusting to the reality of the loss is complicated by children's immature concepts related to dying and death which often give rise to false beliefs and unrealistic fears. This incomplete understanding is often further compounded by the lack of accurate, age-appropriate information given by adults – often with a spurious rationale of 'protecting' them from the truth.
2 Likewise, children have a more limited capacity than adults to experience and tolerate painful affects. Their sadness often occurs in brief bursts, perhaps while playing, and often goes unrecognized by others.
3 Due to their dependency, children are reliant on others to care for them and to help them adjust to their new circumstances. Children adjusting to the physical absence of a dead parent may have to manage the emotional absence and grief of a surviving parent who has been consumed in mourning.
4 Psychological autonomy develops throughout childhood and young children particularly are not so able mentally to separate their own identity and fate from those closest to them. This complicates their task of establishing a new identity because their hopes and aspirations for the future are still tied up with those of the deceased.

Cultural influences on bereaved children

One could argue that these developmental vulnerabilities, and the specific needs which arise from them, transcend cultural differences. However, on closer inspection, it soon becomes clear that each culture has a specific and direct influence on all these areas as well as many factors which play a mediating role in children's experience of and adjustment to death and bereavement (Black and Young, 1995). These include general cultural differences such as child-rearing practices and the status of children, as well as more specific influences such as how children acquire their understanding of death and how they are involved or excluded from mourning practices.

Children's understanding of death and bereavement

Few parents would doubt that children become aware of death from an early age. Each culture provides its own opportunities for children to learn about both the physical facts and the shared beliefs concerning life, death and beyond. In traditional cultures, death is often a natural and familiar, if not everyday, occurrence. Furthermore, the dying and dead are cared for by their own family and children are not only close observers of this but are often active participants in any activities or rituals of the 'death surround'. In this way, they are exposed to and learn from the same realities as adults – no special arrangements are made to shield or exclude them, as they so often are in the West. In contrast, we in the West have removed real death from the public arena and children are more likely to be exposed to death through graphic media images and are more likely to view it as violent, horrific or untimely. These distorted perceptions are compounded by an increasing reliance on medical technology and the overall professionalization of death which, through adopting restrictive hospital and funeral practices, has further reduced children's opportunities for learning about dying and death.

It seems that while we have become busy denying the reality of death, we have also developed an obsession with its explicit and morbid details through crime stories, horror films and war pictures. Western children are not immune to this and can themselves acquire an unhealthy appetite for this 'pornography of death' which seldom gives any realistic account of the effects of death on those left behind. Again, this contrasts with the myths, stories and folk-tales of many traditional cultures which carry profound lessons about life, death and loss. Interestingly, some Western countries, North America in particular, have witnessed the introduction of 'death education' into schools and colleges. In addition, there is an increasing amount of educational literature, both fiction and non-fiction, available for children, parents and professionals on the subjects of death and bereavement.

Religious beliefs about the afterlife can both help and hinder children's understanding about death. Some will find the idea of a loved one being looked after somewhere or keeping watch over them reassuring. Indeed, many children hold these beliefs intuitively, regardless of their parents' religious orientation. At the same time, some may become confused by the difference between physical death and spiritual life or may even feel persecuted by the 'ghost' of someone who can no longer be seen. Likewise, religious explanations about why people die, especially other children, may create more confusion and anxiety than they seek to alleviate.

Children's involvement in mourning practices

Shared mourning practices are as important for children as they are for adults. Before bereavement, just as for dying children, those facing the death of a parent or loved one can benefit greatly from adult support and preparation for their impending loss (Siegel, Mesagno and Christ, 1990). After bereavement, children, even more than adults, need concrete evidence to accept that their loved one is physically absent but they also need concrete reminders to help them recapture and retain their memories of that person (Silverman, Nickman and Worden, 1992). Although some cultures segregate children from certain preparatory and mourning practices, most encourage their participation and may even make special provision for them. However, it is important to ascertain what any particular family beliefs are about this.

It is worth having in mind that the original purpose of many death rituals, such as funerals, was to create auspicious circumstances for the dead person's onward journey into the afterlife. With this are various beliefs about ongoing communication between the worlds of the living and dead. These understandings are 'caught by' rather than 'taught to' children and then incorporated into their belief systems and eventually guide their mourning. Children thereby learn that the dead are remembered and honoured not only because it is natural but also because the dead can exert physical or even supernatural influences on the material world. More importantly, by involving children, many cultures ensure that familiar and trusted adults are available to them – to give emotional support, to explain and teach about the beliefs and practices of their culture, and to act as role models.

The issue of funeral attendance has been a particular concern in the West although the research indicates that children usually benefit not only because it helps to promote their immediate mourning but also since, in later years, children often report that their participation was important, while others regret not having attended (Weller et al., 1988). In many ways, this research is only lending scientific validity to practices which other cultures have 'known' all along, that is, children should be encouraged to attend and even participate in funerals, be prepared for and supported through the event by trusted adults, and be given the opportunity to see and touch the body as a final 'farewell'.

Family support for bereaved children

Many have argued that the ongoing deprivation of a parent is a more significant adversity than the trauma of the loss itself. Certainly parentally bereaved children need to experience as much continuity as possible in relation to their physical and emotional care. From this perspective, the extent to which any surviving adults can meet the child's needs is more important than their gender or parental status. The make-up of the family and the traditional roles of men and women may be important in this respect. For instance, surviving fathers from cultures in which men traditionally have minimal child-care responsibilities may lack the experience or even the desire to take up this new role. In some cultures, older children may be expected to take on additional, even parental, responsibilities. Often female relatives will provide support or even assume care of the children but this may not be possible if the extended family still live in the parent's country of origin and children may even be sent back to be raised there.

Apart from their physical care, children's emotional ability to cope with bereavement depends crucially on the way in which the family as a whole manages the loss (Walsh and McGoldrick, 1991). A family which was previously dysfunctional with poor communication, emotional involvement and problem solving will provide a less tolerant and supportive environment within which a child can express and make sense of their experience. Likewise, previously dysfunctional families are more likely to redistribute roles in anomalous or deviant ways thus exposing grieving children to additional stresses. However, whether or not a family is considered 'dysfunctional' has to be understood in the context of their cultural practices and expectations. This may be very difficult for families which are isolated from their original countries. Some cultures give priority to survival of the family unit and emphasize loyalty, self-sacrifice and private mourning. Others endorse the rights of individuals, including children, to express their grief openly and even publicly. Families from non-Western cultures often choose to invest their own 'ritual specialists' with the necessary magical powers or religious authority to support and guide them through their grief.

In contrast to the stable traditions guiding those in purer cultures, most Western societies have witnessed a decline in the status of established religion and this, along with the dissolution of extended family and community networks, has meant that the beliefs and practices, as well as the institutional structures, which would have supported bereaved adults and children, are now often unavailable or inadequate. Moreover, the socio-political processes of humanization and secularization have shifted attention away from the destiny of the deceased towards an awareness of the fate of the bereaved including, most recently, to the needs of bereaved children. As a result of all these trends, Western society has created its own 'ritual specialists' in the form of bereavement counsellors who have their own set of scientifically developed tools collectively referred to as therapeutic interventions.

Therapeutic intervention

Many voluntary organizations originally set up to provide humanitarian support for bereaved adults, such as Cruse: Bereavement Care in the UK, have increasingly broadened the scope of their work to include bereaved children. Many forms of bereavement counselling employed with adults have been adapted for children with generally positive results. Examples include individual play therapy (Webb, 1993), group and school-based interventions (Dyregrov, 1992) and family counselling (Black and Urbanowicz, 1987).

With children, it may be beneficial to facilitate and possibly accelerate normal grief as this will not only protect a mourning child from the noxious effects of grief, but may also reduce the time period during which they are exposed to all the other stresses children face. In addition, an increasing number of children in Western society are experiencing violent or traumatic deaths which further complicate their grief and mourning. This has resulted in greater attention being made to providing preventive and therapeutic intervention for these and other bereaved children who are considered to be at a higher risk of psychological problems (Harris-Hendriks, Black and Kaplan, 1993).

Some would consider children and families from ethnic minorities also to be at increased risk. They may have become dislocated from their parent culture where help would normally be available. Their concepts and patterns of grief and psychiatric disorder may be unfamiliar to professionals who may either avoid involvement through fear or ignorance or deliver inappropriate forms of intervention. While there is much clinical and research work to suggest that those from ethnic minorities can benefit from counselling, there are often problems in providing accessible and appropriate services for them, particularly if they do not speak the host culture's language. For these reasons and others, families may be reluctant, or even resistant, to allow themselves or their children to receive help from someone outside their culture.

SUMMARY

- [ ] The bond between parent and child is considered to be the most significant, enduring and unparalleled of any other type of relationship. It grows within a specific social and cultural context.
- [ ] Scant attention has been paid to cultural factors in studies of the needs of bereaved parents and children.
- [ ] The ways grief is expressed when a parent or child dies and the way each culture accords value and meaning to these types of bereavement and accommodates the wishes and needs of both the deceased and surviving member, vary widely across cultures.
- [ ] Children, because of their unique vulnerability and strengths, merit specific and separate attention whether they are facing their own death or that of a parent.
- [ ] Culture has a specific and direct impact on child-rearing practices and the status of children, as well as more specific influences such as how children acquire their understanding of death and how they are involved or excluded from mourning practices.
- [ ] The child's age, gender, original position, and cause of death may affect the meaning that is attributed to a loss and determines the rites of passage and norms for 'appropriate' grieving behaviours within a given culture.
- [ ] In countries where rates of mortality are high the death of a child is usually perceived as inevitable and mourning may not last more than a few days.
- [ ] The death of a child in Western societies is perceived as unnatural and leads to more complicated, intense and long-lasting effects than other types of bereavement (shadow grief).
- [ ] When Western parents lose a child they lose hope for the future, meaning in their lives, they feel they have failed as parents and perceive the world as unjust, anomic and out of control.
- [ ] In Western societies parents are expected to grieve in private and return to their work and other activities soon after the child's death.
- [ ] Grief reactions differ greatly in other societies and must be understood within the cultural context they occur, otherwise we run the risk of evaluating them as pathological by our own cultural standards.
- [ ] When male children are valued more highly than female, grief at their loss is correspondingly greater.
- [ ] In several cultures children are considered innocent and their premature death affords them heavenly status. The analogy between

marriage and death is explicitly articulated at the funeral of unmarried individuals and youngsters.

☐ In many societies, childhood deaths are considered 'shameful' and prevent families from grieving openly and receiving social support.

☐ The Yoruba of Nigeria dispose of the dead body of their baby by throwing it into the bush. If buried, a dead baby would be considered as deeply offending the earth shrines which bring fertility and ward off death.

☐ In many Western countries, perinatal deaths are regarded as 'minor' losses or they are completely disregarded by society, and sometimes by parents themselves. This complicates acceptance and adjustment to the loss of an infant, and may lead to psychosomatic problems or complicate the life of a 'replacement' child.

☐ For those who regard abortion as 'murder', grieving is accompanied by intense guilt which is further intensified by social stigma. Even when this is not the case grief is likely to occur and to be related to the length of gestation.

☐ Each culture provides its own explanations for illness and the death of children and determines its own rituals and care of the dying child. In most, these take place in the child's home.

☐ In those societies affected by modern medicine, dying children become patients in an acute, cure-oriented, technology based system which replaces the family and the community in one of their critical functions. This has caused several new psychological, social and ethical problems for families who adopt the Western medical model, but even more so for families that have different cultural beliefs.

☐ When people fail to respond to their questions and fears, and when they assume an attitude of 'pretence', children are emotionally isolated and left unsupported in the face of impending death.

☐ The values, beliefs and practices of Western medicine may clash with those held by families with a different cultural background.

☐ Permission for surgery can be very difficult to obtain from a Hmong family because they hold that persons will live for eternity in the afterlife in the same state they are in at the time of death.

☐ With paediatric home-based care the dying child is in his familiar environment, family members are more involved in care, parents experience reduced feelings of helplessness and guilt, family communication and intimacy is increased and their adjustment following the death of the child is more satisfactory than in those whose child dies in a hospital.

☐ Home care services have advantages over hospital services for many dying children and their families.

☐ Bereaved children have a significantly increased risk of developing psychiatric disorders and may suffer considerable psychological and social difficulties throughout their lives.

☐ Rates of bereavement are considerably higher in developing countries and, of course, in those afflicted by natural disasters and wars.

☐ Adjusting to the reality of the loss is complicated by children's incomplete concepts related to dying and death which often give rise to false beliefs and unrealistic fears and by the lack of or distortion of information that they receive.

☐ Children have a more limited capacity than adults to experience and tolerate painful affects. Their sadness often occurs in brief bursts, perhaps while playing, and often goes unrecognized by others.

☐ Children adjusting to the physical absence of a dead parent may have to manage the emotional absence and grief of a surviving parent while consumed in their own grief.

☐ Children in other countries obtain a more realistic and less horrific view of death than do those in the West.

☐ Children in non-Western cultures learn about the belief systems attending death by participation in ritual and talk rather than formal teaching. Most Western children who attend funerals regard their participation as having been helpful to them. Children should be encouraged but not forced to attend, prepared and supported through the event by trusted adults, and perhaps given the opportunity to see and touch the body.

☐ The deprivation of a parent may be a more significant adversity than the trauma of the loss itself. Adults need to meet the surviving child's needs regardless of their gender and parental status.

☐ In the West, the beliefs and practices, as well as the institutional structures, which would have supported bereaved children, are now often unavailable or inadequate.

☐ Mental health professionals have their own set of scientifically developed tools for the support of bereaved children.

☐ Many forms of bereavement counselling have been developed to help bereaved children.

☐ While those from ethnic minorities can benefit from counselling, such services need to be accessible, appropriate and acceptable to the families they serve.

Chapter 11

Help for the dying and the bereaved

Colin Murray Parkes

For the caring person some of the foregoing chapters make discouraging reading. Given the complexities of communication with people of other races, the doubts which some of the authors have expressed regarding their need for help from outsiders and our own doubts of our ability to give help, we may be tempted to give up altogether: 'Let foreigners and pagans look after their own, we have no right and no need to interfere.'

This attitude might be justified if it was always and necessarily true but there are a number of circumstances in which this is not the case.

1 In many areas help from an immigrant's parent culture may not be available. Immigrants may be isolated from members of the culture they have left behind.
2 Many people from other races and religions seek help from the healthcare and counselling services in their adoptive countries. They may not be satisfied with the care which is available to them from their own ethnic and religious groups and may, indeed, have repudiated these groups. Yet, whether they like it or not, they carry within them many of the habits of thought and assumptions of their parent culture.
3 Members of healthcare services are often involved in the care of people of other races. It is not wise of us to split them in two, to treat the body and ignore the mind. Patients may have sought help from us for treatment of a symptom or disease which they believe to be bodily but which may well be rooted in the mind. Unless we understand enough about their ways of thinking we may end up giving physical treatment for emotional problems.
4 Many people come under medical and nursing care when they are dying. We may be able to provide relief of distressing symptoms but

it is sad if that is all we can offer. At the very least we need to make every effort to allow our patients to die and their families and priests to support them in the ways that seem right to them. We need to understand their needs in order to explain them to hospital authorities, fellow patients and others who may obstruct or misunderstand what is happening.

5 Losses may cause mental illness. Although people from other races and religions often view psychiatric disorders in different ways from us this does not mean that their culture denies the existence of psychiatric disorder. The concept of pathological grief, for instance, is common although it is defined in different ways in different cultures. People who suffer from these reactions expect and need help. It may be that we are the only people available to give it.

The first step in counselling people from other cultures must be to find out what they want and, hopefully, need from us. Their wants may be very different from our assumption of their needs but unless we have taken the trouble to find out what their wants are we cannot even begin to guess at their needs. In order to do this we may have to make use of an interpreter but we should not assume that the sole function of an interpreter is to translate language. Most interpreters are very familiar with the culture as well as the language of the people they serve and can help us to bridge the cultural gap. But they too may have their biasses and we should satisfy ourselves that the interpreter is acceptable to the client as well as to us.

The decision whether or not to refer people on to other sources of help will depend partly on our and their assessment of our ability to help them and partly on the availability of acceptable alternatives. It is usually quite possible to help people from other cultures provided we are willing to take the time and the trouble to learn to see the world through their eyes. When we do this we shall find ourselves less likely to judge them and better able to understand the nature of the problems they face.

Even among people of one's own culture it is usually a mistake for counsellors to give advice. Counselling is not something that one person does to another, it is something that two or more people do together. While our clients are explaining themselves to us they are also explaining themselves to themselves. This can be a very therapeutic thing to do.

At times of death and bereavement people are faced with turning points in their lives. One chapter is coming to an end and another is beginning. Old assumptions about the world have to be given up and new ones figured out. Despite all the differences between cultures in the way in which they express fear or grief, there are certain things which human beings share with each other, and with other social animals, which transcend culture. These have to do with the support and protection which social animals give to each other at times of danger.

Families exist to give support to their members at times of danger and loss. Most of the time they will do this without much help from outsiders, but there are many situations when the family fails in its supportive function. Immigrants may be separated from their families and have no substitute within their new communities, their families may themselves be too traumatized or too alienated to be able to cope. Just when the family is most needed it may become dysfunctional. It is at such times that the help of someone from outside the family is most needed.

It follows that an important task for the would-be counsellor is to discover what familial and other supports exist for the person. If we conclude that no adequate support is available we may need to attempt to provide it ourselves. Again this sounds like a tall order when we have little idea how a family supports its members in the particular culture, but we shall usually be right to assume that an important component is emotional support. This is best expressed by non-verbal rather than verbal means. A smile or a touch of the hand will usually be recognized and responded to as a sign that we care and may have a profound effect on someone who is isolated and afraid. Even if we have got it wrong and broken a taboo we will usually be forgiven and the client's reaction will immediately warn us not to try again. Clients are all too aware that people in a foreign land see things differently and behave differently from themselves and they will tolerate behaviour that would be deplored in a fellow countryman.

All worthwhile communication takes time and even more time is needed if there are barriers to communication. Strange to say the linguistic barrier may be less of a problem than we imagine. The fact that it takes time for someone to explain themselves to us may simply give them the time that they need to check us out at a non-verbal level. Much more of a problem are the expectations which we have of each other. This may come from us or from our clients. We may not take the trouble to ask questions or to listen to what foreign clients are saying because we do not expect to understand; they may give up trying to communicate because they do not expect to be understood. We may imagine that they are more different from us than they really are. They may imagine that we are more different from them than we really are.

Some immigrants have unrealistic expectations that we will solve their problems by magic (or science), others distrust us and expect us to harm them. Some counsellors have unrealistic expectations that a client's cultural supports will solve all of their emotional problems, others regard any culture but their own as ineffectual and inferior.

It is prejudices such as these that we must set aside if we are to be of any help to people of other cultures. If *we* set aside *our* prejudices there is a chance that our clients will respond by setting aside theirs. Openness evokes open responses and when people from alien cultures succeed in crossing the gap the effect can be quite extraordinary. The trappings of cultural diversity can drop away and people have the feeling of meeting 'soul to soul'. It is this that makes cross-cultural counselling so rewarding for the counsellor as well as the client. People who, at first contact, seem to speak poor English often turn out to be very much better at it when we get to know them. Their apparent lack of fluency may have resulted from shyness or reticence rather than ignorance of the English tongue. This is particularly the case among Asian women who usually expect their husbands to speak for them even if they know a language better than he.

Even if we are familiar with the client's culture we would do well to ask them to explain it to us. Are they orthodox adherents of a particular faith, have they repudiated that faith or have they chosen an intermediate path? Do they have clear cut beliefs or are they, like a lot of people in our own culture, agnostics with no commitment to a particular faith. Are they seeking for guidance from us on these issues or do they prefer to let them alone?

Perhaps our most difficult task is to find out whether or not it is permissible to talk at all about issues relating to serious illness, death and bereavement. Unless the clients themselves bring up the issue it is probably advisable not to raise these issues at the first meeting but to take time in getting to know the client and other members of their family who may be better able to educate us regarding these matters. However, we should not be afraid to be honest and frank with people if it is clear that this is what they want, and we should never lie. This is particularly important when people have a terminal illness for usually, sooner or later, the true facts of the case will become obvious.

The best way to find out what people are ready to know is to invite questions. People hardly ever ask questions when they are not ready to hear the answers. It goes without saying that our replies should be in language that they can understand. This is difficult enough in our own culture when words like 'cancer' and 'death' often have connotations for patients which bear little relationship to the illness from which they are suffering or the way this patient can expect to die. In other cultures such communication may be more difficult, although it is also often true that people of other races are more familiar with death and better able to accept and talk about it than we are. Again the use of a good interpreter or family member can make all the difference.

The development of hospices has added another dimension to the care of the dying in the United Kingdom and many other countries. Their undoubted success results from two factors: firstly, their methods of relieving pain and other unpleasant symptoms which have greatly improved the chances of patients with terminal illnesses achieving a peaceful death, and secondly, their psychological, social and spiritual care for patients and their families, the latter continuing after bereavement when necessary. Between them these approaches have greatly improved the quality of the life of people whose lives are affected by cancer, AIDS and other illnesses whose course is predictably 'terminal'.

Hospices rely on sufficient numbers of highly trained staff backed by volunteers to provide close support for family members as well as for patients. This applies to patients at home as well as on the wards of hospices. Research indicates that the provision of adequate home care often enables patients to spend more time at home than they would without this support and many of them will then opt to die at home. It also shows that the strain on the family can be very great when the patient is at home but that most families gladly accept this added burden if they are given the support that they need (Parkes, 1978, and Hinton, 1994).

The success of hospices has led to many other types of specialist Palliative Care Units being set up and has improved the care of patients with terminal illnesses in many settings. The control of pain and other symptoms has easily been transferred to other types of setting but the same cannot be said of the psycho-social and spiritual aspects of care which seldom match that provided in the better hospices (Parkes and Parkes, 1984). The movement owes much to its founder, Dame Cicely Saunders, who after working for seven years in a Roman Catholic hospice, St Joseph's in Hackney, started her own hospice, St Christopher's, in Sydenham, South London (du Boulay, 1984). St Christopher's Hospice is an Anglican foundation but, as Tony Walter pointed out (see p. 183), the staff there adopt a patient- and family-centred, non-dogmatic approach which aims to encourage people of all faiths to find their own spiritual course.

During the last twenty years hospices have sprung up in most parts of the world. While this spread is understandable given the success of hospices in the UK and USA it remains to be seen how successfully the psycho-social and spiritual support which works so well in Judao-Christian countries can be adapted to work with other religious and cultural populations. Because there is no international standard governing the use of the word 'hospice' it has come to mean different things in different places. In the UK, where the movement started, it usually implies a place, with beds, where patients can stay until they die. Home care has been tacked onto this. In the USA, where most medical care is given in clinics and hospitals and general practitioners no longer visit the home, the idea that people might be successfully cared for at home and even die at home needed to be rediscovered. Consequently it was home care that came to be associated with 'Hospice' in the public mind.

At St Christopher's and many other hospices every nurse is trained to draw family trees (genograms) and to assess the psycho-social needs of family members from the time of their first contact with the patient. They are supported in their work by social workers who are also responsible for selecting, training and supporting volunteer bereavement counsellors. These reach out to approximately a third of families after bereavement, the decision being based on a systematic assessment of family need. The method of assessing is derived from research into the prediction of bereavement outcome, most of which was carried out in Western cultures.

Evidence for the value of counselling comes from research in England and Australia which indicates that 'high-risk' bereaved people who are assigned at random to counselling have significantly fewer symptoms of lasting anxiety and tension and consume fewer drugs, and less alcohol and tobacco than those who receive no counselling (Raphael, 1977, and Parkes, 1981). By contrast, several studies in which unselected bereaved people who were given counselling were compared with others who were given no counselling showed little or no evidence that the counselling had any effect (Parkes, 1980). In other words, only when counselling was offered to those most at risk did it prove useful. Despite this the predictive value of risk assessment is not high and there is little reason to believe that those factors which predict bereavement outcome in one society will be equally predictive in another. This is an area in which much research is needed if we are to develop predictive indices which apply across cultural boundaries.

Usually the best single predictor of risk is the 'hunch' or 'gut reaction' which we get when we talk to a bereaved person or someone who is about to be bereaved. But even this may not be a valid measure across cultures. In societies in which people do not easily show emotion, intense distress before or at the time of a bereavement is a predictor of poor outcome. In other societies it may have the opposite connotation. British nurses and doctors often misread the intense distress of a bereaved Italian or other person from a Mediterranean culture as indicating that they are at risk of pathological grief, whereas in fact their reaction is perfectly normal for this particular culture.

Support for families of the dying and for bereaved people can take many forms. These range from individual support to groups of various kinds, reactive (relying on self-referral) to proactive (relying on outreach), hospital-based, hospice-based or community-based, counselling (by professional or volunteer counsellors) or befriending (often by 'veterans' who have experienced similar losses). It may take place in an office or in the client's home, soon after the bereavement or after a lapse of time. To judge from the reports of clients, all of these types of help are likely to be appreciated by those who receive them, but this does not mean that they are all equally effective and there are many who refuse all help or choose one type of help while rejecting another.

Well-conducted comparisons between types of help are few and far between and most of the types listed above have not been scientifically evaluated at all. The random-allocation studies by Raphael (1977) and Parkes (1981), which were referred to above, resembled each other in providing individual help in the home of 'high-risk' bereaved people. In both instances individual counselling was given in the first three months of bereavement to widows and widowers who were predominantly English-speaking, white, people from a nominally Christian culture. They differed in that Raphael's study was carried out in Sydney, Australia and the counselling was given by Raphael herself, a highly experienced psychiatrist with many years of experience in the psychiatric care of bereaved people. It was strictly limited to the first three months of bereavement and included people whose partners had died from many different causes. Parkes's study was carried out in South London, it was confined to the spouses of patients who had died from cancer in St Christopher's Hospice and the counselling was given by volunteers who had been carefully selected and trained by Parkes for the purpose. In many of Parkes's cases counselling continued beyond the first three months.

Perhaps the most reassuring thing about this study is the fact that good results were obtained without the need for the expertise of a highly trained psychiatrist. This is important, not only because of the expense of psychiatric care, but also because it enabled people to get help without being labelled as 'sick'. Grief is not a psychiatric illness and it is not appropriate to treat it as such. We conclude that individual counselling, given by trained persons to those white, 'Western', bereaved people who need it can reduce the trauma of bereavement. At this time there is no substantial evidence for the effectiveness of counselling given to people of other races. Nor is there scientific evidence for the success of other types of counselling and support given in the West, but that does not mean that they are ineffective. Psychodynamic psychotherapies, cognitive therapy, family therapy and other 'treatments' should be reserved for the small minority of bereaved people who suffer manifest psychiatric illness following bereavement.

The model of bereavement care that is common in hospices throughout the world, individual counselling by volunteers who are selected, trained and supported by professionals, is found on a wider scale throughout Britain in the organization, Cruse: Bereavement Care,[1] and various other organizations under the umbrella of the National Association of Bereavement Services. No other countries, to our knowledge, have quite so extensive a network of trained volunteer counsellors. In these others we more often find counselling provided by professional psychologists and social workers who may have received special training for the purpose. Thus in Australia the National Association for Loss and Grief sets standards and provides training for professionals, some of whom work for or closely with funeral directors. A similar organization in the USA is The Association for Death Education and Counselling.

Another model, that of the self-help or mutual help group, originated in Britain with The Compassionate Friends (for parents who have lost a child) and spread to the USA. Soon afterwards a Widow-to-Widow project was set up and spawned a wide range of similar organizations. In all of these the essential qualification for giving help to a bereaved person is the experience of personal bereavement oneself. No other training is thought necessary and no attempt is made to select

1 The name 'Cruse' means a container for oil. In the biblical book of Kings (I Kings 17: 10–16) the story is told how the contents of such a cruse were shared with a stranger, by a widow and her son, who were on the point of starving. The stranger proved to be the prophet Elijah, who blessed the widow's cruse so that it would not run dry while famine remained in the land. The cruse can, however, be seen as a symbol of charity to the bereaved. Cruse: Bereavement Care has no religious affiliation.

counsellors or to make a distinction between counsellor and client. All who come to the organization for help are expected to give as well as to receive. Thus the organization is self-sustaining and makes little or no use of professionals. In fact some self-help organizations become anti-professional. This is particularly likely to occur if members have had bad experiences at the hands of professionals and there is, no doubt, a place for organizations that can act as watchdogs for the rights of patients or others who may be harmed by the professionals who exist to help them. But we should not assume that *all* professionals are harmful to the people they serve and an organization that ignores the help which professionals can give may well find itself in difficulties when people come to it for help who need psychiatric or other medical help. It is as dangerous for untrained persons to attempt to treat psychosis as it is for them to attempt to treat cancer. People at risk of suicide or who may have physical health problems, as well as those who need specific psychological treatment, should be seen and assessed by properly qualified professionals. For this reason we do not recommend people to make use of services that do not cooperate closely with members of the caring professions.

There are, of course, many organizations that provide more than one type of service. Thus The British Association of Cancer United Patients (BACUP) provides a service of information to cancer patients as well as counselling by trained counsellors to patients and family members. Professionals, patients with cancer, family members and volunteers work together to meet a wide range of needs. Similar organizations exist in other countries and it is not possible to list them all here. We would, however, recommend our readers to learn all that they can about the organizations that are available to them and to attempt to set up services where those that exist are not appropriate to the needs.

As we have already seen, religious leaders and ritual specialists provided help to the dying and the bereaved in all countries in the past and in most they continue to do so. It is no coincidence that most hospices and bereavement services have been initiated by people with strong religious commitments. However, as Tony Walter has pointed out, there has been a tendency in the West for them to become independent of particular religions and to make a virtue of their openness. While this may be highly desirable in a multi-cultural society it does run the risk of the attention paid to the spiritual component quietly dwindling.

One group who have paid special attention to this issue is the International Work Group on Death, Dying and Bereavement. This body of international experts from many different disciplines has produced a series of *Statements on Death, Dying and Bereavement* which include the deliberations of a work group on spiritual care (Corr, Morgan and Wass, 1993). Among other things they conclude that 'Caregivers should be aware that they each have the potential for providing spiritual care, as do all human beings, and should be encouraged to offer spiritual care to dying patients and their families as needed.' They also recommend that 'Health care curricula should foster an awareness of the spiritual dimension in the clinical setting.' Quite how these two objectives are to be attained is less clear.

Our experience suggests that people are usually pleased to discuss their own spiritual and religious thinking if encouraged to do so. They are less likely to want to learn about ours. Because death and bereavement raise important questions regarding the meanings which people find in their lives, they may also want to share their doubts and fears. When they do this we shall often find that, far from being undermined by their lack of certainty, people may find a certain dignity and pride in rejecting the simple answers which, previously, they took for granted. 'Don't speak to me of the comforts of religion', said C.S. Lewis in the diary which he wrote after the death of his wife and subsequently published as *A Grief Observed* (1961). Later he speaks of the way in which grief has shattered his idea of God. 'My idea of God is not a divine idea. It has to be shattered time after time. He shatters it Himself. He is the great iconoclast.' This sense of a house of cards collapsing and having to be slowly and painfully rebuilt is a common image of bereavement for, when someone we love dies, we don't just lose someone 'out there', we lose a part of ourselves and a set of basic assumptions about the world. As Peter Marris puts it, 'Losing someone you love is less like losing a very valuable and irreplaceable possession than like finding the law of gravity to be invalid' (1982).

The bereaved only discover that the dead continue to enrich their lives 'in here' *after* they have stopped the desperate search for them 'out there'. Because gain is not possible without loss, love without grief and pleasure without pain, it may be necessary for us to let go of an outside, 'guardian-angel', God, whom we expect to protect us from pain and misery, and settle for an inside, participative God, who enriches our lives. We accept the whole package or none of it. It may be safer not to fall in love and less painful to blot out all consciousness with drugs than to suffer the pangs of grief, but without love or consciousness we are not truly alive. Lessons like these can only be learned by going through grief, suffering, and emerging on the other side.

SUMMARY

- ☐ Support for people from other cultures may be needed because: help from their parent culture may not be available; they may not be satisfied with the care which is available to them from their parent culture; they may want and require Western health care; we may need to explain their needs to hospital authorities, fellow patients and others.

- ☐ It is usually quite possible to help people from other cultures, provided we are willing to take the time and the trouble to learn to see the world through their eyes.

- ☐ It is usually a mistake for counsellors to give advice. Counselling is something that two or more people do together. While our clients are explaining themselves to us they are also explaining themselves to themselves.

- ☐ Despite all the differences in the ways which cultures express fear or grief, the support and protection which social animals give to each other at times of danger transcend culture.

- ☐ At times of death and bereavement people are faced with turning points in their lives.

- ☐ Families exist to give support to their members at times of danger and loss. Most of the time they will do this without much help from outsiders but there are many situations when the family fails in its supportive function. It is at such times that the help of someone from outside the family is most needed.

- ☐ Emotional support is expressed by non-verbal as well as verbal means.

- ☐ All worthwhile communication takes time and more time is needed if there are barriers to communication.

- ☐ Openness evokes open responses and when people from alien cultures succeed in crossing the gap the effect can be quite extraordinary. Cross-cultural counselling can be rewarding for the counsellor as well as the client.

- ☐ Even if we are familiar with the client's culture we would do well to ask them to explain it to us.

- ☐ Our most difficult task is to find out whether or not it is permissible to talk at all about issues relating to serious illness, death and bereavement.

- ☐ The best way to find out what people are ready to know is to invite questions. We should not be afraid to be honest and frank with people, if it is clear that this is what they want, and we should never lie.

☐ The use of a good interpreter or family member can make all the difference.

☐ Hospices have sprung up in most parts of the world. It remains to be seen how successfully the psycho-social and spiritual support, which work so well in Judaeo-Christian countries, can be adapted to work with other religious and cultural populations.

☐ The bereavement counselling provided by most hospices derives from research which was carried out in Western cultures.

☐ In societies in which people do not easily show emotion, intense distress before or at the time of a bereavement is a predictor of poor outcome; in other societies it may have the opposite connotation.

☐ In the past, religious leaders and ritual specialists provided help to the dying and the bereaved in nearly all countries and in most they continue to do so.

☐ Individual counselling for the bereaved by volunteers who are selected, trained and supported by professionals, is found on a wide scale throughout Britain. In other Western countries we more often find counselling provided by professional psychologists and social workers or by mutual help groups.

☐ People are usually willing to discuss their own spiritual and religious thinking if encouraged to do so.

☐ The bereaved only discover that the dead continue to enrich their lives 'in here' *after* they have stopped the desperate search for them 'out there'. Because gain is not possible without loss, love without grief and pleasure without pain, it may be necessary for us to let go of an outside, 'guardian-angel', God who will protect us from pain and misery, and settle for an inside, participative God who enriches our lives.

Chapter 12

Conclusions I: Implications for practice and policy

Pittu Laungani and Bill Young

It is now time to take stock. Before we start to consider the implications for practice and policy, let us briefly summarize the main themes with which the book has been concerned. As the title suggests, the book's main concern has been to examine the ways in which people from different cultures conceive of death, handle the disposal of their dead, mourn for the dead, and, over time, overcome the sad loss which the death of a loved one brings. We have also examined the range of social (and professional) networks which swing into action to enable the bereaved to overcome their sorrow and come to terms with their loss.

PUBLIC AND PRIVATE EVENT

In some cultures – such as India (see Chapter 4), Nepal and China (see Chapter 5), Pakistan (see chapter 8), Greece (see Chapter 10) and many of the small group societies dotted around the world (see Chapter 3) – we noticed that death when it occurs affects not only the immediate family but one's community, of which one is an integral part. The disposal of the dead and the accompanying mourning then becomes a social, if not public affair. Crying, weeping, sobbing, wailing in public – in fact, expressing all the emotions in public, in the presence of all the mourners who themselves make no attempts to conceal their own emotional expressions – is an accepted part of the social ritual in such cultures. In fact, the bereaved family is encouraged, even exhorted to display grief openly. Such expressions of public grief are often seen as being cathartic for the bereaved and hence therapeutic. However, in the absence of any carefully controlled studies, one cannot make unequivocal claims that that is the case.

We also saw that funerals are public events and anyone who is in any way related to the deceased or to the bereaved family attends the funeral and participates in most of the ensuing rituals and ceremonies. The family members of the deceased accept and welcome such visitations and look upon them as part of the acceptable cultural norms.

In many of the North European societies on the other hand – particularly in Britain (see Chapter 7), America and the Scandinavian countries – death, to a very large extent, is viewed as a private event, affecting mainly the immediate members of the family. Even the funeral ceremonies are seen as private events and only those expressly invited to the funeral are expected to attend and offer their condolences. We noticed too that in such societies the free expression of emotions, although not expressly discouraged, is by no means encouraged. In some instances, as Hockey (1993) points out, the clergy may frown upon the display of what are considered as excessive emotional feelings. In general therefore, funeral ceremonies proceed with restraint, in a quiet and what is considered a dignified manner.

There is a social expectation that those who were not invited to the funeral – the social acquaintances, work associates and colleagues, distant relatives of the deceased etc. – will write to the family members of the bereaved and offer their written condolences. The bereaved family members usually look forward to receiving such letters, which often contain eulogies of the deceased, accompanied by an expression of grief and sorrow at the loss experienced.

The emotional expression of one's grief, which is thus kept in check during the public ceremony, may find an outlet in the privacy of one's home and in solitude. One is, by the nature of social customs, inhibited, if not prevented, from sharing openly one's loss with the rest of the community.

ACQUAINTANCE AND FAMILIARITY WITH DEATH

In Western societies the spectacular advances in the medical sciences have raised hopes in people of longevity. Such advances have given rise to the belief that death can be put off, postponed, held in check, or even conquered permanently. Modern medicine, by regarding death as a medical failure, may have unwittingly perpetuated this image. The belief in longevity allows one to distance oneself from one's own death and those of one's loved ones. It is not an event about which one needs to concern oneself unduly. Yet people die everyday, everywhere, and not all die of old age. No society has discovered the elixir of life. Nor has any society found a profoundly satisfactory way of dealing with one's own death or the death of one's near ones.

As Rosenblatt (see Chapter 3) points out, each society, large or small, each culture, developed or developing, acquires its own way of dealing with death. In contemporary Western society, when death occurs, it usually does so outside the home, most often in a hospital, where of course, it is *medicalized,* a term favoured by sociologists. The involvement of the family is kept to a bare minimum – or in some instances, not at all. The entire process involved in the handling of the dead, the laying out of the body, its eventual transportation to the crematorium or cemetery, the arrangement of the funeral service, the cremation or the burial of the body, etc., is done by outsiders, funeral directors. The Western family in that respect is protected from inviting 'death' home. In keeping death away from one's home, in absolving oneself from all the rituals related to the handling, laying out and dressing of the body, Western society to a large extent has succeeded in 'distancing' itself from death. One learns of death, one is cognitively (and no doubt emotionally) aware that one's loved one has died, one mourns for the dead, but one does not and is not expected to deal physically with the dead. That is left to paid outsiders. In fact the process of distancing starts in hospital, where death is handled with clinical efficiency by the hospital staff. There is little that the bereaved can do other than to let the hospital staff and then the undertakers deal with the deceased.

One might contend that in Western society one learns of death in the abstract, so to speak. One acquires a cognitive awareness of death. One learns that it is the final event in every individual's life. But the knowledge of death is in the head; neither the heart nor the eye experiences it directly. When death does occur, as is inevitable, one is distanced from the dead, both physically and psychologically. The reality of death once again turns into an abstraction.

The process of distancing is accelerated by the dread of death from which no society appears to be exempt. This is articulated by Shakespeare:

> Of all the wonders that I yet have heard,
> It seems to me most strange that men should fear,
> Seeing that death, a necessary end,
> Will come when it will come.

> *(Julius Caesar,* Act 2 Scene 2)

In the West the fear of death can be attributed to several factors. Most Western societies have witnessed a decline in the status of established religion. At a psychological level this has resulted in diminishing beliefs in an afterlife, rebirth, and heaven and hell. This, along with the dissolution of the extended family and community networks, has meant that the beliefs and practices, as well as the institutional structures which would have supported the bereaved are now often unavailable or inadequate. In addition, the socio-political processes of humanization and secularization have shifted our attention away from the destiny of the deceased towards the fate of the bereft.

However, Walter (Chapter 9) points out that the tenets of humanism and secularization may in fact assist persons to overcome their fears of death. He argues that, to a humanist, death equals extinction and therefore it is not to be feared. Because we can never know about any life beyond the grave, there is no point in worrying about it now. Therefore one learns to accept the inevitable with a sense of equanimity. What matters is not one's death, for that is inevitable and unavoidable, nor what lies beyond death; what matters most is how one lives one's life. A humanist is concerned more about living and life than about dying and death.

But it should be pointed out that this is a rationalist view of life and death which is unlikely to be shared (and acted upon) by the majority of people – not just people in Western societies, but all over the world – some of whom, despite their professed allegiance to a philosophy of liberalism and humanism, nonetheless experience the primeval terrors associated with death and extinction.

To many people death is seen as a period of transition. Upon death a person does not become extinct. Although the human body, if left unattended, will rot, decompose and decay, the spirit or the soul remains free and unaffected. One goes, according to one's beliefs, to heaven, to an everlasting afterlife, or (heaven forbid!) to hell. Such beliefs, which helped and still help many people to come to terms with their own impending death and with that of their loved ones, appear to have declined significantly.

The attempts to distance oneself from death start early. Not only do parents protect themselves from encountering death, they take special pains to prevent their children from witnessing death. The child, it is believed, must be shielded from the trauma of beholding a dead body. There is, in this cultural norm, a rather curious paradox. As Young and Papadatou (Chapter 10) point out, awareness of death and bereavement starts in early childhood. Such an awareness is made sharper by the fact that both adults *and* children are exposed to a virtually inexhaustible diet of violence and death in its gory and graphic detail through the media of televison, films, video-games, etc. The appetite for violence, if one is to judge by the number and the type of films which are produced and released in any one year, appears to be insatiable: it grows by what it feeds on – as is evidenced by the eagerness with which the consumer industry produces and promotes electronic, mechanical, plastic and computerized 'role-models' of the avenging heroes who deal in indiscriminate death and destruction. But although children are socialized into a culture of violence, destruction and death, they are insulated from death in reality. Death on television, despite its graphic detail, is make-believe; death in the home is real. While parents may let their children – willingly or unwillingly – indulge in the former, they insulate them from the latter. Clearly on the one hand we deny the reality of death and, on the other, show an obsession with its morbid details through crime stories, horror films and war pictures – a contemporary 'pornography of death'.

Why are young children on the one hand prevented from seeing a dead body and on the other allowed to watch (albeit grudgingly in many cases) gratuitous violence and death at home? Is it that children can see through make-believe and reality, and whereas they find the former exciting, they may perceive (or are they led to perceive?) the latter as being traumatic? That young, innocent children will be severely traumatized when exposed to real death is a popular Western belief which lacks any firm empirical evidence. Yet it has been elevated to the status of a myth.

However, when one turns to non-Western cultures (see Chapter 4) one learns that in those cultures children are not consciously protected from witnessing a dead body. In third-world countries, most people die at home, not in hospitals, as is normally the case in the West. Even those who die in hospitals are invariably brought home. The funeral arrangements are undertaken by the members of the family and not by professional undertakers. And as has been pointed out earlier, most people in third-world countries live within an extended family network which includes the father, the mother, their unmarried daughters, their sons and their spouses, and their children, all living together. Under those crowded living conditions, it would be difficult to prevent (even if one wanted to) a child from witnessing the dead body of another member in the family. If indeed the perception of a dead body has 'traumatizing' psychological effects on a young child, as is believed in the West, one might expect over the years the entire population in third-world countries to have grown up with a terrible unresolved trauma. But of course this is not the case.

It should also be pointed out that death in non-Western cultures is not (at least not as yet) *medicalized,* as it is in Western countries. Most people die in their homes and not in hospitals. Also, the rates of mortality for infants, children and adults is far higher than in the West. As a result, death is seen as a common, everyday phenomenon, and although it may hold the same private terrors as it does for people in the West, such close proximity makes its denial a virtual impossibility.

CROSS-CULTURAL ATTITUDES TOWARDS DEATH

We have seen that, to a large extent, people in Western societies resort to a variety of strategies by which they 'distance' themselves from death, whereas people from most third-world countries tend not to, or are unable to do this. These different practices are often related to the attitudes which people of different cultures and religions have towards death. The preceding chapters, each in its own way, have shown that the attitudes which people hold toward death vary within and between groups. Each culture has its own sets of rites, rituals, taboos and practices concerning death.

In some cultures death may be seen as a subject to be talked about freely. There is an acceptance of mortality and there are very few restrictions which prevent a person from raising the topic of death in day-to-day conversation. In many non-Western societies – India being a prime example – death is not considered a taboo subject, although Muslims tend not to discuss it openly. There are very few taboos related to talking about death, except on certain auspicious occasions, such as during weddings, christenings, and during religious festivities, etc. The theme of death occurs in daily conversations; among friends, among relatives, within families, between strangers; people do not shy away from talking about death. Death is around one, it is part of the human condition, and there is an acceptance of its eventuality. The elderly in India talk openly of dying, of their approaching time of death. In social conversations, it is not unusual to see the elderly openly turn their gaze heavenwards and remark that it is time for them to die; it is time for God to 'call them', and for them to leave the illusory world of *maya,* in which, as a result of their past karmic actions, they have become entangled.

At a psychological level, however, the expression of such sentiments may serve two different functions. The constant reference to death may come to acquire the quality of a talisman, which one rubs in order to ward off death. (The more one talks about it the less are the chances that it will happen.) Also, it may serve the function of preparing the individual concerned for the final eventuality and in so doing, blunt the edges of primeval fears which death might otherwise arouse.

CROSS-CULTURAL ATTITUDES TOWARD AN 'AFTERLIFE'

Is death the end of life, or the beginning of a new one? A serious answer to this question requires us fully to understand how individual beliefs are related to notions of heaven, hell, resurrection, Armageddon, afterlife, transmigration of the soul, rebirth, reincarnation, etc. All the chapters in this book have attempted to tackle these extremely serious issues. Let us briefly summarize some of their arguments, beginning at one extreme and slowly tracing our steps to the other.

Tony Walter (Chapter 9) argues that death to the humanist is primarily a human problem. God and religion do not enter into it. He also goes on to stress that *death is the end of life*. And since no one knows and there is no way of knowing what lies beyond death – if anything – it makes no sense to speculate (and as a result create an industry of beliefs and practices) on the unknowable. Upon death therefore one merely ceases to be. However, he injects some purpose – although not in a teleological sense – into his stark thesis by suggesting the dead 'live on' in the memory of the living they have left behind. Thus one survives extinction in the memory of others and in the 'human products' one leaves behind. It follows therefore that questions related to the existence of the soul, the tenability of an afterlife, or re-birth, etc. are questions which are almost entirely devoid of meaning for a humanist. They have no part to play in their funeral services, which are non-religious, non-sectarian, and are initiated (or led) by persons specially trained to hold such informal and open services. This is not to suggest that humanists do not mourn and grieve for the dead. The loss of a loved one arouses pain, sorrow and regret. Grieving and mourning are a *natural* human process.

The humanist attitude to dying, death and bereavement is primarily a Western European development. It is difficult to state with any degree of certainty the present number of adherents to this philosophy, or whether their number is increasing or decreasing.

Moving on, we come to the arguments presented by Rosenblatt (Chapter 3) in his studies of small-scale societies dotted around the world. 'Each culture', Rosenblatt writes, 'has its own approaches to dealing with loss'. He argues that to understand how each culture deals with loss requires a sensitive understanding of the manner in which people of all cultures – large or small – conceptualize death within their own culture. Notwithstanding the rarefied and rather tedious medical debates concerning what constitutes clinical death, Euro-American societies generally see life and death in dichotomous terms: one is *either* dead *or* alive. There are no gradations between life and death. That, as Rosenblatt points out, may not be the case in many small-scale societies, where there may be an assortment of categories and gradations of 'dead'. A person deemed alive in Britain may be regarded as being dead in other societies; similarly, a person seen as being dead in Britain, may be perceived as being alive in other societies. Moreover, a person may even participate in his or her own 'funeral' rites. (This was true in the case of the author's elderly cousin who, being dubious as to the quality of the funeral rites which his sons would perform upon his death, arranged for all his funeral rites to be performed while he was alive. It so happened that upon his death, his sons outdid their father in the 'lavish' funeral rites which they performed!)

It is, as Rosenblatt points out, important to note that, in most societies, death is not a transition into nothingness, but to some other state. To ensure that the process of transition proceeds unimpeded, it is incumbent upon the bereaved to perform all the culturally determined rituals, which may last for several days, weeks, months and, in some instances, even years. The people in those societies may be expected to get in touch with 'ritual specialists' whose job it is to help the bereaved to perform all the rituals appropriately and in accordance with cultural norms and expectations. The performance of these time-honoured rituals not only ensures the successful transition of the deceased but also enables the bereaved to part from their dead in gradual stages.

To those Westerners to whom such rituals may seem bizarre, crude, childish, insensitive, irrational or illogical, Rosenblatt asserts that the Westerner's rituals are no more universal or deserving of respect. For there is no universally right or wrong way of dealing with the dead.

Here it needs to be pointed out that occasionally the term 'cultural differences' tends to be used indiscriminately – as a 'waste-basket phenomenon' to explain away any anomalous experiences. Yet a closer examination may reveal that the differences in question turn out in fact to be superficial, such as differences in terminology, semantics and/or perspectives. It is a myth that the Western world sets a universal standard against which all other societies all over the world are to be evaluated. Consequently, those societies which come close to achieving (or mimicking) Western standards are to be applauded and those which don't. derided.

Rosenblatt offers two inter-related suggestions to practitioners: first, to engender a spirit of tolerance and respect for the beliefs, values and practices of peoples of other cultures; and second, a willingness to learn from other cultures. And as Rosenblatt points out, there are valuable lessons to be learnt. Immigrants of other cultures living in the West ought not to be made to conform to and abide by the standards of practice operative in Western societies. They should be allowed to engage in their own culturally meaningful mourning practices.

Where the religious beliefs of the members of small-scale societies are concerned there are no clear parallels to be drawn. The variation within and between diverse groups does not permit a clear analysis of the impact of their religious beliefs and attitudes on death and bereavement. However, as Rosenblatt points out, many small-scale societies accept the idea that the spirits of the dead act upon the world of the living and are present in the world of the living – an idea which is not entirely alien to Westerners who, although they may not refer directly to the spirit, do not shy away from referring to what Rosenblatt calls a 'sense of presence' of the deceased. And the fact that it is not uncommon among Westerners to talk about the powerful controlling influences which the dead exercise over their lives, and may continue to exercise over their lives, merely transforms the term 'spirit' into a metaphor. However, the essence of the beliefs may remain unchanged.

Let us now briefly turn to Hinduism (Chapter 4) and Buddhism (Chapter 5). The reader could not have failed to notice the strong similarities between both religions. But this is hardly surprising when one realizes that Buddhism grew out of Hinduism. Gautama, who eventually came to be known as the Buddha – The Enlightened One – came from a princely Hindu family in India during the sixth century BC.

Gielen points out that over the centuries Buddhism has come to be accepted as a religion. But strictly speaking it is not a religion. It does not advocate devotion and prayer and the emotional joy and bliss (*anand*) associated with prayer – which in Hinduism is one of the ways by which a Hindu may attain salvation. Although Buddhism grew out of Hinduism, it is not a reformist movement (de Riencourt, 1960). Buddha was not really concerned about forming a new religion (Radhakrishnan, (1979). Buddhism was – and continues to be – a practical and profoundly rational philosophy concerned with understanding and finding solutions to the perennial problems of human existence.

Both Buddhists and Hindus propound the view that the world in which we live is a world of sorrow. This, according to the Buddhists, is part of the human condition. The members of the human race are spiritually unhealthy; they carry on their shoulders the burden of sorrow. The sorrow and suffering does not end with death: death in that sense brings no relief to the sufferer. Suffering begins afresh with each new birth. For death is not the end of human life, but the beginning of a new one. Thus the cycle of birth and death, birth and death, continues inexorably, until such time as an individual is able to free him/herself from the cycle and attain salvation. Hindus refer to this as *moksha* and the Buddhists as *nirvana*. The precise meanings of the words *moksha* and *nirvana* remain unclear. Nor is it clear in which ways the meanings of the two words differ. All we know is that *nirvana* does not refer to the soul; unlike the word *moksha*, it does not have a religious connotation. But does *nirvana* refer to extinction, to a state of non-being, to a 'void'? Coomaraswamy and Nivedita suggest that *nirvana* is best understood as 'a freeing from the fetters of individuality' (1967, p. 249).

Hindus and Buddhists often share the view that the world in which we live is false and illusory. They say it is *maya*: by this they do not mean that the 'real' world is a phantasm. In an empirical sense of course the world is real. It is bound by time and space. Yet it is an ever-changing world and is subject to all the forces of decay. And since that is the case, it serves no purpose to explore this changing, transient, illusory world nor to pursue the 'rewards' which we, in our ignorance (*avidya*), believe the world has to offer.

What is the cause of human suffering and sorrow? Sorrow, both for the Buddhists and the Hindus, is a result of ignorant craving (*trishna*). We are driven by false desires and we pursue false goals. In so doing we mistake illusion for reality. To the Buddhists the ills of the individual cannot be understood in terms of the individual's mistakes because this ignorant craving which leads to sorrow is the natural function of the life process. No metaphysical explanations are offered. To the Buddhists the causes of suffering are to be seen at a practical, psychological level. Hindus on the other hand explain human suffering and sorrow in metaphysical terms: as a consequence of their own actions (karma) in their past lives.

Yet such a condition, both for the Hindus and the Buddhists, is not ineradicable. The suppression of suffering can be achieved by those who follow what is described in Buddhist philosophy as the eightfold 'middle path'. A middle path is one which avoids extremes. One needs to be unswerving in one's attempts to follow the middle path, the pursuance of which will ultimately lead to salvation. In Hinduism too there is the belief that one can overcome one's false desires, in which one is entangled by the process of living, and transcend the illusory nature of the world. This can be achieved by following one of the three paths open to Hindus: the path of devotion and prayer (*bhakti marga*); the path of true knowledge (*gyana marga*) and the path of right action or duty (*karma marga*). The ultimate aim of life – both for Hindus and Buddhists – is to free oneself from the burden of life, from the bondage of the cycle of birth and rebirth.

The two chapters have shown how the beliefs of both Hindus and Buddhists concerning the cycle of birth, death and rebirth translate themselves into understanding their attitudes to death and bereavement. Death is not the end of life: it is the beginning of a new one. Birth, which in one sense leads to rejoicing, in another leads to sorrow and suffering throughout the life of the person who is born. Such a belief has a profound impact upon the psyche of Hindus and Buddhists. It tends to engender among both Hindus and Buddhists – at a psychological and existential level – a temperament of fatalistic acceptance of the vicissitudes of life and death.

SUGGESTIONS AND RECOMMENDATIONS

As a result of the trends away from established religion and towards humanization and secularization, new structures are emerging within society to deal with the unmet needs of the bereaved. For instance, whereas 'ritual specialists' used to be invested with the necessary magical powers or religious authority to ease the pain of grief, society now delegates this responsibility to others. In many ways, mental health professionals and bereavement counsellors are today's 'ritual specialists' who have their own set of scientifically developed tools.

Awareness of death and bereavement begins in childhood. Unfortunately, children are even further removed from real death than adults. We choose to expose ourselves to death through graphic media images depicting it as a violent or untimely event. On the one hand, we deny the reality of death. How can such preoccupations be counterbalanced? Young and Papadatou have already noted the increasing tendency to bring death education into school settings. The most recent British National Curriculum gave attention to this area as well as to cultural differences. While this might seem appropriate to many teachers and parents, there are also many who would express reservations about such institutionalized instruction, or even resist such developments. There are similarities between the introduction of sex education into schools and that of death education. Both involve aspects of private lives, both carry taboos and neither has universally accepted norms or values. Furthermore, if teachers were to undertake education in such sensitive areas, they would need guidance, and perhaps additional training. While such initiatives are occurring with increasing frequency, there is little in the way of policy-making to support them.

Whereas the debate about bringing death education into schools is ongoing, few would dispute the need for such training within the core health professions as well as many allied professions. Nevertheless, the evidence would suggest that this is still a neglected area of post-graduate training programmes. This may be based on assumptions that it is 'common sense' or that one can only learn through actual experience. It is also true that those involved in the training of professionals tend not to be from minority cultures, perhaps to an even greater extent than the professionals themselves.

Whether by anecdote, principle or empirical findings, every author in this book has emphasized the crucial importance of recognizing that not only are there different cultural needs between groups but also within groups. The dangers of stereotyping are as serious as entrenched ethnocentrism. Even the concept of 'help' has different meanings across cultures. Several authors note that the needs of any cultural group may not be made explicit to the practitioner, who has to be constantly vigilant about imposing their own assumptions about what is 'right', 'best', 'normal', 'healthy' or 'appropriate', particularly when the wishes of the individual or family are not obvious or forthcoming.

The original purpose of many death rituals, such as funerals, was to create auspicious circumstances for the dead person's onward journey into the afterlife. With this were various beliefs about communication beween the worlds of the living and dead. Young and Papadatou highlight how such understandings were 'caught by' rather than 'taught to' children and then incorporated into their own worldviews and mourning process. They learned that the dead are remembered and honoured not only because it is natural but also because the dead were thought to exert supernatural influences on the material world.

Laungani's account of a Hindu funeral vividly demonstrates how the dying and dead were cared for by their own kin and were not passive observers but active participants in the practicalities and rituals of the 'death surround'. Even for young children, no special arrangements were made to shield or exclude them from these experiences. In contrast, with the massive escalation in medical technology and the professionalization of death, we are all more removed from the natural event of death. Several authors, particularly Laungani and Walter, show

how this professionalization has extended to modern undertaking, itself a concept from Euro-American culture.

Parkes tackles the important question of whether or not counselling is really appropriate or necessary for the majority of the bereaved. To some extent, this question can be approached by considering three potentially different aims of bereavement counselling; humanitarian -providing human comfort and support; preventive – facilitating mourning and readjustment; and therapeutic – ameliorating pathological grief.

Many voluntary agencies and self-help groups follow a humanitarian prerogative to offer counselling to the bereaved, if only to help relieve their burden of suffering. While there is no firm evidence that counselling 'speeds up' the mourning process itself, many can testify that their grief is ameliorated by sharing it with another. Another way that a counsellor may be particularly helpful to those from minority, and often economically disadvantaged, clients is by arranging and providing practical support. Alongside the emotional turmoil of grief, bereavement often brings many other changes and associated losses in its wake. A counsellor who is familiar with statutory provisions and other community resources is often in the best position to direct the bereaved towards these sources of support and may, in certain situations, act as their advocate in obtaining entitlements.

What kind of support networks are now available for minority cultures? The stable traditions guiding them in the past may not be available to them for a variety of reasons (Neuberger, 1987, and Irish, Lundquist and Nelson, 1993). They may have become dislocated from their parent culture where help would normally be available. Their concepts and patterns of grief and psychiatric disorder may be unfamiliar to professionals, resulting in their either avoiding involvement through fear or ignorance or delivering inappropriate forms of intervention. While there is much clinical and research work to suggest that those from ethnic minorities can benefit from counselling, there are often problems in providing accessible and appropriate services for them, particularly if they do not speak the host culture's language (Lago and Thompson, 1989). Through his seminal account of adult grief, Parkes established a firm scientific basis for the organization and delivery of support to the bereaved (Parkes, 1980). He noted that many professionals do not receive any formal training in bereavement counselling and that trained volunteers with a year or more's experience in bereavement work may exceed the expertise of these professionals. The value of trained volunteers is borne out by organizations such as Cruse: Bereavement Care who provided counselling support for nearly 20,000 people in the year 1993–4.

Despite the ubiquity of bereavement, the status of a bereaved person and the expression of grief seems to vary widely across cultures. Indeed, a vigorous debate is opening up amongst workers in the field of bereavement research about the validity of many of our hypotheses about how individuals cope with loss. Many cite a lack of empirical support for many 'commonly held myths' while others (Stroebe, Stroebe and Hansson, 1995) assert that untested and untestable assumptions are not representative of the current state of knowledge or research efforts. Hence, there is probably much to be gained from studying how different cultures deal with death and bereavement.

SUMMARY

☐ Expressing all the emotions of grief in public is an accepted part of the social ritual in many cultures. Such expressions are often seen as being therapeutic.

☐ In many North European societies death is viewed as a private event, and people are inhibited, if not prevented, from sharing openly their loss with the rest of the community.

☐ The spectacular advances in the medical sciences have given rise to the belief that death can be put off, postponed, held in check, or even conquered permanently.

☐ By keeping death away from the home, absolving themselves from all the rituals related to the handling, laying out and dressing of the body, Westerners have succeeded in 'distancing' themselves from death.

☐ Humanization and secularization have shifted our attention away from the destiny of the deceased towards the fate of the bereft.

☐ Beliefs in a life after death appear to have declined significantly.

☐ Although children are socialized into a culture of violence, destruction and death, they are insulated from death in reality. In third-world countries, however, children are frequently exposed to the reality of death without, apparently, suffering great trauma.

☐ In many non-Western societies death is not considered a taboo subject.

☐ A humanist attitude to dying, death and bereavement is primarily a Western European development. To the humanist there is no afterlife although people may live on in the memory of others.

☐ In most societies, death is not a transition into nothingness, but to some other state. To ensure that the process of transition proceeds unimpeded, the bereaved must perform all the culturally determined rituals. This not only ensures the successful transition of the deceased but also enables the bereaved to part from their dead in gradual stages.

☐ It is a myth that the Western world sets a universal standard against which all other societies all over the world are to be evaluated. We need tolerance and respect for the beliefs, values and practices of peoples of other cultures and a willingness to learn from them.

☐ The fact that Westerners commonly experience a sense of the presence of a dead person and talk about the powerful controlling influences which the dead exercise over their lives, merely transforms the term 'spirit' into a metaphor. But the essence of the beliefs may remain unchanged.

☐ Buddhism is a practical and profoundly rational philosophy concerned with understanding and finding solutions to the problems of human existence.

☐ To Buddhists the cycle of birth and death continues inexorably, until the individual is able to free him/herself from the cycle and attain salvation which, to some, is understood as 'a freeing from the fetters of individuality'. This is the ultimate aim of life.

☐ Hindus and Buddhists often share the view that the world in which we live is false and illusory. We are driven by false desires. We pursue false goals. In so doing we mistake illusion for reality. These beliefs engender a temperament of fatalistic acceptance of the vicissitudes of life and death.

☐ In the West mental health professionals and bereavement counsellors are today's 'ritual specialists' who have their own set of scientifically developed tools for helping the bereaved.

☐ The problems of helping children to learn about death and bereavement are being met by an increasing tendency to bring death education into school settings.

☐ Not only are there different cultural needs between groups but also within groups. The dangers of stereotyping are as serious as entrenched ethnocentrism. Practitioners have to be constantly vigilant about imposing their own assumptions about what is 'right', 'best', 'normal', 'healthy' or 'appropriate', particularly when the wishes of the individual or family are not obvious or forthcoming.

☐ The aims of bereavement counselling are: humanitarian – providing human comfort and support; preventive – facilitating mourning and re-adjustment; and therapeutic – ameliorating pathological grief.

☐ While those from ethnic minorities can benefit from counselling, there are often problems in providing accessible and appropriate services for them.

☐ There is much to be gained from studying how different cultures deal with death and bereavement.

Chapter 13

Conclusions II: Attachments and losses in cross-cultural perspective

Colin Murray Parkes

Our review of the beliefs, customs and rituals attending death and bereavement and the light which these throw on the beliefs, customs and rituals of the West has repeatedly revealed the problems which we in the West now face.

Death remains a mystery. Any reader of this book who has tried to approach it with an open mind will have been both fascinated and frustrated by the many contradictions and the bewildering variety of the beliefs and rituals attending death and bereavement. In the cold light of reason many of them seem silly, some cruel and others inconsistent. Certainly they cannot all be true. Yet each one of them brings a perspective on death that is different from our own and that beckons us to look again at our own basic assumptions about life as well as death. Most of these beliefs and rituals seem to meet the emotional needs of their adherents. In this respect they may have a symbolic or poetic truth that transcends reason. Since each culture has different symbols it would be surprising if the symbols that have deep meaning to Indians had the same meaning to people of other races. To many Westerners it seems strange to revere the cow, yet we have our own symbols which may seem just as silly to Indians. (For example, other races are surprised by our tendency to worship fashionable beauty to the extent that we inflict first degree burns on ourselves and risk skin cancer every summer.)

Our review of the beliefs and practices that are held by most people across the world raises important issues. Secularism emerges as the belief system that is sweeping the Western world. We tend to assume that it is automatically in conflict with religions but is this necessarily the case? Given that secularism is gaining ground, is it either possible or desirable to attempt to stem the tide? Although most people would be surprised to be called secularists, for secularism is not a religion and has no formal status, the beliefs and assumptions that distinguish it are held to by most in the West, whatever formal religious affiliations they may claim. What are these assumptions?

1 Secularism is essentially rational; it is the faith that we must rely on our reason in all matters, and that reason must take precedence over other ways of perceiving reality. It is not reasonable to set reason aside, irrationality is the arch heresy. Reason takes precedence over tradition, it questions received knowledge and casts doubt on the 'wisdom' of forefathers. When the heart and the head are in conflict it is the head that must succeed.

Four further assumptions arise from this:

2 Distrust of strong emotions of all kinds, since these are seen as the enemies of reason.
3 A tendency to agnosticism: we reserve judgement on all issues that lie outside the grasp of reason.
4 We divide sacred from secular and treat the sacred with suspicion.
5 We distrust ritual and divest those rituals that persist of emotional significance.

These beliefs have enabled Westerners to achieve the wonders of the scientific revolution that has changed the world and reduced suffering in many ways. In this it has been so successful that people all over the world are jumping onto the bandwagon. Countries that are not yet industrialized are labelled as 'under-developed' and pitied. The advantages of scientific development are undoubted and it seems niggardly to raise doubts.

Our attitudes to death, as we have seen, are profoundly affected by these secularist assumptions. Throughout this book it has become clear that people in the West, and many of those in other countries who are now becoming industrialized, are attempting to ignore death. Even in societies such as Spain, where the actual spectacle of death by violence in the bull ring is commonplace, confrontation with death by cancer or other disease in the form of television programmes about hospices have been banned on the grounds that they are 'too disturbing'.

When real death forces itself on our attention we become greatly distressed, for we have no schema, no system of belief that can make sense of it. The bereaved experience this as a breakdown in the meaning of life. They easily come to see grief as an illness for which treatment is needed. We turn to bereavement counsellors and psychotherapists in the hope of obtaining a cure. The counsellors, who should know better, sometimes collude with this tendency. To some extent the counsellors and psychotherapists are taking over from the priests and becoming the 'ritual specialists' of our age. The only difference is that the priest sees death as a transition for the dead whereas the psychotherapist sees it as a transition for the bereaved.

What are the alternatives? The editors of this book think that counsellors and other carers have important roles to play and will be much more effective if they have opened their minds to a wider view of life and death. To do this we must set aside our own basic assumptions and listen to the 'poetry' of other cultures and religions. One alternative to secularism is Humanism. As Tony Walter has pointed out, this is the current belief system which comes closest to secularism. Yet secularism conflicts with Humanism, for Humanism recognizes the sacred nature of life and of humanity and Humanists have devised their own rituals. Humanists reject the possibility of life beyond death, but secularists are agnostic on this issue and most people think that there must be *something* beyond this life. This may account for the fact that formal commitment to Humanism is still rare.

If we can, for the time being, ignore the logical contradictions between faiths, what can we learn from the main systems of belief that are current in the world today? Hinduism, the oldest of the current great religions, exhibits a wide tolerance of belief. Hindus can be atheists or theists and the differences between the formal beliefs of Hindu sects often seem greater than the points of similarity. Their great strength lies in their respect for the family and the rich variety of rituals which have evolved over the years and which attend all of the turning points of life. These are most obvious at times of death when the rituals to induct the dead into the next phase of existence, whatever that may be, are seen as right and proper. That they also help to ameliorate the pains of grief is undoubted, but we should not allow that consideration to blind us to the fact that these rituals are intended to reassure the dying and help the dead rather than the bereaved.

In recent years psychologists have begun to use rituals in support of personal change at times of crisis and loss. Reports indicate that these are powerful tools which can do harm as well as good. Great caution will be needed if these tools are introduced untried into cultures in which they are not traditional. With all their disadvantages the priesthood does have the benefit of long experience and it may be more appropriate for psychologists to work with the priests rather than to compete with them.

In most religions, prayers and other rituals at the bedside of a dying person help them to achieve peace of mind in the face of a situation that most find daunting. There is a possible conflict here between the needs of the dying, who may want and need quiet and peace, and those of the family who may need to grieve in anticipation of the loss that is to come. These differences are reflected in different religions; thus Buddhists may exclude family members from the bedside if they cannot remain calm, while certain Arab sects expect all of the family to come and to wail loudly. Systematic cross-cultural studies are needed to clarify the advantages and disadvantages of each approach.

One of the most puzzling and controversial issues is still that of the expression of grief. What evidence there is supports the notion that emotional expression is usually therapeutic and that people come through the grieving process more quickly if they express their feelings than they do if these are 'bottled up'. However, this does not mean that grief needs to be continuous and unrestrained. In fact the dangers of unrestrained expression become very obvious in societies where anger is directed to the punishment of supposed witches, or the law of vendetta still holds. This is an area in which systematic cross-cultural studies are urgently needed if we are to explore the reasons why some cultures seem to inhibit grief without suffering lasting harm while others pay a high price.

The rituals attending death and bereavement are, of course, very much more than occasions for the expression of emotion. Funerals are usually important social events which allow all of those whose lives are touched by a death to meet together. They help to make real the fact of death, to identify the mourners, to restate the beliefs that make sense of death, to launch the dead into the next phase of their existence and to prescribe a set of roles to be performed by the bereaved who may be suffering from the loss of their previous roles and functions.

One of the psychological difficulties that faces the bereaved is the suddenness of death. One minute a loved person is alive, the next they are dead. All in a moment a married woman becomes a widow or a child becomes an orphan. In many cases they may have had no warning of this huge transition and no time to prepare themselves for it. The funeral itself comes too soon after death to represent a satisfactory ending to a relationship.

We have seen in this book that, in many societies, death is spread out in time. The souls of the dead remain earthbound for a while and the bereaved are expected to continue to relate to them. For most people in these societies, and many others in the larger-scale religions, it appears that for the dead as well as the living there may be a period of transition during which the dead remain close by and the living are under an obligation to mourn them. Research into the psychology of bereavement in Western countries has shown how frequently newly bereaved people experience a strong sense of the presence of the dead person near at hand and continue to treat them as if they were present. They do not necessarily mention this behaviour for fear of being thought 'odd'.

Part of the problem of bereavement is to find a satisfactory location for the dead for there are few who can accept the idea that they are nowhere. For many bereaved Westerners the cemetery does not constitute a satisfactory location – sometimes they will locate the dead person in a favourite chair or bed – sometimes it is a more numinous place, such as the sea or the open sky, that becomes associated with the dead person.

Others drift uncertainly from one location to another finding no comfort in any of them. Their problem seems to be the lack of any social sanction for locating the dead. In current Shinto and Buddhist belief in Japan and in other countries, shrines to the dead become the chosen location and the bereaved find it comforting to visit them and to commune with the dead person.

Although most wedding ceremonies make it clear that the obligation of fidelity to a partner ends with the partner's death, this is not the way most widows and widowers see it. For some time afterwards they feel an obligation to remain sexually faithful whatever feelings they may have towards others. Similarly mothers who have lost a child continue to place the wishes of their dead child on a par with those of their surviving children.

Rosenblatt's account of numerous small-scale religions in Chapter 3 reveals how frequently people feel the need for a second ceremony some time after the funeral. Second rituals help to signal the passage of time and allow for the idea that the bereaved may have fulfilled any obligation to mourn and are now free to move on to the next chapter of their lives. Requiem Masses are deeply moving occasions which can serve a similar function. Likewise, several hospices now hold memorial services, followed by a social meeting, for the relatives of patients who have died six months to a year previously.

Whatever the course of the transitions of death and bereavement there comes a time when it makes sense for the dying and the bereaved to accept the reality of their loss and approach the next passage of their lives. Acceptance of the will of God is an important aspect of Islamic and Buddhist faiths and is made easier if people's investment in the perishable aspects of this life is not too great. The idea that nothing lasts and that there is a flux between dark and light, birth and death, loss and gain, Yin and Yang, is a powerful and potentially helpful concept that can prepare us for the losses that are to come.

It may seem ungrateful to view this life as a vale of tears in which sorrow outweighs happiness, yet this is the view of the world accepted by orthodox Buddhists and Hindus. To make matters worse this misery is not relieved by death, for most will only go on to be reborn into another miserable existence. This pessimistic view, however, is not without hope. The cycle of death and rebirth can be broken, for when people succeed in freeing themselves from the illusion of their own individuality, they thereby attain peace (*moksha* or *nirvana*).

Pessimism is less justified in the comfortable circumstances of the first world where, for much of our lives, we can ignore the dark side of life and delude ourselves with the belief that every day, in every way, life is getting better and better. This view is encouraged by the endless stream of new discoveries and other sources of pleasure that our industrial world is currently able to produce. It does not take much prescience to recognize that there are limits to industrial growth and that the current boom cannot last. In fact, for many young people today, whose expectations of 'success' are crumbling, a new vision is already needed. Instead of finding satisfaction in foreign holidays and luxurious possessions, the next generation may have to find other sources of self-esteem. The time may well be ripe for us to review the meanings of our lives and to reduce our expectation that science will find a solution to all our problems.

We tend to assume that consciousness is a function of the mind but it is equally possible that consciousness is present in all matter and that all a mind does is to act as a channel for it. In the transition from inorganic molecule to organic, from organic molecule to living organism, from single cell to multi-cellular foetus and from foetus to adult human being we undergo a process of differentiation which separates us off from other matter. When, in death, the cycle is reversed, it may be that we are reunited with the ground of our being. It is at least possible that the Buddhist injunction to us to accept the loss of individuality, hard though this is, is a reasonable preparation for death. Far from being reunited as separate persons who come together we may simply lose the differentiation that separated us from each other in the first place.

This brings us to the heart of the matter. For many people it is not so much the loss of individuality that we fear but the loss of others to whom we are attached. Current psychology has much to say about attachments (see Parkes, Stevenson-Hinde and Marris, 1991 and Parkes, 1996, for more details). These are seen as behavioural and feeling tendencies which are rooted in instinct but modified by learning from the time of their inception in infancy. They are found in all social animals, some reptiles, most fish and many insects. The urge to attachment, which is necessary to survival, develops in babies and their parents during the first year of life in order to keep children safe in the world until they become capable of surviving without parental support. In the course of childhood, attachments are made to a wider and wider range of other people and, during adolescence and early adult life, the strong attachment to parents usually diminishes and a new strong attachment is made to a person who is not related by blood and is most often of the opposite sex. This attachment provides both partners with the mutual support that they need in order to rear children of their own. Attachments need to be powerful if they are to keep us and our children safe.

The urge to seek for and to find those from whom we have become separated transcends most other drives and is felt as the most passionate of emotions, separation distress or pining. Loss by death, like other losses, evokes intense pining for the lost person and an urge to stop all other activities in order to find them. The fact that we know this to be a fruitless endeavour does not prevent the feelings from emerging and the pain of grief is probably the most powerful psychological pain that we experience. No appeal to reason will wish it away although it will gradually diminish with the passage of time. Even then severe grief remains liable to recur for many years.

The fact that attachments are modified by learning makes them susceptible to cultural influences. One such is the availability of 'parent figures'. The young child who is reared by a number of 'mothers', as in the Long House culture in Malaysia, will suffer less if one of them dies than will a child who only receives parenting from one 'mother'. ('Mother' is here placed in quotes to indicate that mothering is a matter of behaviour not blood relationship. Men as well as women can fulfil this role.) Similarly the repertoire of attachment behaviours is moulded by the interactions between parents and children and this in turn influences the way people feel and behave when separated, in adult life, from those they love. In some situations of danger it is essential for children to keep quiet if they are to survive, in others it may be essential for them to cry loudly. This simple observation explains why children are so sensitive to the example of the familiar adults, particularly their parents, who will indicate to them the behaviour that they deem appropriate in the present circumstances. Children who are brought up to believe that crying is dangerous soon learn to inhibit their tears.

If attachments serve the function of enhancing our chances of survival, what function do they serve us when we are dying? The answer in Buddhist thinking is 'none'. They see it as spiritually appropriate to sever all of our attachments at this time. By the time that we have reached adult life all of us will have developed a sophisticated range of attachments, not only to people but to places, objects and even ideational systems. Thus I become attached to everything that I call 'mine'; 'my country', 'my home town', 'my car' and even 'my profession', 'my legal system', 'my language' and 'my God'. Each of these contributes to my sense of security, of knowing my place in the world and being, to some degree, in control. Each of them will be a cause for grief if they are lost. Again cultural factors help to determine not only the rules of kinship and other ties to people but also the ties to objects, social systems and ideas. Those whose security remains intimately dependent on a particular person or a small family are more vulnerable than those who spread their attachments over an extended network. Those who invest more in their job, their body, their physical prowess or their God, will suffer more if they should lose these and less if they should lose other, less salient, objects of attachment than the rest of us. And since it is our culture which usually determines who and what we love, we should not be surprised if cultural influences play a large part in our reactions to loss and change.

Even the attachments we make to other individuals are not as simple as they seem. I may be attached to my partner because he or she is physically attractive, is very strong, has wealth or status, is knowledgeable or wise. Most often it will be a mixture of these attributes. When my partner dies I shall lose some but not all of these things. I shall no longer have the physical presence of a beautiful person but I may inherit wealth and there is a very real sense in which the people we love do 'live on' in the memory of those who survive them. 'I only have to think, "What would my husband have done about this?" and it is almost as if I had him inside my head telling me what to do', said one widow. In this sense the wisdom and knowledge of the people we love does transcend their mortal life and may help to mitigate the grief that we feel when we lose them.

A culture such as that prevalent in the West, which idealizes achievement and physical and mental prowess is likely to engender more problematic grief when these attributes are lost than one, such as Buddhism, which fosters detachment, acceptance of God's will and humility. These issues become particularly difficult for Westerners during the latter part of life. Those who are sick or ageing can no longer compete with the young; their physical and mental status is declining and there are some who having lost employment think, with some justification, that they are on the 'scrap heap' from the age of forty.

It makes sense for us to expect the transition from the second to the third age of life to be just as challenging as the transition from childhood to adult life. Having completed the transition, if we have the good fortune to live in a society in which a decent standard of security and medical care for the aged can be assured, we should be able to stop worrying and striving and enjoy the chapter that remains to us. The fact that there are a thousands and one things we can no longer do does not mean that there are not still a hundred and one that we can enjoy. We need to attune our minds to relinquish those things that are now beyond our grasp in order to enjoy those that are not. Independence is no longer a virtue and we may need to be prepared to give others the pleasure of using their strength and skills on our behalf.

And in the end, when even those things that remained are taken away, we embark on the greatest adventure of all. One thing seems certain, we will undergo an extra-ordinary transition: in the immortal words of Monty Python, 'And now for something completely different.'

SUMMARY

- [ ] Most of the multiplicity of beliefs and rituals seem to meet the emotional needs of their adherents. They may have a symbolic or poetic truth that transcends reason.
- [ ] Secularism emerges as a powerful set of assumptions that is sweeping the world. It is essentially rational, it distrusts strong emotions as the enemy of reason, it favours agnosticism, separates sacred from secular and distrusts ritual.
- [ ] People in the West, and many of those in other countries that are now becoming industrialized, are attempting to ignore death.
- [ ] When death forces itself on our attention we become greatly distressed, for we have no schema, no system of belief that can make sense of it. The bereaved experience this as a breakdown in the meaning of life.
- [ ] Counsellors and other carers have important roles to play and will be much more effective if they have opened their minds to a wider view of life and death.
- [ ] Rituals are powerful and can do harm as well as good. We are wary of the prospect of psychologists taking them over from priests.
- [ ] There is a wide range of variation, with some societies expecting

and fostering emotional expression at times of death and bereavement and others limiting or inhibiting it. Emotional expression is usually therapeutic but this does not mean that grief needs to be continuous and unrestrained.

☐ Funerals help to make real the fact of death, to identify the mourners, to restate the beliefs that make sense of death, to launch the dead into the next phase of their existence and to prescribe a set of roles to be performed by the bereaved, who may be suffering from the loss of their previous roles and functions.

☐ In many societies, death is spread out in time. The souls of the dead remain earthbound for a while and the bereaved are expected to continue to relate to them. Shrines to the dead become the chosen location and the bereaved find it comforting to visit them and to commune with the dead person.

☐ Second rituals help to signal the passage of time and allow for the idea that the bereaved may have fulfilled any obligation to mourn and are now free to move on to the next chapter of their lives.

☐ The idea that nothing lasts and that there is a flux between dark and light, birth and death, loss and gain, Yin and Yang, is a powerful and potentially helpful concept that can prepare us for the losses that are to come.

☐ To Buddhists the cycle of death and rebirth can be broken when people succeed in freeing themselves from the illusion of their own individuality.

☐ The time may well be ripe for us to review the meanings of our lives and reduce our reliance on science for a solution to all our problems.

☐ We tend to assume that consciousness is a function of the mind but it is equally possible that consciousness is present in all matter and that all that a mind does is to act as a channel for it. If so, it may be that, when we die, we are reunited with the ground of our being. Far from being reunited as separate persons who come together we may simply lose the differentiation that separated us from each other in the first place.

☐ For many people it is not so much the loss of individuality that we fear but the loss of others to whom we are attached. Attachments serve the function of enhancing our chances of survival but they serve no function when we are dying. Buddhists see it as spiritually appropriate to sever these ties at this time.

☐ A culture such as that prevalent in the West, which idealizes achievement and physical and mental prowess is likely to engender more problematic grief when these attributes are lost than one, such as Buddhism, which fosters detachment, acceptance of God's will, and humility. These issues become particularly difficult for Westerners when we are sick or ageing.

Bibliography

Abu Lughod, L. (1993) 'Islam and the gendered discourses on death', *International Journal of Middle Eastern Studies*, 25, 187–205.

Adams, K.M. (1993) 'The discourse of souls in Tana Toraja (Indonesia): indigenous notions and Christian conceptions', *Ethnology*, 32, 55–68.

Anesaki, M. (1963) *The History of Japanese Religion, with Special Reference to the Social and Moral Life of the Nation*, Rutland VT: Charles E. Tuttle.

Arney, W.R. and Bergen, B.J. (1984) *Medicine and the Management of Living*, Chicago, IL: University of Chicago Press.

Ashford, S. and Timms, N. (1992) *What Europe Thinks: A Study of Western European Values*, Aldershot: Dartmouth.

Beattie, J. (1964) *Other Cultures: Aims, Methods and Achievements in Social Anthropology*, London: Routledge & Kegan Paul.

Becker, C.B. (1989) 'Rebirth and afterlife in Buddhism', in A. Berger, P. Badham, H. Kutscher, J. Berger, M. Perry and J. Beloff (eds) *Perspectives on Death and Dying: Cross-cultural and Multi-disciplinary Views*, Philadelphia: Charles.

Black, D. and Urbanowicz, M.A. (1987) 'Family intervention with bereaved children', *Journal of Child Psychology and Psychiatry*, 28 (3), 467–76.

Black, D. and Young, B. (1995) 'Bereaved children: Risk and preventive intervention', in B. Raphael and G. Burrows (eds) *Handbook of Studies on Preventive Psychiatry*, Amsterdam: Elsevier.

Blackham, H.J. (1968) *Humanism*, Harmondsworth: Pelican.

Blueblond-Langner, M. (1978) *The Private Worlds of Dying Children*, Princeton, NJ: Princeton University Press.

Boaz, F. (1911) *The Mind of the Primitive Man*, New York: Macmillan.

Bock, P.K. (1980) *Continuities in Cultural Anthropology: A Historical Introduction*, San Francisco, CA: Freeman.

Boehnlein, J.K. (1987) 'Clinical relevance of grief and mourning among Cambodian refugees', *Social Science and Medicine*, 25, 765–72.

Brauen, M. (1980) *Feste in Ladakh* [Festivals in Ladakh], Graz, Austria: Akademische Druck-und Verlagsanstalt.

—— (1982) 'Death customs in Ladakh', *Kailash*, 9 (4), 319–32.

Brener, A. (1993) *Mourning and Mitzvah: A Guided Journal for Walking the Mourner's Path Through Grief to Healing*, Woodstock, VT: Jewish Lights Publishing.

Brison, K.J. (1992) *Just Talk: Gossip, Meetings, and Power in a Papua New Guinea Village*, Berkeley, CA: University of California Press.

Bulka, R.P. (1980) *As a Tree by the Waters. Pirkey Avoth: Psychological and Philosophical Insights*, Jerusalem: Feldheim Publishers Ltd.

Burgoine, E. (1988) 'A cross-cultural comparison of bereavement among widows in New Providence, Bahamas and London, England'. Paper read at International Conference on Grief and Bereavement in Contemporary Society, London, July 12–15.

Chalmers, A.F. (1985) *What is This Thing Called Science?*, 2nd edn, London: Open University Press.

Chaudhuri, N.C. (1979) *Hinduism*, New York: Oxford University Press.

Chorlton, W. (1982) *Cloud-dwellers of the Himalayas: The Bhotia*, Amsterdam: Time-Life.

Corlin, C. (1988) 'The journey through the Bardö. Notes on the symbolism of Tibetan mortality rites and the Tibetan Book of the Dead', in S. Cederroth, C. Corlin and J. Lindstrom (eds) *On the Meaning of Death: Essays on Mortuary Rituals and Eschatological Beliefs*, Uppsala Studies in Cultural Anthropology 8, Stockholm: Almquist & Wiksell.

Corr, C.A., Morgan, J.D. and Wass, H. (1993) *Statements on Death, Dying and Bereavement*, International Work Group on Death, Dying and Bereavement, Ontario: King's College.

Crain, M.M. (1991) 'Poetics and politics in the Ecuadorean Andes: women's narratives of death and devil possession', *American Ethnologist*, 18, 67–89.

Davies, D. (1990) *Cremation Today and Tomorrow*, Nottingham: Grove Books.

de Riencourt, A. (1960) *The Soul of India*, Honeyglen Publishing, United Kingdom.

du Boulay, S. (1984) *Cicely Saunders*, London: Hodder.

Dyregrov, A. (1992) Grief in Children, London: Jessica Kingsley.

Encyclopedia of Islam, Leyden: Brill.

Epstein, L. (1982) 'On the history and psychology of the "Das-log"', *The Tibet Journal*, 7 (4), 20–85.

—— (1990) 'A comparative view of Tibetan and Western near-death experiences', in L. Epstein and R.F. Sherburn (eds) *Reflections on Tibetan Culture: Essays in Memory of Turren V. Wylie*, Lampeter: Edwin Mellen.

Evans-Wentz. W.Y. (1960) *The Tibetan Book of the Dead or the After-Death Experiences of the Bardö Place According to Lama Kazi Dawa-Samdup's English Rendering*, 3rd edn, London: Oxford University Press.

—— (1969) *Tibet's Great Yogi Milarepa*, Oxford: Oxford University Press.

Fields, R. (1986) *How the Swans Came to the Lake*, 2nd edn, Boston: Shambhala.

Firth, S. (1993) 'Approaches to death in Hindu and Sikh communities in Britain' and 'Cross-cultural perspectives on bereavement', in D. Dickenson and M. Johnson (eds) *Death, Dying and Bereavement*, London: Sage.

Folta, J.R. and Deck, E.S. (1988) 'The impact of children's death on Shona mothers and families', *Journal of Comparative Family Studies*, 19, 433–51.

Frazer, J.G. (1890) *The Golden Bough* (republished 1922), London: Macmillan.

Freemantle, F. and Trungpa, C. (1975) *The Tibetan Book of the Dead*, Boulder, CO: Shambhala.

Gielen, U.P. (1993) 'Traditional Tibetan societies', in L.L. Adler (ed.) *International Handbook on Gender Roles*, Westport, CT: Greenwood.

Gielen, U.P. and Chirico-Rosenberg, D. (1993) 'Traditional Buddhist Ladakh and the ethos of peace', *International Journal of Group Tensions*, 23 (1), 5–23.

Glascock, A.P. and Braden, R.W. (1981) 'Transitions of being: death and dying in cross-cultural perspective', unpublished paper presented at the annual meeting of the American Anthropological Association, Los Angeles, CA, December 1981.

Gorer, G. (1965) *Death, Grief and Mourning in Contemporary Britain*, London: Cresset.

Govinda, L.A. (1960) *Foundations of Tibetan Mysticism*, London: Rider.

—— (1970) *The Way of the White Clouds: A Buddhist Pilgrim in Tibet*, Boulder, CO: Shambala.

Graham, B. (1987) *Facing Death and the Life After*, Milton Keynes: Word.

Grollman, E. (1995) *Bereaved Children and Teens: A Support Guide for Parents and Professionals*, Boston: Beacon.

Guillaume, A. (1956) *The Life of Mohammed* [translation of Ishaq, *Sirat Rasul Allah*] with an introduction and notes, XXXX, Oxford, Lahore, Karachi and Dacca.

Harris, M. (1968) *The Rise of Anthropological Theory: A History of Theories and Culture*, London: Routledge & Kegan Paul.

Harris-Hendriks, J., Black, D. and Kaplan, T. (1993) *When Father Kills Mother: Guiding Children through Trauma and Grief*, London: Routledge.

Harvey, A. (1983) *A Journey in Ladakh*, Boston, MA: Houghton-Mifflin.

Herrnstein, R. and Murray, C. (1994) *The Bell Curve: Intelligence and Class Structure in American Life*, New York: The Free Press.

Hill, A.M. (1992) 'Chinese funerals and Chinese ethnicity in Chiang Mai, Thailand', *Ethnology*, 31, 315–30.

Hinton, J.M. (1994) 'Can home care maintain an acceptable quality of life for patients with terminal cancer and their relatives?' *Palliative Medicine*, 8, 183–96.

Hockey (1993) 'The acceptable face of human grieving: the clergy's role in managing emotional expression during funerals', in D. Clark (ed.) *The Sociology of Death*, Oxford: Blackwell, 129–48.

Hoffman, Y. (1986) *Japanese Death Poems Written by Zen Monks and Haiku Poets on the Verge of Death*, Rutland, VT: Charles E. Tuttle.

Holck, F.H. (1974) *Death in Eastern Thought*, Nashville, TN: Abingdon.

Hollan, D.W. (1992) 'Emotion, work and value of emotional equanimity among the Toraja', *Ethnology*, 31, 45–56.

Hollan, D.W. and Wellenkamp, J.C. (1994) *Contentment and Suffering: Culture and Experience in Toraja*, New York: Columbia University Press.

Houghton, A.A. and Boersma, F.J. (1988) 'The loss–grief connection in *susto*', *Ethnology*, 27, 145–54.

Idleman Smith, J. and Yazbeck Hadad, Y. (1981) *The Islamic Understanding of Death and Resurrection*, New York.

International Work Group on Death, Dying and Bereavement (1993) *Death Studies*, 17 (3), 227–80.

Irish, D.P., Lundquist, K.S. and Nelson, V.J. (1993) *Ethnic Variations in Dying, Death and Grief: Diversity in Universality*, London: Taylor & Francis.

Jahoda, G.A. (1970) 'A cross-cultural perspective on psychology', *The Advancement of Science* (Sept.) 27 (31), 57–70.

James, N. and Field, D. (1992) 'The routinization of hospice: charisma and bureaucratisation', *Social Science and Medicine*, 34 (12), 1363–75.

Johnson, P. (1976) *A History of Christianity*, London: Weidenfeld & Nicolson and London, NY, Victoria and Ontario: Penguin.

Jonker, G. (1996a) 'The knife's edge: Muslim burial in the diaspora', *Mortality*, 1 (1), 27–45.

—— (1996b) 'Die Totenklage in der Migration: interkonfessionelle Bewertungen einer traditionsreichen Praxis', in G. Jonker and G. Höpp (eds) *In Fremde Erde: Islamische Bestattung in Deutschland*, Berlin: Das arabische Buch.

Kalish, R.A. (1980) *Death, Grief and Caring Relationships*, Monterey, CA: Brooks Cole.

Kapleau, P. (ed.) (1971) *The Wheel of Death: Zen Perspectives on Death and Dying*, New York: Harper & Row.

Kolatch, A.J. (1990) *The Jewish Home Advisor*, Middle Village, NY: Jonathan David Publishers, Inc.

Kselman, T. (1993) *Death and the Afterlife in Modern France*, Princeton, NJ: Princeton University Press.

Kübler-Ross, E. (1970) *On Death and Dying*, London: Tavistock.

—— (ed.) (1975) *Death: The Final Stage of Growth*, Englewood Cliffs, NJ: Prentice Hall.

—— (1991) *On Life After Death*, Berkeley, CA: Celestial Arts.

Lago, C. and Thompson, J. (1989) *Counselling and Race (Handbook of Counselling in Britain)*, London: Routledge.

Lamm, M. (1969) *The Jewish Way in Death and Mourning*, New York: Jonathan David Publishers, Inc.

Landis, D.J. (1991) 'Dying among children: a clash of cultures', in J.D. Morgan (ed.) *Young People and Death*, Boston: Charles.

Lati, R. and Hopkins, J. (1979) *Death, Intermediate State and Rebirth in Tibetan Buddhism*, Valois, NY: Gabriel/Snow Lion.

Lauf, D.I. (trans. G. Parkes) (1989) *Secret Doctrines of the Tibetan Books of the Dead*, Boston: Shambhala.

Laungani, P. (1992) 'Cultural variations in the understanding and treatment of mental disorders: India and England', *Counselling Psychology Quarterly*, 5 (3), 231–44.

—— (1993a) 'Cultural differences in stress and its management', *Stress Medicine*, 9 (1), 37–43.

—— (1993b) 'Cultural influences on learning: contrasting Indian and English experiences', *New Quest*, July–August, 202–11.

—— (1994) 'Cultural differences in stress: India and England', *Counselling Psychology Review*, 19 (4), 25–37.

—— (1995) 'Patterns of bereavement in Indian and British Society', *Bereavement Care*.

Levine, S. (1982) *Who Dies?* New York: Anchor/Doubleday.

Lewis, C.S. (1961) *A Grief Observed*, London: Faber (first published as by N.W. Clerk).

Lo-drüp, Lama (trans. Lama Geshe Wangyal) (1982) *The Prince who Became a Cuckoo: A Tale of Liberation*, New York: Theatre Arts Books.

Lutz, C. (1985) 'Depression and the translation of emotional worlds', in A. Kleinman and B. Good (eds) *Culture and Depression: Studies in the Anthropology and Cross-Cultural Psychiatry of Affect and Disorder*, Berkeley, CA: University of California Press.

Marris, P. (1982) 'Attachment and society', in C.M. Parkes and J. Stevenson-Hinde (eds) *The Place of Attachment in Human Behaviour*, London: Tavistock, and New York: Basic Books.

Martin, D. (1978) *A General Theory of Secularisation*, Oxford: Blackwell.

Martinson, I.M. and Papadatou, D. (1994) 'Care of the dying child and the bereaved', in B.J. Beraison and R.K. Mulhern (eds) *Paediatric Psychology*, New York: Oxford University Press.

Mathew, K.M. (ed) (1994) *Manorama Year Book*, Thiruvanathapuram, India: Malayala Manorama.

McClowry, S.G., Davies, E.B., May, K.A., Lulenkamp, E.J. and Martinson, I.M. (1987) 'The empty space phenomenon: the process of grief in the bereaved family', *Death Studies*, 11, 361–74.

McManners, J. (1981) *Death and the Enlightenment: Changing Attitudes to Death among Christians and Unbelievers in Eighteenth-century France*, Oxford: Clarendon.

Messenger, D.R. (1979) *Ceremonies for Today*, Armadale, Victoria, NSW: Brian Zouch Publications.

Middleton, W., Moylan, A., Raphael, B., Burnett, P. and Martinek, N. (1994) 'An international perspective on bereavement-related concepts', *Australian and New Zealand Journal of Psychiatry*, 27, 457–63.

Mullin, G.H. (1987) *Death and Dying: The Tibetan Tradition*, London: Arkana.

Munson, H., Jr. (1984) *The House of Si Abd Allah. The Oral History of a Moroccan Family*, New Haven, CT and London: Yale University Press.

Neuberger, J. (1987) *Caring for People of Different Faiths*, London: Austen Cornish.

Orofino, G. (1990) *Sacred Tibetan Teachings on Death and Liberation*, New York: Unity, and Bridgeport, CT: Prism.

Osterweis, M., Solomon, F. and Green, M. (1984) *Bereavement: Reactions, Consequences and Care*, Washington DC: National Academic Press.

Pallis, M. (1974) *Peaks and Lamas*, 3rd edn, London: Woburn.

Papadatou, D. and Papadatos, C. (1991) *Children and Death*, New York: Hemisphere.

Parkes, C.M. (1970) 'The first year of bereavement: a longitudinal study of the reaction of London widows to the death of their husbands', *Psychiatry*, 33, 442–67. (Reprinted in J.M. Bardwick (ed.) *Readings on the Psychology of Women*, New York and London: Harper & Row.)

—— (1972, 3rd edn 1996) *Bereavement: Studies of Grief in Adult Life*, London: Tavistock/Routledge; Harmondsworth; Pelican and New York: International Universities Press.

—— (1978) 'Home or hospital? Terminal care as seen by surviving spouses', *Journal of the Royal College of General Practitioners*, 28, 19–30.

—— (1980) 'Bereavement counselling: does it work?' *British Medical Journal*, 281, 3–6.

—— (1981) 'Evaluation of a bereavement service', *Journal of Preventive Psychiatry*, 1, 179–88.

Parkes, C.M. and Parkes, J.L.N. (1984) '"Hospice" versus "hospital" care – reevaluation after 10 years as seen by surviving spouses', *Postgraduate Medical Journal*, 60, 120.

Parkes, C.M., Stevenson-Hinde, J. and Marris, P. (eds) (1991) *Attachment Across the Life Cycle*, London and New York: Routledge.

Pascal, B. (1670) *Pensées*, IV, 277.

Pepper, L.G. (1989) 'Grief and elective abortion: implications for the counsellor', in K.J. Doka, (ed.) *Disenfranchised Grief: Coping with Human Sorrow*, Lexington, NY: Lexington.

Perry, H.L. (1993) 'Mourning and funeral customs of African Americans', in Irish, D.P., Lundquist, K.F. and Nelsen, V.J. (eds), *Ethnic Variations in Dying, Death and Grief*, Washington DC and London: Taylor & Francis.

Petech, L. (1977) *The Kingdom of Ladakh c. 950–1892 AD*, Rome: Istituto Italiano per il Medio ed Estremo Oriente.

Popper, K.R. (1963) *Conjectures and Refutations*, London: Routledge & Kegan Paul.

—— (1972) *Objective Knowledge: An Evolutionary Approach*, Oxford: Clarendon.

Porter, R. (1989) 'Death and the doctors in Georgian England', in Houlbrooke (ed.) *Death, Ritual and Bereavement*, London: Routledge.

Racy, A.J. (1985) *Laments of the Lebanon*, Ethnic Folkways Library FE 4046 [with photos, text, and music].

—— (1986) 'Lebanese laments: grief, music and cultural values', *World of Music* 28 (2), 27–40.

Radhakrishnan, S. (1923/1989) *Indian Philosophy*, vol. 2, centenary edition, Delhi: Oxford University Press.

Ramble, C. (1982) 'Status and death: mortuary rites and attitudes to the body in a Tibetan village', *Kailash*, 9 (4), 333–59.

Rando, T.A. (1986) *Parental Loss of a Child*, Champaign, IL: Research Press.

Raphael, B. (1977) 'Preventive intervention with the recently bereaved', *Archives of General Psychiatry*, 34, 1450–4.

Reat, N.R. (1994) *Buddhism: A History*, Berkeley, CA: Asian Humanities Press.

Reischauer, E.O. (1988) *The Japanese Today: Change and Continuity*, Tokyo: Charles. E. Tuttle.

Ribbach, S.H. (1940) *Drogpa Namgyal. Ein Tibeterleben* [Drogpa Namgyal: Life of a Tibetan], Munich: Barth-Verlag.

—— (1986) *Culture and Society in Ladakh* (trans. J. Bray), New Delhi: Ess Ess.

Rizvi, J. (1989) *Ladakh: Crossroads of High Asia*, Delhi: Oxford University Press.

Rosaldo, M.Z. (1984) 'Toward an anthropology of self and feeling', in Richard A. Shweder and Robert A. LeVine (eds) *Culture Theory: Essays on Mind, Self, and Emotion*, New York: Cambridge University Press.

Rosenblatt, P.C., Walsh, R.P. and Jackson, D.A. (1976) *Grief and Mourning in Cross-Cultural Perspective*, Washington DC: HRAF Press.

Sachdev, D. (1992) 'Effects of psychocultural factors on the socialisation of British born Indian children and indigenous British children living in England', unpublished Ph.D. thesis, South Bank University, London.

Samuel, G. (1993) *Civilised Shamans: Buddhism in Tibetan Societies*, Washington and London: Smithsonian Institutional Press.

Sangay, T. (1984) 'Tibetan rituals of the dead', *Tibetan Medicine*, 7, 30–40.

Santayana, G. (1905–6) *The Life of Reason*, vol. 1, ch. 12.

Schmidt, L. (1987) 'Working with bereaved parents', in T. Kulrick, B. Holaday and I.M. Martinson (eds) *The Child and Family Facing Life-Threatening Illness*, Philadelphia, PA: Lipincott.

Siegel, K., Mesagno, F.P. and Christ, G. (1990) 'A prevention program for bereaved children', *American Journal of Orthopsychiatry*, 60 (2), 168–74.

Silverman, P., Nickman, S. and Worden, W. (1992) 'Detachment revisited: the child's reconstruction of a dead parent', *American Journal of Orthopsychiatry*, 62, 494–503.

Sloane, D.C. (1991) *The Last Great Necessity: Cemeteries in American History*, Baltimore, MD: Johns Hopkins University Press.

Smith, H. (1991) *The World's Religions*, San Francisco, CA: Harper.

Smith, J.I. and Hadad, Y.Y. (1981) *The Islamic Understanding of Death and Resurrection*, New York.

Snelling, J. (1991) *The Buddhist Handbook: A Complete Guide to Buddhist Schools, Teaching, Practice and History*, Rochester, VT: Inner Traditions.

Sogyal Rinpoche (1992) *The Tibetan Book of Living and Dying*, P. Gaffney and A. Harvey (eds) San Francisco: Harper.

Stroebe, M., Gergen, M.M., Gergen, K.J. and Stroebe, W. (1992) 'Broken hearts or broken bonds: love and death in historical perspective', *American Psychologist*, 47, 1205–12.

Stroebe, M.S., Stroebe, W. and Hansson, R.O. (1993) *Handbook of Bereavement: Theory, Research, and Intervention*, New York: Cambridge.

Stutley, M. (1985) *Hinduism: The Eternal Law*, Northamptonshire: The Aquarian Press.

Thurman, R.A.F. (1994) *The Tibetan Book of the Dead*, trans. of Padma Sambhava, *The Great Book of Natural Liberation through Understanding the In-between*, New York: Bantam.

Triandis, H.C. (1980) 'Introduction to Volume 1', H.C. Triandis and W.W. Lambert (eds) *Handbook of Cross-Cultural Psychology*, Boston: Allyn & Bacon, pp. 1–14.

Tucci, G. (trans. J.E. Stapleton-Driver) (1967) *Tibet: Land of Snows*, New York: Stein & Day.

—— (1980) *The Religions of Tibet*, London: Routledge & Kegan Paul.

Walsh, F. and McGoldrick, M. (1991) *Living Beyond Loss: Death in the Family*, New York: Norton.

Walter, T. (1990) *Funerals: And How to Improve Them*, London: Hodder.

—— (1994) *The Revival of Death*, London: Routledge.

—— (1996) *The Eclipse of Eternity: A Sociology of the Afterlife*, Basingstoke: Macmillan.

Webb, N.B. (1993) *Helping Bereaved Children*, London: Guilford.

Wellenkamp, J.C. (1988) 'Notions of grief and catharsis among the Toraja', *American Ethnologist*, 15, 486–500.

—— (1991) 'Fallen leaves: death and grieving in Toraja', in D.R. Counts and D. Counts (eds) *Coping with the Final Tragedy: Cultural Variation in Dying and Grieving*, Amityville, NY: Baywood.

Weller, E.B., Weller, R.A., Fristand M.A., Cain, S.E. and Bowes, J.M. (1988) 'Should children attend their parent's funeral?', *Journal of American Academic Child Adolescent Psychology*, 27, 559–67.

Wikan, U. (1980) *Life Among the Poor in Cairo*, London: Tavistock.

—— (1990) *Managing Turbulent Hearts: A Balinese Formula for Living*, Chicago, IL: University of Chicago Press.

Wilson, B.R. (1966) *Religion in Secular Society*, London: Watts.

Wolfson, R. (1993). *A Time to Mourn, A Time to Comfort*, New York: The Federation of Jewish Men's Clubs.

Worden, W. (1991) *Grief Counselling and Grief Therapy*, London: Routledge.

Wynne Willson, J. (1989) *Funerals Without God – A Practical Guide to Non-Religious Funerals*, London: British Humanist Association.

Zimmer, H. (1989). *Philosophies of India*, Bollington Series XXVI, Princeton, NJ: Princeton University Press.

Zotz, V. (1993) *Buddha* (2nd edn), Reinbeck, Germany: Rowholt [in German].

Index